Albert H. Markham

The Great Frozen Sea

Seventh Edition

Albert H. Markham

The Great Frozen Sea
Seventh Edition

ISBN/EAN: 9783337323424

Printed in Europe, USA, Canada, Australia, Japan

Cover: Foto ©Andreas Hilbeck / pixelio.de

More available books at **www.hansebooks.com**

THE
GREAT FROZEN SEA

A PERSONAL NARRATIVE OF THE VOYAGE OF THE "ALERT"

DURING THE ARCTIC EXPEDITION OF 1875-6

BY

REAR-ADMIRAL ALBERT HASTINGS MARKHAM, R.N.

(LATE COMMANDER OF H.M.S. "ALERT")

AUTHOR OF "A WHALING CRUISE TO BAFFIN'S BAY AND THE GULF OF BOOTHIA,"
AND "THE CRUISE OF THE 'ROSARIO'"

> "There's a flag on the mast, and it points to the north,
> And the north holds the land that I love;
> I will steer back to northward, the heavenly course,
> Of the winds guiding sure from above."
> — FRITHIOF'S "SAGA"

SEVENTH EDITION

LONDON
KEGAN PAUL, TRENCH, TRÜBNER & CO., Ltd.
1894

TO

𝔗𝔥𝔢 𝔐𝔢𝔪𝔬𝔯𝔶 of

REAR-ADMIRAL SHERARD OSBORN, C.B.,

WHO, WHILE HE LIVED,
WAS THE MOVING SPIRIT IN SECURING THE DESPATCH OF
THE ARCTIC EXPEDITION, AND WHOSE PAST DEEDS
IN THE SAME FIELD REFLECTED A BRIGHT RAY OF HOPEFUL LIGHT
ON THOSE WHO STROVE TO EMULATE HIS EXAMPLE
WHILST FOLLOWING IN HIS FOOTSTEPS,

𝔗𝔥𝔦𝔰 𝔩𝔦𝔱𝔱𝔩𝔢 𝔚𝔬𝔯𝔨

IS REVERENTLY AND AFFECTIONATELY INSCRIBED BY

THE AUTHOR.

PREFACE TO THE FIRST EDITION.

The History of the Arctic Expedition of 1875-76, and the record of its results, will be found in the work of Sir George Nares. My object in publishing the present volume is to furnish a popular narrative of memorable events as they presented themselves to an individual member of the Expedition, and especially of the work of sledge travelling over the frozen polar ocean. It was written a few months after our return to England, but its appearance has been purposely deferred until the publication of the work by Sir George Nares.

The same reasons still exist for continuing the work of Arctic exploration as were adduced for commencing it in 1875.

It is impossible to complete so great a work in one campaign, and the results of the late Expedition ought only to whet our appetites, and stimulate us to undertake further discoveries.

The narrative of Sir George Nares will show the

completeness of the work accomplished, so far as the route by Smith Sound is concerned, and with the appendices containing the numerous and valuable scientific results, will prove the importance of Arctic discovery. But there are other routes remaining to be explored, which will yield equally useful results.

Behring Strait is a portal leading to a vast region, the history of which has hitherto been as a sealed book.

An expedition to the east coast of Greenland for the purpose of connecting our discoveries at Cape Britannia with those of the Germans at Cape Bismarck, and thus solving the interesting geographical problem regarding the insularity of Greenland, would be of the greatest importance.

The exploration of Jones and Hayes Sounds offer a rich field; but that which, in my opinion, would yield the most profitable harvest, is the continuation of the discoveries of the Austro-Hungarian expedition in Franz-Josef Land. Once reach in a ship the position attained by Lieut. Payer and his sledge party, and such a measure of success would follow as would prove satisfactory even to the most sanguine. Although the flags of Holland, Sweden, and America will this year float in the Arctic Regions, that of England will be unrepresented.

It is hardly to be expected, in the present critical state of affairs, that our Government can afford to give either time or attention to the subject of Arctic exploration, but when the existing differences are all happily settled, there will really be more reasons for following up the work than were brought forward for undertaking it in 1875. We were never in a better position for doing so than at the present time. We possess a couple of ships whose capabilities for Arctic navigation have been already thoroughly tested, and found perfect; we have officers and men experienced in the navigation of those icy seas and in sledging, and we have stores and provisions ready to equip another expedition.

The expense, seeing that the ships and stores are lying idle, would be insignificant, and would hardly be more than equal to that of keeping a couple of small gun-boats in commission. Surely this great nation could easily afford, in the interests of science and for her own honour, to incur such an expenditure. I trust so; and I, for one, look forward with confident hope to the despatch, in a few years, of another Arctic expedition as well equipped as the one of which I was lately a member.

A. H. M.

21, Eccleston Square,
March, 1878.

OFFICERS AND SHIP'S COMPANY OF H.M.S. "ALERT."

OFFICERS.

Captain, GEORGE S. NARES, F.R.S.
Commander, ALBERT H. MARKHAM, F.R.G.S.
Lieutenant, PELHAM ALDRICH.
　　" 　　ALFRED A. CHASE PARR.
　　" 　　GEORGE A. GIFFARD.
　　" 　　WILLIAM H. MAY.
Sub-Lieutenant, GEORGE LE C. EGERTON (promoted to Lieutenant during the absence of the expedition).
Fleet Surgeon, THOMAS COLAN, M.D.
Surgeon, EDWARD L. MOSS, M.D.
Engineer, JAMES WOOTTON.
　　" 　　GEORGE WHITE.
Naturalist, Captain H. WEMYSS FEILDEN, R.A., F.G.S., F.Z.S.
Chaplain, Rev. W. H. PULLEN.

SHIP'S COMPANY.

Joseph Good, chief boatswain's mate.
John R. Radmore, chief carp. mate.*
Geo. Burroughs, ship's steward.
Vincent Dominic, ship's cook.
David Deuchars, ice quartermaster.
John Thores, ice quartermaster.
James Berrie, ice quartermaster.

Edward Lawrence, 1st cl. P.O.†
Daniel Harley, 1st cl. P.O.‡
Thomas Stuckberry, 1st cl. P.O.
Thomas Rawlings, 1st cl. P.O.
James Doidge, 1st cl. P.O.§
Thomas Jolliffe, 1st. cl. P.O.
Spero Capato, captain's steward.
George Kemish, W. R. steward.
Frederick Cane, armourer.
John Hawkins, cooper.

* Promoted to carpenter.
† First class petty officer.
‡ Lost in H.M.S. "Eurydice."
§ Promoted to boatswain.

SHIP'S COMPANY.

William F. Hunt, W. R. cook.
Robert Joiner, leading stoker.
John Simmons, 2nd cl. P.O.
Adam Ayles, 2nd cl. P.O.
William Ferbrache, A.B.
George Cranstone, A.B.
William Lorrimer, A.B.
George Winstone, A.B.
Reuben Francombe, A.B.
Thomas H. Simpson, A.B.
David Mitchell, A.B.
Alfred R. Pearce, A.B.
James Self, A.B.
William Woolley, A.B.

John Pearson, A.B.
William Maskell, A.B.
William Malley, A.B.
Robert Symons, A.B.
Henry Mann, shipwright.
William Gore, stoker.
John Shirley, stoker.
Edward Stubbs, stoker and blacksmith.
George Norris, carpenter's crew.
Neil Christian Petersen, Danish interpreter and dog driver.*
Frederic, Eskimo dog driver and hunter.

MARINES.

William Wood, colour-sergeant R.M.L.I.
William Ellard, private R.M.L.I.
Thomas Smith, private R.M.L.I.

John Hollins, private R.M.L.I.
Elias Hill, gunner R.M.A.
George Porter, gunner R.M.A.†
Thomas Oakley, gunner R.M.A.

The following sledge crew from H.M.S. "Discovery" wintered on board the "Alert":—

Lieutenant Wyatt Rawson.
George Bryant, 1st cl. P.O.‡
George Stone, 2nd cl. P.O.
Michael O'Regan, A.B.

James Hand, A.B.§
Thomas Chalkley, A.B.
Alfred Hindle, A.B.
Elijah Rayner, private R.M.L.I.

The following "means" of ages, weights, and chest capacities of those belonging to the "Alert" may be of interest:—

	Age.	Weight.	Chest Capacity.
Officers	32·1 years	149·8 lbs.	266
Men	27·4 ,,	146·6 ,,	245·1
General Mean	28·4 ,,	147·3 ,,	249·5

* Died on May 14th from the effects of frost-bite whilst sledging.
† Died on the 8th of June of scurvy whilst sledging.
‡ Promoted to boatswain.
§ Died in June of scurvy whilst sledging with Lieut. Beaumont.

CONTENTS.

	PAGE
DEDICATION	v
PREFACE	vii
OFFICERS AND SHIP'S COMPANY OF H.M.S. "ALERT"	xi

CHAPTER I. FITTING OUT.

Description of ships, 2; special fittings, 3; selection of officers and men, 5; kindness of friends, 6; games and musical instruments, 7; visitors to the ships, 8; departure, 9; arrival at Bantry Bay, 12; the voyage commenced, 13.

CHAPTER II. THE VOYAGE TO DISCO.

Tests of physical capacity, 15; regular issue of lime-juice, 16; gales of wind in the Atlantic, 17; slow progress, 19; whales, 20; the first ice, 22; the Land of Desolation, 22; seals, 23; the Greenland coast, 25; fishing for cod, 25; arrival at Godhavn, 26.

CHAPTER III. THE GREENLAND SETTLEMENTS.

An Eskimo dance, 28; Eskimo dogs, 29; amusements at Godhavn, 30; ascent of the Lyngenmarkfjeld, 31; aid from the "Valorous," 33; tradition of Disco, 34; Ritenbenk, 35; part company with "Valorous," 36; the Waigat Strait, 36; dangers in the Waigat, 37; Proven, 38; Hans Hendrik engaged, 39; "Sanderson, his hope," 39; Upernivik, 41.

CHAPTER IV. MELVILLE BAY AND THE NORTH WATER.

Preparations for a nip, 43; the middle ice, 44; a bear hunt, 46; the North Water, 47; Cary Island depôt, 49; approaching Smith Sound, 50; enter Smith Sound, 51.

CONTENTS.

CHAPTER V. SMITH SOUND.

Life-boat Cove, 53; visit winter quarters of "Polaris," 54; Littleton Island, 55; Cape Isabella, 56; stopped by the ice, 57; Payer Harbour, 58; first experiences in sledging, 59; Twin Glacier Bay, 60; an Arctic paradise, 61; tidal observations, 62.

CHAPTER VI. STRUGGLES WITH THE ICE.

Open water, 64; in danger of a nip, 65; vigilance of Captain Nares, 66; wanderings of the Eskimo, 68.

CHAPTER VII. A WALRUS HUNT. DOG DRIVING.

Grinnell Land, 72; glaciers, 73; a walrus hunt, 74; amusements on the ice, 77; the Eskimo dogs, 78; dog sledging, 80.

CHAPTER VIII. SLOW PROGRESS THROUGH THE ICE.

Cape Hawks and Dobbin Bay, 83; discovery of an ancient cairn, 85; cutting a dock, 87; struggles through the ice, 90; dangerous position, 91; Cape Fraser, 92; junction of two tides, 92; Cape John Barrow, 93; Cape Collinson, 94; heavy squalls, 95; increasing thickness of floes, 96; icebergs decreasing in number, 96.

CHAPTER IX. KENNEDY CHANNEL.

Cape Constitution, 98; difference in appearance of coast-lines, 99; Hall Basin blocked with ice, 100; Bessels Bay, 100; Hannah Island, 101; cross Kennedy Channel, 103; musk-oxen, 104; winter quarters of "Discovery," 107; the two ships part company, 107.

CHAPTER X. THE CROSSING OF THE THRESHOLD.

Robeson Channel, 110; stopped off Cape Beechey, 113; Shift-Rudder Bay, 114; floe-bergs, 114; the first lemming, 115; marine shells above sea-level, 116; depôt established at Lincoln Bay, 117; a fortunate escape, 119; crossing the threshold, 119; finally stopped by ice, 121; the Frozen Ocean, 122.

CHAPTER XI. FLOE-BERG BEACH.

Saved by floe-bergs, 125; precarious winter quarters, 126; a reconnaissance in dog-sledges, 128; habits of Eskimo dogs, 130;

Dumb-bell Bay, 131; eider-ducks, 132; two boats advanced northwards, 133; a severe march, 134; danger of the ship, 134; unable to move, 135; autumn sledging commenced, 136.

Chapter XII. Autumn Travelling.

Autumn travelling, 138; discomforts, 139; liability to frost-bites, 142; difficulties, 145; cheerfulness of the men, 146; highest position reached in the autumn, 147; frost-bites, 147; return of travellers, 149; results, 150.

Chapter XIII. Winter Quarters.

Preparations for winter, 152; observatories, 153; snow houses, 154; the ship "housed" in, 154; interior arrangements, 156; winter clothing, 159; precautions against fire, 161; observations for temperature, 162.

Chapter XIV. The Royal Arctic Theatre.

Printing-office, 164; school, 166; amusements, 167; Thursday pops, 168; lectures, 169; the Royal Arctic Theatre, 170; the prologue, 172; conjuring entertainment, 175; magic-lantern exhibition, 176.

Chapter XV. Winter Occupations and Amusements.

Departure of the sun, 178; Guy Fawkes' Day, 179; scientific observations, 180; the moon, 181; open-air exercise, 181; inconvenience from drip, 182; fluctuations of temperature, 183; movement of the ice, 184; celebration of birthdays, 185; bill of fare, 185; fresh meat, 186; Divine service, 187; medical inspections, 187; tabogganing, 187; Nellie, 189; a lost dog, 190.

Chapter XVI. An Arctic Christmas.

Preparations for Christmas Day, 193; Christmas presents, 194; Christmas Day, 195; retrospect, 197; frost-bite patients, 198; precautions against frost-bite, 199; the Palæocrystic Sea, 200; a brilliant meteor, 200.

Chapter XVII. A Happy New Year.

New Year's Day, 202; mustard and cress, 205; heavy snow-drifts, 206; returning light, 207; severe cold, 208; an alarm in the observatory, 209; condition of the Eskimo dogs, 210; Nellie and the lemmings, 212; Rawson's snow hut, 212; the last school meeting, 213; the last dramatic performance, 214; the last "pop," 215; grand palæocrystic sledging chorus, 216.

CHAPTER XVIII. RETURN OF THE SUN.

Cairn Hill, 220; the sun's return, 221; intense cold, 223; experiments on various substances during extreme cold, 223; daylight, 225; alarm of fire, 226; dismantling the observatories, 227; the sledge-crews exercised, 228; a wolf, 229.

CHAPTER XIX. DETAILS OF SLEDGE TRAVELLING.

Preparations for sledging, 231; weights, 232; auxiliary sledges and depôts, 234; tents, 235; cooking apparatus, 236; scale of provisions, 237; lime-juice, 238; medical instructions, 238; sledging costume, 239; precautions against snow-blindness, 240; programme of sledging work, 241; boats to be carried by northern division, 244; names of sledges, 245.

CHAPTER XX. THE JOURNEY OF EGERTON AND RAWSON.

Decide to communicate with "Discovery," 247; departure of Egerton and Rawson, 248; their return, 249; Petersen frost-bitten, 249; heroic conduct, 251; efforts to save Petersen, 251; difficulties of the return journey, 253; Egerton's second start, 255; death of Petersen, 255.

CHAPTER XXI. THE ROUTINE OF SLEDGE TRAVELLING.

Departure of the sledges, 258; first camp, 260; intense cold, 262; arrival at the autumn depôt, 263; the parties separate, 264; duties of cook, 265; sledging breakfast, 266; luncheon, 266; halting for the night, 268; evenings in the tent, 270.

CHAPTER XXII. THE NORTHERN DIVISION—TRAVELLING IN APRIL.

Heavy ice encountered, 273; road-making over the ice, 275; struggling over hummocks, 278; daily routine, 279; continued cold, 280; excellence of the sledges, 281; first symptoms of disease, 282; a gale of wind, 283; heavy snow-drifts, 285; disease increasing, 286; excellent conduct of the men, 286; resolve to abandon one boat, 288; increased weight to drag, 289; intense cold, 290; state of the floes, 291; cross the 83rd parallel, 292; enormous hummocks, 293; hummocks and snow-drifts, 294; tracks of a hare seen, 296; young ice, 296; enforced rest, 297.

CONTENTS.

CHAPTER XXIII. THE MOST NORTHERN POINT EVER REACHED BY MAN.

Scurvy, 299; difficulties increasing, 300; struggling northwards, 301; hummocks discoloured by mud, 301; condition of party, 303; issue of lime-juice, 304; scorbutic symptoms, 305; the last advance, 306; most northern encampment, 307; soundings obtained, 308; the most northern position ever reached by man, 309.

CHAPTER XXIV. RETURN OF THE NORTHERN DIVISION.

Homeward bound, 312; increased sufferings, 314; courage of the men, 316; extreme weakness of the men, 316; abandonment of the second boat, 318; a snow-bunting seen, 319; the land reached, 321; Parr despatched for succour, 322; a stray dog, 322; death of Porter, 323; his burial, 323; saved, 325; return on board, 326.

CHAPTER XXV. RETURN OF ALL THE SLEDGE TRAVELLERS.

Causes of scurvy, 329; anxiety for Aldrich, 331; May sent to his rescue, 331; return of Aldrich, 332; care of the sick, 333; the welcome back, 335; decide to return to England, 337; muskoxen, 338; shooting parties, 338; liberation of the ship, 341; under weigh, 342.

CHAPTER XXVI. THE RETURN VOYAGE IN THE ICE.

Preparations for abandoning ship, 344; communicate with "Discovery," 345; discovery of Eskimo relics, 347; a severe nip, 348; critical situation of ship, 349; Discovery Harbour, 349; return of Beaumont, 350; a frozen cave, 350; "Alert" forced on shore, 351; struggles with the ice, 352; pass Cape Fraser and Dobbin Bay, 353; a seal and fox shot, 354; reach the open sea, 354.

CHAPTER XXVII. HOMEWARD BOUND.

Cape Isabella, 357; letters from home, 358; bad weather, 359; Whale Sound, 359; off Lancaster Sound, 360; reappearance of fulmar petrels, 361; reach Godhavn, 362; receive letters from England, 363; leave Godhavn, 363; Egedesminde, 364; sight the "Pandora," 366; arrive at Valentia, 367; at Queenstown, 367; welcome home, 368.

INDEX . . . . *Page* 371

LIST OF ILLUSTRATIONS.

FULL-PAGE PLATES.

	PAGE
"Alert" and "Discovery"	*Frontispiece*
Polar Bears	*To face* 46
Winter Quarters H.M.S. "Alert" . . .	,, 151
Highest Northern Camp	,, 308
Reducing a Floe-berg	,, 349
H.M.S. "Alert" forced on Shore . . .	,, 351

SMALLER WOODCUTS.

Seals basking on the Ice	23
Eskimo Women	28
Walruses	75
Cape Hawks	84
Plan of Ice Dock	88
"The Moaning of the Tide"	89
Musk Oxen	105
Knots	111
Dog-sledge in difficulties	131
Start of the Autumn Sledges	143
Diagram of Magnetic Observatories	153
Flag-staff Point (Cape Sheridan)	155
Royal Arctic Theatre—Scene from "Aladdin and the Wonderful Scamp"	170

LIST OF ILLUSTRATIONS.

	PAGE
NELLIE	189
LEMMINGS	212
CAIRN HILL	220
SLEDGE UNDER SAIL	231
DOGS AND SLEDGE	247
GETTING READY TO "BAG"	269
CHART OF OUTWARD AND RETURN TRACKS	274
INTERIOR OF TENT	280
A PACKED SLEDGE	281
SNOW-BUNTING	319
BRENT-GOOSE AND EIDER-DUCKS	340
ALLMAN BAY	355
FULMAR PETRELS ("MOLLIES")	361
FAREWELL!	369

MAP SHOWING THE DISCOVERIES OF THE ARCTIC EXPEDITION, 1875–6 . . . . *To face* 1

ARCTIC EXPEDITION
1875-76
(Capt. Sir George Nares, R.N., K.C.B.)
Reduced from an Admiralty Chart

Scale 1:2.200,000

0 10 20 30 40 50 Nautical Miles
0 10 20 30 40 50 Statute Miles

————————— Track of H M S Alert Outwards
— — — — — Tracks of Sledges

Glaciers

THE GREAT FROZEN SEA.

CHAPTER I.

FITTING OUT.

> "Vitailled was the shippe, it is no drede,
> Habundantly for hire a ful long space:
> And other necessaries that shuld nede
> She had ynow, heried be Godde's grace:
> For wind and weather, Almighty God purchace,
> And bring hire home, I can no better say
> But in the see she driveth forth hire way."
> CHAUCER (*Man of Lawe's Tale*).

THE above quaint lines, written five hundred years ago, well describe the scenes that were being enacted during the months of April and May, 1875, in Portsmouth Dockyard.

Busy as this great naval depôt of England almost always is, it is seldom, in peace time, that so much interest is shown in the equipment of two small steam-vessels as was the case with regard to those that were then lying "all a taunto" in the steam basin of that extensive yard.

The names of those comparatively small ships were

the "Alert" and the "Discovery," their destination the unknown North.

Although of insignificant size, in comparison with the huge ironclad monsters by which they were surrounded, yet a close observer would readily detect signs of great strength in these two business-like looking vessels. And very necessary was it that they should possess strength and powers of resistance of no ordinary kind, for they were destined to grapple and fight with the heavy and unyielding ice floes of the Polar Ocean.

The two ships had been very carefully selected and fitted for the important work in which they were about to engage. The "Alert" was a 17-gun sloop, and had already served two or three commissions on foreign stations before she was converted for Arctic service. The "Discovery" was built in Dundee for the whaling and sealing trade, in which she had been engaged for a short time off the coast of Newfoundland, before she was purchased for the Arctic expedition.

The "Alert" was thoroughly strengthened, and, under the supervision of the Admiral Superintendent of the Dockyard (Sir Leopold McClintock), adapted in every way for the hazardous service on which she was about to be employed.

After a complete overhaul of her hull, all defective timbers and beams were removed, and replaced by sound ones; extra beam power was introduced; an external sheathing of seven inches of teak, tapering from amidships to four inches forward and three inches aft, extending from the keel to the waterways, was put on; whilst a longitudinal beam, placed between the shelf-piece and the lower-deck waterway internally, bound and strapped the whole ship together. Extra iron knees were introduced in order more effectually to resist the enormous pressure of the ice; and the stem was fortified outside with half-inch iron plates extending to about ten or twelve feet aft, whilst inside the bow was strengthened by numerous diagonal beams and dead-wood.

Between the inside planking and the lining were placed sheets of felt for the promotion of warmth. New waterways, of a most substantial form, were added; and the ship was divided into watertight compartments.

Two large davits projected over each quarter of the vessel, by the aid of which the rudder, some three tons weight, was easily shipped and unshipped when in danger of being damaged by the ice. On these occasions it would be suspended horizontally over the stern from the davits.

Around the galley-funnel was an ingenious contrivance for making water, consisting of a large reservoir to receive either snow or ice; this, being dissolved by the heat from the fire underneath, is drawn off through a tap at the bottom, thus providing our water supply. Like all vessels employed in the whaling trade, both ships were fitted with Pinkey and Collins' patent reefing and furling topsails; and each possessed a steam-winch on the upper deck, capable of being utilized for many purposes.

At the maintop-gallant-mast-head of each vessel was a large barrel-like object. This was the crow's nest, a very necessary item on board all ships destined to navigate the icy seas. Both ships were barque-rigged, and were supplied with the ordinary contrivances used on board short-handed merchant vessels to facilitate the work.

They formed, indeed, a curious contrast to the heavily rigged but trim men-of-war, which, with their tapering spars and faultlessly squared yards, lay in the harbour near them.

Each vessel was supplied with nine boats of various shapes and sizes, specially designed and constructed for the service peculiar to Arctic waters. Two of these were completely equipped for whaling, so as to be able to follow and capture walruses and narwhals. They were both fitted with harpoon-guns fixed on swivels in the bows. The ice-boats were three in number for each ship, and were built as light as it was possible to make them. Paddles were supplied, by which they could be propelled, as well as oars. They were all carvel-built boats, and the bows of each were armed with a broad sheet of copper as a protection from the ice.

The figure-heads of each ship, like their fittings, were exactly similar. They were what are commonly called "fiddle-heads," having the Union Jack painted on them, and underneath the word *Ubique;* and to no flag can that word be more truly and more appropriately applied. *Everywhere* is it to be found, even beyond the limits of the abode of man!

The clothing and provisions supplied to the ships were in a great measure regulated according to the establishments by which preceding expeditions had been fitted out, and were almost identical in texture and quality.

Great care was taken in the selection of both officers and men, and none were appointed until they had undergone a searching medical examination as to their fitness for Arctic service, several being rejected who had the appearance of being fine and eligible young fellows. The slightest defect, such as bad teeth or old wounds, was a sufficient pretext for refusing the services of otherwise apparently strong and healthy men. Numerous were the volunteers that came forward, rendering the task of selecting a few from the number of eager willing men that presented themselves one of no little difficulty.

Their social and moral qualifications were as strictly inquired into as was their physical condition; and men of a happy and genial disposition were selected in preference to others who appeared morose and taciturn.

"Can you sing or dance? or what can you do for the amusement of others?" were questions invariably addressed to candidates for Arctic service by the board of officers appointed to select from the numerous applicants who presented themselves.

The ray of pleasure that lighted up the faces of those individuals who were informed that they were to be of that small chosen band, indicated most clearly the popularity of the enterprize amongst the men of the Royal Navy; whilst the disappointed ones, and they were many, showed only too plainly the mortification they experienced at being rejected. As an instance of the eagerness evinced by the men to be employed in the expedition, a gallant captain commanding a ship at Portsmouth called at the office where the men were being entered, and requested advice. He said, "An order has come on board my ship, directing me to send volunteers for Arctic service to this office. What am I to do? The whole ship's company, nearly eight hundred men, have given in their names!"

This is merely mentioned in order to show the

amount of interest taken by the whole navy in the cause for which the ships were being equipped.

The ships' companies being completed, officers and men were unremittingly engaged in the various duties incidental to fitting out. Provisions and stores, sufficient to last for three years, had to be received on board and stowed away. There was no waste space on board either vessel. Every little nook and corner was destined to be the receptacle of some important article. The ships gradually settled down in the water as the weights on board accumulated, until they appeared to be alarmingly deep, whilst much yet remained unstowed. The Admiralty had, however, provided for this emergency. The "Valorous," an old paddle-wheel sloop of good carrying capabilities, was ordered to convey all surplus stores, that could not be stowed on board the two exploring vessels, as far as the island of Disco, on the west coast of Greenland.

This was a very wise and necessary precaution, as it would be obviously unsafe to cross the Atlantic in boisterous weather, laden as the two ships undoubtedly would have been if they had received no assistance from a third vessel in the conveyance of their stores.

Through the kindness and generosity of our friends, and of those who more especially interested themselves in the progress of Arctic discovery, we received many useful and valuable gifts. Her Majesty and the members of the Royal Family testified, in a substantial manner, the deep interest they took in the enterprize. The name of her Imperial Majesty the Empress Eugénie must always be associated with the expedition as one of its warmest friends.

Her kind and considerate present, consisting of a fine woollen cap for each individual, contributed materially to our comfort whilst engaged in the onerous duties of sledging.

To mention the names of all our generous benefactors would require a chapter to itself. Books, magic lanterns, a piano, pictures, and money came pouring in from all sides; but smaller and less valuable, though not the less appreciated, gifts were also received. A small case, with the superscription, "A Christmas box for my friends on board the 'Alert,'" and containing four bottles of excellent punch, and a little parcel of well-thumbed books and periodicals, showing undoubted signs of having been well perused, but which came with the "best wishes of a warrant officer, himself an old Arctic explorer," were accepted with as much pleasure and gratitude as were the more costly presents.

Games of all descriptions, to while away the long evenings of a dark and monotonous winter, were purchased; whilst a complete set of instruments for a drum-and-fife band was also added to the long list of our necessaries.

In devoting a certain sum of money to the purchase of musical instruments and games, wherewithal to amuse ourselves, we were only following an example set us many years ago; for when Sir Humphrey Gilbert sailed in 1583, for the purpose of discovering new lands, and planting Christian colonies upon those large and ample countries extending northward from Florida, we read that, "for the solace of our people, and allurement of the savages, we were provided of musicke in good varietie; not omitting the least toyes, as morris dancers, hobby horses, and many like conceits, to delight the savage people, whom we intended to winne by all faire meanes possible."

We also hear, when that brave old navigator John Davis undertook his first voyage in 1585, with his two frail little barks, the "Sunneshine" and the "Mooneshine," that in the first-named vessel were twenty-three persons, of whom four were musicians— a large band in proportion to the complement of officers and men.

In spite of the bustle and confusion that are inseparable from the preparation of such an expedition, in spite of fresh paint and tarry ropes, several thousands of visitors came on board before sailing, to the no small hindrance of the work; but it is feared that many others, owing to the stringent regulations that it was necessary to issue in order to have the vessels ready by the appointed time, were compelled to return to their homes without having the satisfaction of saying that they had been on board the Polar ships. Amongst those who honoured the vessels with a visit were his Royal Highness the Prince of Wales, his Royal Highness the Duke of Edinburgh, and her Imperial Majesty the Empress Eugénie.

The entertainments given in our honour were very numerous; many were almost regarded as *farewell* banquets.

We were looked upon as public property; our hospitable countrymen, in the generosity of their hearts, never thinking that we should like to spend our last few days in England in peace and quietness amongst our own friends, wished to feed us on the fat of the land, and send us to sea suffering from that worst of all complaints, dyspepsia, accompanied perhaps by *mal de mer*.

At length all preparations were completed. The day originally assigned for the sailing of the expedition, the 29th of May, dawned grey and misty, with dashes of rain falling and lying in little pools on our freshly painted deck. During the forenoon we were honoured by a visit from the Lords Commissioners of the Admiralty, who came to bid us farewell and success on our mission. This was the last official visit paid to the vessels. At its termination officers and men were left pretty much to themselves, so that their last few hours in England might be spent with their own relatives. Four o'clock in the afternoon was the hour named for the departure of the ships, and punctual to the very minute they cast off from the dockyard jetty. The last embrace had been taken, the last fervent farewell had been wished, and, a good omen for the coming voyage, as the vessels steamed out of Portsmouth Harbour, all clouds cleared away, and the sun shone out bright and joyous. During the day crowds had been flocking from all parts of England in order to add their voices to those of other well-wishers to the enterprize. Seldom before in that famous seaport town, although the centre of many stirring events, had such a scene been witnessed. Thousands of spectators were congregated along the sea-face extending from the dockyard to Southsea Castle, and on the opposite shore of Gosport, to witness our departure; and cheer after cheer pealed forth from the assembled multitude as we slowly threaded our way amongst the numerous yachts and pleasure boats that had collected to bid us Godspeed. A small thin line of red, hardly to be distinguished amidst the more sombre hue of the holiday seekers' dresses, denoted the troops of the garrison drawn up to do honour to their comrades of the sister service, whilst their bands, breaking forth with the soul-stirring strains of "Auld lang syne," found an echo in the hearts of all connected with the expedition.

It was, indeed, a proud moment for us as we witnessed this unmistakeable demonstration, and felt that we, a small but chosen band, had been selected to carry out a national enterprize of such importance.

If anything was required to assure us of the popularity of our undertaking, the spectacle that afternoon on Southsea Common was surely a convincing proof.

There was but one responsive feeling in the hearts of every member of the expedition, namely, a determination to deserve this confidence, and to achieve, with God's help, such a measure of success as would prove satisfactory to the country and creditable to the navy.

It will be long before that scene is effaced from our memories. Our last view of Portsmouth was across a bright blue sea to a shore thronged with an enthusiastic and cheering crowd waving a last farewell; whilst the last glimpse our friends had of us was across the same blue sparkling sea, the snow-white sails of our ships being lit up by the rays of the setting sun.

Our feelings appeared to be reflected in the changes of the weather on that, to us, memorable day. The rain and mist in the morning were emblematical of the sorrow of parting; while when the sun burst forth bright and joyous in the afternoon, we all felt assured that the work on which we were about to be employed would be achieved, and that the enterprize commenced under such bright auspices would terminate as well and happily.

Nothing occurred to mar the departure; one incident only happened that might have terminated disastrously and thrown a gloom over the little squadron. Immediately after the pilot had been discharged, one of the men of the "Alert," in the excitement and ardour of responding to the cheers with which we were on all sides greeted, lost his balance in the rigging and fell overboard. He was, however, quickly picked up and brought on board none the worse for his immersion, although the consternation excited by this mishap to a boatload of men and women, who happened to witness the accident, nearly resulted in fatal consequences. The half-drowned and thoroughly drenched man being restored to his shipmates, the squadron having been joined at Spithead by the "Valorous," rounded the Nab-light vessel, and before a fine fresh north-easterly breeze spread their sails and steered down channel.

For many hours, however, they were escorted by a little yacht containing the relatives of some few of the officers of the expedition, which following in their wake reluctantly parted only when all further communication was impracticable.

This, and a visit we received on the following morning from the brave old admiral, the Commander-in-chief at Plymouth, when passing the port, was the last sight of friends we were destined to enjoy for many a long month.

We all felt that we had bidden them a long farewell,

and from thenceforth, as far as they were concerned, we could only live in the happy memories of the past, buoyed up by hopes and aspirations as to the future.

Experiencing fine weather, the anchors were dropped on the third day in the snug little harbour of Berehaven, in Bantry Bay. The object of this visit was to obtain our last supply of fresh meat, and our last budget of letters from home. A farewell ramble on shore amongst green fields and picturesque little farmhouses, where we were regaled with delicious fresh milk, was also enjoyed, and a visit paid to some Druidical remains near the long straggling village of Castletown.

And here, amongst the long green grass and by the side of clear rippling rivulets, we gathered the last flowers of spring that would gladden our eyes until after our return to our native shore. Carefully were these floral treasures hoarded until an opportunity offered of transmitting them to dear friends at home. It is related of one officer, who was so fortunate as to gather several sprigs of "forget-me-not," and whose home ties were, perhaps, not so attractive as those of others, that he offered to barter small tufts of this precious little plant for a bottle of beer, or a pot of cocoa and milk, the two latter articles being excessively scarce on board the Arctic ships, and proportionately valuable.

On the 2nd of June, the day following their arrival, the little squadron once more put to sea. From that date the receipt of all letters ceased. No more telegrams; no loving missives; all intelligence from home must come to an end. We could live only for the future, and pray for a happy and speedy return.

Before nightfall the high and rugged coast of Ireland had sunk below the eastern horizon, leaving nothing visible on the apparently boundless ocean but our three ships as they were lazily rocked by the long rolling swell of the broad Atlantic.

> "The vessel gently made her liquid way;
> The cloven billows flashed from off her prow,
> In furrows formed by that majestic plough;
> The waters with their world were all before."

CHAPTER II.

THE VOYAGE TO DISCO.

> "Now from the sight of land, our galleys move;
> With only seas around, and skies above.
> When o'er our heads descends a cloud of rain,
> And night with sable clouds involves the main,
> The ruffling winds the foaming billows raise,
> The scattered fleet is forced to several ways.
> . . . . And from our shrouds
> We view a rising land like distant clouds,
> The mountain tops confirm the pleasing sight."
>
> VIRGIL.

THE next morning we found that on leaving England we had also left behind bright sunshine and blue skies, and in their place gloomy grey clouds were spread over us, while rain fell sullenly through the murky air. This, with head winds, was our normal condition for many days. Steam was occasionally raised during any lengthened periods of calm; but the report from the engineer that steam was ready was, as a rule, followed by a report from deck that a breeze was springing up, but invariably from an adverse quarter.

On the 5th of June, in order to expedite our movements, the "Valorous" received permission to ignore the presence of a senior officer and make the best of her way to Disco; the "Alert" and "Discovery" continuing their course together.

We were not many days together at sea before we discovered the good qualities of our ship's company. There was a willingness about them that could not fail to be appreciated, whilst the thorough good feeling that seemed to exist was highly satisfactory. As a proof of the desire of each one to assist his neighbour, it may not be out of place to mention that the petty officers of the "Alert," a day or two after leaving harbour, requested permission to take turns with the able seamen in steering the ship, a duty from which, by their position, they are usually exempt. It need hardly be said their wish was immediately gratified.

During the passage our medical staff was busily engaged in ascertaining the physical capacities of every individual member of the expedition. These experiments were by some jokingly resented as an unauthorized system of mental and bodily torture. Every one's age was carefully noted; height and weight accurately ascertained; dimensions round the chest measured; and by means of an instrument called a spirometer the capacity of the chest was also obtained; a clinical thermometer was inserted into the mouth and kept there for an apparently interminable time for the purpose of ascertaining the temperature of the blood. The treatment we were subjected to in the cause of science was thus described by one whose acquaintance with the Royal Navy was only of a few days' standing: "I was unceremoniously laid hold of and measured, forced into a chair and weighed, was compelled to answer the most impertinent questions regarding my age and connections; a horrid instrument was kept in my mouth for an hour or more, and I was forced to blow into a machine until not a breath of wind was left in my body!" The results of all these experiments were duly registered, the intention being to compare them with a similar examination on the return of the expedition, in order to ascertain the effects of an Arctic life upon the physical development of our bodies.

The appetites of the officers, rendered doubly keen by the fresh sea air, were so inordinate as to cause serious anxiety in the mind of our worthy caterer, who was fearful that the allowance of provisions would never last the specified time, at the rate they were then being consumed.

From the fifth day after leaving port lime juice was regularly issued to every officer and man in the expedition. Being considered an indispensable antiscorbutic, it was essential that precautions should be adopted to ensure the certainty of each man drinking it daily. It was therefore the practice to serve it out on the quarter-deck every forenoon in the presence of an officer. This was never omitted during the whole period that our expedition was absent from England. With one or two exceptions the lime juice was drunk with pleasure by the men, and the exceptions were gradually educated, by taking it in small quantities, until their dislike was cured.

In consequence of the limited stowage capacity on board, the officers were unable to provide themselves with a large stock of beer. A considerable quantity of wine and spirits, however, was laid in; but as an anticipated absence of three years had to be provided for, we were restricted to an allowance of two glasses of sherry per diem, a glass of port or madeira once a week, and a bottle of brandy or whiskey about every fourteen or fifteen days. On birthdays or fête days we were also indulged in a glass of port wine after dinner.

Ten hogsheads of Allsopp's ale, brewed especially for the Arctic Expedition, were provided by Government and formed part of the ship's stores. It was grand stuff—"strong enough," as one of the men observed, "to make our hair curl!"

We were not destined to enjoy fine weather long, and our passage across the Atlantic was by no means a pleasant or a comfortable one. Gale followed after gale. If they had only blown from the right quarter we should have been happy, but we had no such luck, they were sure to come ahead!

What a lively ship was the "Alert"! making it utterly impossible to keep anything in its place. It was decidedly annoying, one day, when I entered my cabin to find my nice smart crimson table-cloth drenched with ink; but it was no use repining, and I could only exclaim, with Lord Dorset—

"Our paper, pens, and ink, and we,
Are tumbled up and down at sea."

Liveliness was not her only peculiarity, she was likewise excessively wet, and although battened down carefully it was impossible to keep the water from going below. To those who are uninitiated in nautical terms it must be explained that "battening down" means the careful closing and covering with a tarpaulin of every skylight and hatchway, in order to prevent the water from finding its way below. In spite, however, of these precautions, it is excessively difficult to keep the lower deck of a small ship dry during heavy weather.

On the 13th it was blowing furiously with a terrific sea, and we were compelled to "lay-to" under very reduced canvas. During the night a large steamer, supposed to be bound for Quebec, passed close to us, so close indeed that we were compelled to burn blue lights in order to denote our position, so as to avoid collision.

On the same night a heavy sea struck us, and washed away our starboard whale boat. Our consort also suffered the same loss. Nearly all our fowls, which were in hen-coops on the upper deck, were drowned; only two escaping! Fresh meat being scarce the manner of their death did not prevent their appearance on our table for some days. This gale had the effect of dispersing our little squadron, nor did we again assemble together until our arrival at Disco.

No sooner had we recovered from the effects of one gale, than we were assailed by another. Our only consolation was, the very poor one of trying to believe that these storms would eventually be the means of assisting us in our passage through Melville Bay, by breaking up the ice and blowing it out of Davis Straits!

The discomforts entailed by the perpetual bad weather did not in any way check the ardour of some of the officers in their praiseworthy endeavours to add to the scientific collections of the expedition. It is related, but I will not vouch for the authenticity of the story, that on one occasion, when the ship was labouring heavily, a hugh sea washed on board, finding its way down through the skylight into the wardroom, where it splashed about from side to side with every roll of the ship. An officer, a most zealous and enthusiastic collector in all branches of natural history, being in bed at the time, thought that he detected by the dim light of a lantern some interesting, and perhaps unknown, specimens of zoology in the water. His landing net was immediately called into requisition, and, from his bed, he succeeded in fishing up some of these supposed wonderful organisms. The microscope was instantly produced for the purpose of ascertaining the nature of his find, when, to his great disappointment, he discovered they were simply grains of buckwheat—part of the stock that had been laid in for our unfortunate fowls!

Our progress was tardy. On more than one occasion we were actually farther off Cape Farewell, the point of land we were striving to make, than on the day previous!

As we approached Davis Straits, speculations were rife as to when and where we should meet our first ice. The greatest eagerness was shown by all on board to become acquainted with the enemy whose fastnesses we were preparing to attack and from which we hoped to return victorious.

On the 25th of June, being still at some distance to the southward of Cape Farewell, a vessel was sighted steering in the opposite direction to ourselves. We passed at too great a distance to avail ourselves of such a favourable opportunity of sending letters to England, though there were many on board who showed an intense anxiety to communicate. We suspected, and our reasoning proved correct, that this would be the last vessel we should see for many a long day, and she was consequently watched with a great deal of interest. She was, in all probability, a homeward bound Peterhead vessel laden with *cryolite*. The cryolite is a rare mineral and the sole one which has become an article of trade in Greenland. It is found only in one single spot called Ivigtut in 61° 10′ N., imbedded like a massive body in the granitic rock, and not in veins or strata. In 1857 a licence was granted to a private company for working the cryolite, and in the first nine years 14,000 tons were exported in 80 ship-loads. During the next nine years the total export amounted to 70,000 tons. Cryolite is converted by a chemical process into soda and an alumina unequalled as regards purity and fitness for the art of dyeing.*

As we neared the waters of Davis Straits, whales were observed in great numbers. They were principally what are called by the whalers " bottle-noses." This species of cetacean is the *Hyperoodon rostratus*, and is from twenty to twenty-six feet long, with teeth in the lower jaw. The "bottle-noses" are seldom sought and captured by the whalers owing to the small amount of oil that they yield, not more than a few hundred-weight of blubber being derived from each one of this species. A dead whale of the "right" or "Greenland" sort was also passed. What a prize for a whaler this would have been; worth about £1,000! but of no value whatever to us, so it was allowed to float by untouched. How the mouths of our ice quarter-masters, all hailing from those essentially whaling ports Dundee and Peterhead, watered as they beheld what by them would have undoubtedly been considered a god-send! The evident look of wonder, not unmixed with contempt, that showed itself upon their countenances was truly ludicrous when they found that we were about to pass

* See Dr. Rink's "Greenland," p. 79.

so valuable a prize unheeded. This fish—for all "right" whales (*Balæna mysticetus*) are denominated "fish" by those engaged in their capture—had probably been struck by some whaler and, having succeeded in evading its persecutors, had since died of its wounds; or else it had been killed by the inveterate enemy of the whale the *Orca gladiator*, or "grampus," sometimes called "sword-fish," which pursues and harasses these harmless unoffending leviathans of the deep whenever opportunities offer. The rorqual, or "finner" (*Physalus antiquorum*), was also seen; it is easily distinguished from the right whale by the dorsal fin peculiar to this cetacean, and from which it derives its name. The rorquals are seldom captured, great difficulty being experienced in killing these huge monsters, which are frequently known to measure as much as ninety feet in length. Scoresby mentions one measuring one hundred and twenty feet. Great as is their size, however, the amount of blubber to be obtained from them is very insignificant. They feed upon cod-fish (as many as eight or nine hundred have been found in the stomach of one of these whales) and are constantly seen off the south and west coast of Greenland.

A falling temperature on the 27th of June, and a peculiar light blink along the horizon, gave us due notice of the immediate proximity of ice. As the weather was thick and foggy extra precautions were adopted in order to guard against coming into serious collision with any icebergs, for, however beautiful these floating islands of ice may be during bright clear weather, they are dangerous and formidable foes when near and unseen.

True to the warning received, an iceberg was

shortly afterwards sighted, and by 4 P.M. the ship was steaming through loose detached fragments of heavy floe ice.

It is impossible to describe the excitement that prevailed on board on this first introduction of many among us to that icy world in which we afterwards lived for fifteen months. To me it gave rise to reminiscences of old times, but to the uninitiated it was an exciting scene, and was gazed upon with intense interest.

The officer of the watch, desirous of having the honour of making the ship first touch ice, and being also under the impression that a reward of a bottle of champagne would be given to him who should first succeed in doing so, steered straight for a heavy piece nearly submerged. His efforts were crowned with success, but they were also accompanied by a gentle admonition that for the future he should be a little more careful of her Majesty's property, and avoid all such fragments as were likely to knock a hole in the bows of the ship.

On the following morning we sighted the high, bold, and snow-capped hills in the neighbourhood of Cape Desolation. This headland was so called by that sturdy navigator, brave old John Davis, during his first voyage of discovery in the year 1585. In his quaint manner he describes "the land being very high and full of mightie mountaines all covered with snowe, no viewe of wood, grasse, or earth to be seene, and the shore for two leages into the sea so full of yce as that no shipping cold by any meanes come neere the same. The lothsome viewe of the shore, and irksome noyse of the yce was such as that it bred strange conceipts among us, so that we supposed the place to be wast and voyd of any sencible or vegitable creatures, whereupon I called the same Desolation."

Icebergs were now constantly seen, some being of very considerable dimensions, and looming in the distance like real islands. As one of our men wittily remarked on seeing his first iceberg, it reminded him strongly of the Isle of Wight (white)!!

The streams of ice through which the vessel was navigated were composed of fragments of heavy pack ice, that had in all probability drifted down the east coast of Greenland, and had been swept round Cape Farewell. They were of very deep flotation, and great care had to be taken in steering the ship through, so as to avoid striking these pieces more than was absolutely necessary; so heavily laden was the ship, that the force of the blows in some instances was very seriously felt.

Seals were seen basking lazily and dreamily on the ice, or following in our wake, staring inquisitively at

SEALS BASKING ON THE ICE.

us with their large round eyes, looking for all the world like human beings. The fabulous merman and mermaiden seemed to us easily accounted for. The seals observed were of two descriptions—namely, the *Pagomys fœtidus*, or "floe-rat;" and the *Pagophilus Grœnlandicus*, the "saddle-back," or common Greenland seal.

Birds, common to these regions, hovered around, following us for days together and breaking the solitude that surrounded us with their joyous and gladsome presence.

The 1st of July was a beautiful, bright, clear, sunny day, and to us was doubly welcome after the continuous bad weather which until now had been our lot. Not a ripple disturbed the calm surface of the sea as it lay blue and gleaming in the sunshine. Here and there a few small patches of ice reminded us of our proximity to the Arctic circle, while a certain sharp-bracing crispness in the air, together with a rather low temperature, served to assure us that the high snow-covered land in the distance was in reality "Greenland's icy mountains"—no hymnal myth as supposed by many, but grand ranges, devoid of all verdure, wrapped in their snowy mantle, and rising to an altitude of from two to three thousand feet above the level of the sea, a majestic and sublime reality.

By noon we were off the little Danish settlement of Fiskernaes, and shortly afterwards passed that of Godthaab, but at too great a distance to make out the buildings or any signs of inhabitants. It was at Godthaab that Hans Egede landed on July 3rd, 1721, with his wife and children, and commenced his noble and disinterested labour of love among the Eskimos. The missionary institutions founded by Hans Egede and the Moravians have gradually incorporated the whole population of Greenland into Christian communities.

The appearance of this part of the coast of Greenland was very striking, especially to those who were strangers to Arctic scenery. The mountains, with their peaks so pointed as scarcely to admit of the snow resting on their steep and almost precipitous sides, intersected by grand fiords and gorges penetrating for miles into the interior, formed a magnificent landscape.

To the great relief and joy of all, we were on this day rejoined by our consort the "Discovery," who, like ourselves, had been roughly handled by the tempestuous weather since we lost sight of her in the Atlantic.

Expecting to pass over the "Torske" banks, the dredge was prepared, and fishing lines served out; every one busy stretching and fitting their lines, and smacking their lips over an anticipated dinner of fresh cod and halibut. Soundings in thirty fathoms having been obtained on one of these banks, the ship was stopped and permission given to fish. Immediately fifty or sixty fishing lines were over the side; but, although our eager fishermen persevered for a couple of hours, no capture rewarded their patience. The "wily cod" remained sullen at the bottom, and could not even be induced to "nibble."

The dredge was also put over, and hauled in with unimportant results, only a few echinoderms being obtained.

During the night an iceberg of curious shape was passed. When first seen it was reported as a sail; on approaching it a little nearer it assumed the appearance of a huge column-shaped basaltic rock, and then that of a lighthouse; for some time it was really believed to be the former.

On the 4th of July the Arctic circle was crossed. From this date, for some weeks, we were to have continuous day. The nights had for some time past been getting gradually shorter: now they had ceased altogether—candles and lamps were no longer necessary, bright sunlight reigned paramount.

Two days afterwards the expedition was safely anchored in the bay of Lievely, off the little Danish settlement of Godhavn. Although small, it is the most important establishment in the Inspectorate of North Greenland, for here resides the Royal Inspector, who controls, with absolute authority, the large mixed population of Danes and Eskimos who inhabit this the most northern civilized land in the world.

A salute of nine guns, from a small battery of three diminutive specimens of ordnance, welcomed our arrival, the smoke from which had scarcely blown away before Mr. Krarup Smith, the Inspector, came on board, anxious to offer assistance, and desirous of extending the hospitalities of his house to the members of the expedition.

Nothing could be more kind than the reception accorded us by the inhabitants of this little settlement. Their sole desire was to please and aid us in every way, and we were soon firm and fast friends with the innocent and simple-minded residents.

CHAPTER III.

THE GREENLAND SETTLEMENTS.

" Behold I see the haven nigh at hand,
To which I meane my wearie course to bend;
Vere the maine shete and beare up with the land,
The which afore is fayrly to be kend,
And seemeth safe from stormes that may offend."
SPENSER.

IT was with a very pleasing sensation of relief that we found the ship once more at rest, after thirty-four days of such knocking about as is seldom experienced at sea for so long a time without a break. The rolling and pitching to which a small ship is subjected in a heavy sea are never altogether agreeable, and the quiet and repose of a snug well-protected harbour are welcomed even by the " veriest old sea-dog." But, although free from the turmoil of the "angry waste of waters," our short stay at Godhavn can scarcely be called a period of rest. Much had to be done, coals had to be taken on board, and a nondescript quantity of stores and provisions received from the " Valorous " and stowed away.

The days were long, however. We had arrived in the region where the midnight sun shone almost as brightly and gave as much light as at noonday; and if, in consequence, the men were kept longer at work than they otherwise would have been, they felt themselves amply compensated for their extra labour by the indulgence of a run on shore in the evening, and an open-air dance with the dusky and light-hearted beauties of the land.

Never did the deck of a man-of-war present such an untidy and confused appearance as ours did after

ESKIMO WOMEN.

receiving the last cask from the "Valorous." Casks and cases lay higgledy-piggledy amongst coals and ropes. Such a scene as our upper deck presented would have been sufficient to drive a smart first lieutenant distracted. We were, however, all much too practical to think of appearances, our sole thought was to be provided with enough of everything to guard against all accidents. Between decks was a repetition of the scene above, and it was with the greatest difficulty we could move from one part of the ship to the other. To add to the pleasing state of the vessel twenty-four Eskimo dogs—the number was afterwards augmented to thirty—were received on board, to be used in our sledging operations. Such a howling lot! No sooner did they arrive than a regular battle ensued, and we were compelled for some days to tie up a few of the most pugnacious, in order to secure anything like peace.

This state of affairs, namely, the incessant fighting and squabbling amongst the dogs, continued until one had gained the acknowledged supremacy by thrashing the whole pack. This happens in all well-regulated dog communities. The conqueror is henceforth styled the "king" dog; he rules his subjects with despotic sway, frequently settling a quarrel between a couple of pugilistic disputants, reserving for himself the best of everything in the shape of food, the other dogs yielding their tit-bits with cringing servility, exerting a complete mastery over his canine subjects, and exacting from them the most abject homage. The dogs were kept as much as possible in the fore part of the ship, and soon became great favourites with the men.

To take charge of this unruly pack, we obtained the services, through the kindness and assistance of Mr. Krarup Smith, the Inspector, of a native Eskimo, who with his gun and kayak was duly installed on board in the capacity of dog-driver and interpreter. He rejoiced in the name of Frederic, and had the reputation of being a keen and successful hunter. Although he could not boast of good looks, his bright cheerful face and unvarying good temper soon made him a friend to all on board.

The novelty of a never-ending day, for the first time experienced by so many in the expedition, sadly interfered with the natural time for rest and sleep. Long past midnight would the sounds of music and mirth be heard from the shore, as the dances were kept up with unabated vigour; while shrieks of laughter and merriment would be heard afloat, as the officers, indulging in aquatic tastes, would be seen rowing races in small collapsible boats, or trying their skill for the first time in the frail kayak. For the management of these latter fairy-like canoes great caution is required—indeed, it is hardly possible to manage them without much practice.

Our first lieutenant was, however, an exception to this rule, for owing to experience acquired in canoes in various parts of the world, he succeeded in the management of the kayak so admirably as to excite the surprise and admiration of the natives. W——, another of our officers, not to be outdone by his messmate, also tried his skill in one of these little barks, but he had not paddled many yards before it capsized, leaving him head down in the water, with his legs firmly jammed in the boat. He would undoubtedly have been drowned before assistance could arrive had he not shown a wonderful degree of presence of mind. So securely was he fixed in his kayak, that it was only by unbuttoning his braces and getting out of his trousers that he succeeded in extricating himself from his dangerous predicament, leaving that article of dress inside the kayak!

In spite of the multifarious duties connected with the ship, which kept every one fully occupied, the pursuit of science was not neglected. Several complete series of observations were obtained for the determination of the magnetic force. Photographs were taken, and geological and botanical collections were extensively made, whilst a boat with the first lieutenant and our energetic naturalist proceeded some little distance up the coast to a place called Ovifak for the purpose of obtaining information regarding some "meteorites" reported to have fallen there.

The desire of "stretching one's legs" after being cooped up on board ship for so long was universally felt, and officers and men alike enjoyed a scramble over the lofty volcanic cliffs which overlie the gneiss in this part of the island of Disco.

The difficulty of the ascent of the Lyngenmarkfjeld, a range of hills about two thousand feet in height, situated on the northern side of the harbour, was amply compensated for by the view from its summit. Landing in a pretty little bay, in which lay the remains of an old steam whaler, the "Wildfire," that had fallen a victim to the ice some years ago, and emerging from the rather dense, though stunted, vegetation that grows luxuriantly at the base of these hills, the way led over precipitous basaltic cliffs, until by dint of hard climbing the snow-clad heights were reached.

The accomplishment of this task, however, was both arduous and perilous, in consequence of the action of the frost on the rocks of which the cliffs were composed; for on the slightest touch they often crumbled away, rolling with a mass of *débris* many hundreds of feet to the bottom.

From the summit a glorious scene was revealed to us. The mainland of Greenland, that land so "wonderfull mountaynous, whose mountaynes all the yeare long are full of yce and snowe," was distinctly brought to our view, whilst immediately at our feet was the picturesque settlement of Godhavn, and the three vessels, resembling miniature toy-ships, lying at anchor in its snug little harbour. The Whale-fish Islands, a group in Disco Bay, lay spread out as it were on a map. Hundreds of icebergs dotted the perfectly placid sea, and beyond them we could plainly discern the great ice fiord of Jacobshavn with its gigantic discharging glacier behind, and the mouth of its fiord almost choked with huge fragments of ice, children of that same glacier. At brief intervals a noise as of thunder or distant artillery announced the disruption, or creation, of one of these wonderful islands of ice.

We were not, however, allowed to enjoy this glorious scene in quietness. Our pleasure was marred by the attacks of swarms of musquitoes. These irritating insects assailed us on first landing, and persecuted us incessantly until we were again afloat.

> "A cloud of cumbrous gnattes doe us molest,
> All striving to infixe their feeble stinges,
> That from their noyance we nowhere can reste."

It was indeed hard to meet so far in the icy north our implacable enemies of the tropics!

The descent was as dangerous, though perhaps not so laborious as the ascent. Occasionally we were able to avail ourselves of patches of snow, down which we slid, much to the astonishment and discomfiture of my dog Nellie, who was at a loss to understand the means of our rapid progress, and who rushed down after us barking frantically.

We were excessively fortunate in our weather during

our brief stay at Godhavn. We rejoiced in ceaseless sunshine, which lit up the surrounding hills with a golden light, throwing deep dark shadows into the valleys and ravines by which they were intersected, whilst the bright rays of the sun glittering on the ice-strewn surface of the sea formed a scene at once novel and sublime.

Our short stay at Godhavn will, I think, always be regarded with pleasure by the members of the expedition. Nothing could exceed the kindness we received and the hospitality that was extended to us by the good people on shore, who appeared to vie with each other in their endeavours to render our visit an agreeable one. Nor was it only from the inhabitants that we received so much kindness. The captain, officers, and indeed I may say the ship's company of the "Valorous" were unremitting in their exertions to provide us with every necessary that it was in their power to supply, for the furtherance of the arduous service in which we were so soon to be engaged, depriving themselves of many things that they thought would add to our comfort.

Although the Eskimos, according to Dr. Rink, and we can have no better authority respecting the natives of Greenland, have a pretty fair talent for writing and drawing, scarcely any traces of sculpture belonging to earlier times remain, with the exception of a few small images cut out in wood or bone, which had probably served children as playthings. Notwithstanding the want of means for handing down to posterity and retaining historical events amongst this interesting people, many traditions and legends have been preserved. Among the number is one relating to this island of Disco. It was supposed to have been situated off the southern coast of Greenland, and in consequence of its cutting off the inhabitants of the mainland from the open sea, a great dislike was entertained for it; for, to live comfortably, an Eskimo must be in the vicinity of the sea, so as to follow his usual avocation of seal hunting.

The story relates that two old men, having set their wise heads together, determined to attempt the removal of the island with the aid of magic. A third old gentleman, however, desired to retain it in its position. The first two, launching their kayaks, fastened the hair of a little child to the island wherewith to tow it by; whilst the other, from the shore, attempted to keep it back by means of a sealskin thong. Desperately did the two kayakers labour at their paddles in their endeavours to move the island, chanting their spells as they tugged at the hair. But as resolutely did the third man hold on to his thong, straining every nerve to render their exertions abortive; suddenly, to his chagrin, the thong parted, and the island floated off, and was towed away triumphantly to the northward, where it was deposited in its present position.

Another tradition says it was removed from Baal's River to its present site by a famous angekok, or magician, and that the harbour of Godhavn is the actual hole in the island to which the tow rope was fastened.

On the afternoon of July the 15th, amidst much firing of guns and dipping of flags, the little squadron steamed out of the harbour, threading its way through innumerable icebergs, and passing along the high snow-clad hills that adorn the southern end of the island of Disco, proceeded towards the settlement of Ritenbenk, at which we arrived the following morning.

The scenery as we approached the anchorage was truly magnificent. Lofty hills encompassed us on either hand, down whose steep sides the water was pouring in rapid cascades, produced by the thawing of the snow on their summits. How full of life and joy appeared these bright sparkling streams as they seemed to chase each other in wanton sport, skipping from rock to crag in their headlong career, until lost in one large sheet of glistening spray that poured over the edge of a precipitous cliff into the clear still water at its base!

Thousands of birds congregate along the inaccessible ledges of these cliffs, perched in such precise order, and having such a uniformity of colour, that they resemble regiments of soldiers drawn up in readiness to defend their fortresses from the attacks of ruthless invaders. But fresh food was at a premium, and the wretched looms were doomed to suffer a long assault at the hands of our energetic sportsmen.

Other and more weighty matters also required our attention. We were to bid farewell to the "Valorous" on the following morning. And with her we should lose the last connecting link with home.

Letters had to be hurriedly finished, and then we had to bid adieu to one to whose untiring energy the departure of the expedition was due, who had been mainly instrumental in obtaining the sanction of Government for its dispatch, and who, leaving the comforts of a home life, had accompanied us thus far on our journey, sharing our discomforts, but adding to our knowledge from his rich fund of information, and enlivening our mess-table with his conversation and presence.

We felt, whilst he was on board, that we were not

quite separated from the civilized world. His departure made a chasm that it was difficult for some time to bridge over, but the memory of him lived long amongst us, and served to recall many a pleasant and happy hour.

At four o'clock on the morning of the 17th the "Valorous" steamed away from us on her way to the coal quarries on the north side of the island of Disco, and, two hours after, the "Discovery" and ourselves put to sea, having increased the number of our dogs by purchasing several from the natives at Ritenbenk.

The scenery in the Waigat, a strait separating the island of Disco from the mainland of Greenland, is very grand. The channel was rendered almost impassable from the number of icebergs of every fantastic form and shape that lay scattered about, and which, although adding materially to the beauty of the scene, made the passage one of no little intricacy: indeed we very narrowly escaped losing all our boats on one side of the ship by shaving a large iceberg a little too closely!

On one side were the high snow-clad hills of Disco, intersected by deep and narrow ravines, whilst on the opposite side was a bold and lofty coast with precipitous headlands ending in needle-shaped peaks and separated by glaciers and fiords. Passing the beautiful large discharging glacier of Itivdliarsuk, many minor ones opened to our view as we sailed slowly past, presenting a panorama such as it would be impossible to depict faithfully on canvas.

Several remarkable red patches, apparently of basalt, were observed on the bare gneiss hills in the vicinity of Point Kardluk, which is noted for the large quantity of vegetable fossils that have been found there, and close to the petrified forest of Atanekerdluk.

Catching sight of the "Valorous" at anchor, busily engaged in procuring coal, we endeavoured to reach her, for the purpose of sending a few stray letters that had been inadvertently left behind; but a thick fog overtaking us, we were very reluctantly compelled to relinquish all idea of communicating, and had to be satisfied with reading the signal of "farewell" and "good wishes" that she threw out. It was fortunately distinguished before the vessels were effectually concealed from each other by an impervious fog which crept over the surface of the sea, hiding everything around us, though high above our heads the mountain tops were clearly to be seen.

So dense did it become that we were, after a time, obliged to make the ships fast to icebergs to await a more favourable opportunity of advancing.

Whilst attempting to secure the ships an alarming catastrophe occurred. The boat had been dispatched containing three men with the necessary implements, such as an ice drill and anchor, for making the vessel fast.

As soon as the first blow of the drill was delivered the berg, to our horror, split in two with a loud report, one half with one of our men on it toppling completely over, whilst the other half swayed rapidly backwards and forwards. On this latter piece was another of our men, who was observed with his heels in the air, the violent agitation of the berg having precipitated him head foremost into a rent or crevasse. The water alongside was a mass of seething foam and spray; but curious to relate, the boat with the third man in it was in no way injured. They were all speedily rescued from their perilous position and brought on board, sustaining no further harm than that inflicted by a cold bath. Their escape appeared miraculous.

By the next morning we were through the Waigat Strait. Much to our disappointment the weather remained thick, and we were in consequence unable to gratify ourselves with a sight of the truly grand scenery to be found at the mouth of the Omenak fiord, which possesses some of the largest discharging glaciers in Greenland.

On the night of the 19th both vessels came to an anchor off the Danish settlement of Proven.

The harbour, which is small, is formed by two islands. On the western side of the easternmost of the two is situated the quaintest of quaint little settlements. It consists of a neat little church, the Governor's residence, the storehouse, boiling down establishment, smithy, about two other wooden habitations, and some igdlus, or Eskimo huts. Of course it boasts its flagstaff and battery of three guns. The Governor, who, in his endeavour to be civil, had boarded us before anchoring, apologized for not saluting, saying "that though he had the guns he had no artillerists." Although it was midnight before we arrived, the inhabitants were lining the side of the hill as we entered, the white boots and fur jackets and short trousers of the women affording a very novel though picturesque scene.

The dogs on shore, evidently annoyed at being disturbed in their slumbers, set up a fearful howling, which, being answered by the dogs in both ships, produced a most unpleasant and discordant concert. The natives have a saying, when the dogs make this noise, "that they are holding their parliament." This is hardly flattering to the Greenland senate!

During our short stay at this place a rough survey of the harbour was taken, and a number of scientific observations were made.

Nothing could be kinder or more friendly than the reception met with from all on shore. In the Governor's good wife I recognized an old acquaintance whom I had had the pleasure of meeting on a former occasion during a cruise in a whaler to these regions.

Here also we succeeded in engaging the services of Hans Hendrik, an Eskimo, as dog-driver and hunter. This man had been employed in the same capacity in all the American expeditions to Smith's Sound, and was an invaluable acquisition.

Our men enjoyed themselves every evening during our stay, dancing to their hearts' content.

My black retriever, Nellie, was a great object of admiration amongst the inhabitants, one man especially being very pertinacious in his request that she might be presented to him. On inquiring to what use he would put her, I was informed that my faithful companion would be converted into food for the man's oily-faced family, whilst her beautiful black curly coat would serve to adorn his wife's person. Nellie, I think, had some notion of the designs on her life and skin, as in future she always regarded with disfavour not only the Eskimos themselves, but also their dogs and everything belonging to them.

Leaving Proven on the evening of the 21st of July, we arrived on the same night off a remarkable headland called "Sanderson, his hope." It was so named by old John Davis, after his friend and patron, Mr.

W. Sanderson, in 1587, and was the extreme northern point reached by him during his third voyage.*

This prominent and precipitous cliff is a famous place for looms, as those white-breasted guillemots are termed, which are considered such rare delicacies on an Arctic table. They are the *Uria Brunichii* of naturalists, and are numerous in sub-Arctic regions. Their favourite breeding-places are along these terraced cliffs, where they assemble in large quantities.

Of course so favourable an opportunity of procuring fresh food was not to be disregarded. The ships were hove to, and the boats, crammed with eager sportsmen, dispatched for the purpose of shooting for the "pot."

Myriads of these birds were congregated along the face of the steep precipitous cliffs, in some places almost overhanging, which rose abruptly to an altitude of about a thousand feet. Owing, however, to the unsteadiness of the boats, caused by the roughness of the sea, our "bag" did not realize our anticipations. Many of the birds that were shot remained on the inaccessible ledges of the rocks, and were therefore lost to us; and many fell into the sea beyond, and were no more seen.

The midnight sun was shining brightly during this *battue,* and we returned to the ship, after a couple of hours' sport, the richer by one hundred and seventy birds, each equal in weight to a fair-sized duck. For the succeeding three or four days we revelled in "loom soup," "loom pie," or "roast loom," and

---

* On his return to England he wrote to his friend, saying, "I have been in 73°, finding the sea all open and forty leagues between land and land. The passage (the N.W.) is most probable, the execution easie, as at my coming you shall fully knowe."

looms cooked in every imaginable form. No matter how they were served up, they were always pronounced to be delicious. Indeed, one of my messmates went so far as to say that he had never tasted anything better in his life. In fact, for the purpose of thoroughly enjoying a good dinner, a trip to the Arctic regions is indispensable!

On the following morning we anchored off Upernivik,* the most northern settlement but one in Greenland. It is situated on one of the Woman Islands, so named by Baffin in 1616. The usual kindness and hospitality were extended to us here, as at all the other Danish settlements visited. We also received important information concerning the state of the ice to the northward, with a tabulated statement of all the meteorological observations obtained during the previous winter, a study of which would be of the greatest importance to us.

In the evening, taking the "Discovery" in tow, we again put to sea, this time finally bidding farewell to civilization. From henceforth our energies and our thoughts must turn Polewards.

As the last glimpse of the little church was shut out from our view, many a prayer was silently offered to Him in his infinite mercy to protect and guide us in our endeavours, and to vouchsafe us a safe return again to home and civilization.

---

* It is sometimes spelt Uppernavik. But Upernivik is the correct form. See Rink, p. 354. It means spring in the Eskimo language. Upernivik is in 72° 48′ N. The most northern Danish station is Tasiusak, in 73° 21′ N.

CHAPTER IV.

MELVILLE BAY AND THE NORTH WATER.

"Embark with me, while I new tracts explore,
With flying sails and breezes from the shore.
Not that my song, in such a scanty space,
So large a subject fully can embrace.
Not though I were supplied with iron lungs,
A hundred mouths, filled with as many tongues.
But steer my vessel with a steady hand,
And coast along the shore in sight of land.
Nor will I try thy patience with a train
Of preface, or what ancient poets feign."
VIRGIL.

THREADING our way through narrow passages between numerous islands that lay to the eastward of Upernivik, and trusting to the knowledge and guidance of an Eskimo pilot, we felt at length that we had in reality, seen the last for some time, of our fellow men, and that our struggle with the almost insuperable difficulties of the frozen north was about to commence.

Preparations for an unsuccessful combat with the ice were made, and every precaution was adopted necessary to ensure the safety of the men, in cases of extreme emergency. The boats were prepared for immediate service, each man having his allotted station, so that little or no confusion would ensue if the abandonment of the ships should be decided upon—an event that was by no means improbable. Ice-saw crews were organized in readiness for cutting a dock, in case such a proceeding should become necessary for the protection of the vessels. Provisions and clothes were so arranged along the upper deck that they could easily and readily be thrown out on the ice at a moment's notice. Knapsacks, each containing two pairs of blanket wrappers, one pair of hose, one pair of stockings, one pair of mitts, one pair of drawers, a Welsh wig, a jersey, a comforter, a pair of moccasins, a towel and small piece of soap, were packed and placed in some handy position where they could be reached without delay. The necessary tackles for lifting the screw and unshipping the rudder were provided: in fact every preparation was made that could possibly be thought of to guard against accidents and to promote success in the forthcoming conflict.

On the morning after leaving Upernivik, on account of a dense fog, it was determined to anchor off one of the small islands composing a group through which we were passing, in order to wait for finer weather.

Our pilot, getting into his kayak, offered to pioneer us into a little bay with which he was intimately acquainted. Being totally unable to realize the difference of size between the large unwieldy "Alert" and his own frail little bark, and probably imagining that where he was able to go in his tiny boat, we also could do the same, he led us close in to the land, which, on account of the thick fog, was hidden from our view, and we soon had the annoyance of finding our ship hard and fast on shore. Fortunately we were going very slow at the time, so that no injury was sustained; but we remained immoveable for many hours until the flood-tide floated us and enabled us once more to proceed.

The dangers connected with a passage through Melville Bay are now so well known to all who have taken any interest in Arctic affairs, or who have devoted any time to the perusal of Arctic literature, that it is needless for me either to explain or dwell upon them at any length. Many a well-equipped ship has been caught in the fatal embrace of this bay. What tales of woe and disaster could its icy waters unfold, coupled, however, with deeds of heroic daring, endurance, and suffering!

Captain Nares, determining to avoid the ordinary passage through this once dreaded bay, the dangers of which in these days of steam have been so materially lessened, pushed his ships boldly through what is generally termed the " middle ice." This, at such a late season of the year, is undoubtedly a wise course; but woe to the unfortunate ship that at an earlier period should be caught in this moving pack, and be there detained for thirteen or fourteen months, as the little " Fox " was, under the command of Sir Leopold McClintock!

If the pack is composed of loose light ice, such as we found it to be, rendering a passage through it one of no difficulty, it may also be presumed that the ice in Melville Bay at the same time would be of the same consistency, thereby also affording an easy and safe passage through.

The reason that the passage by Melville Bay is always taken by the whalers is the existence of fixed land ice, which is found adhering to the shores, and

in which it is easy to cut a dock for the preservation
of the ship if the heavy pack is forced by wind, or
otherwise, towards it, thereby endangering any vessel
that may happen to be between the two. Directly
the pack moves off the vessel is liberated and proceeds
on her voyage.

It would be very different if the ship was caught in
the pack. Then she would, in all probability, be
severely handled, and being beset would drift to the
southward with the ice and thereby lose all the
hard-fought ground gained with so much labour and
fatigue.

One of the most important maxims in ice navigation, which is strictly followed out by the whalers, is
" stick to the land-ice."

We were certainly extremely fortunate in finding
the pack so "loose" as to give us little trouble or
difficulty in making progress. The ice was of a soft
"brashy" nature, apparently only of one year's
formation, and only from one to three feet in thickness. The weather being fine and calm, advantage
was taken of it to steam full speed, for there was no
saying how quickly the ice might pack with even a
light breeze. The tow rope was accordingly cast off,
and we proceeded at our highest rate of speed with
the "Discovery" following close at our heels.

Occasionally our progress would be checked by a
stream of ice extending across the lane of water
through which we were steering; but through these
obstructions we bored, or charged them at full speed,
and thus cleared a way. A walrus and a few seals
were seen on the ice, but their capture did not hold
out sufficient inducement to detain the ship.

Very different from the apathy shown on passing

these animals was the excitement exhibited when a bear, a veritable Polar bear, was seen on the ice. Such a rush for rifles and weapons of all descriptions! It was the first and only bear seen, and therefore the excitement its presence caused was natural. Every one appeared to share in it. Bear-skins were certainly on that day at a premium, for all were eager and anxious to become the fortunate possessor of such a prize. Master Bruin, however, did not reciprocate this feeling, and evinced an equal amount of anxiety to retain his nice warm coat.

The engines were immediately stopped, and the boats crammed with volunteer hunters. These landing on the ice, advanced upon their quarry in skirmishing order, while the ship, steaming round to the opposite side of the floe, endeavoured to cut off his retreat. All was ineffectual. Bruin's strategic abilities were of too high an order for us to cope successfully with him in his own territories, and he escaped. Many rounds of ammunition, however, were fired at him both from the party on shore and also by those on board the ship, in the faint hope that a lucky shot might bring him down. To this day there are many who seriously believe that he carried away with him a portion of the bullets they so lavishly expended. So keen were some in the ardour and excitement of the chase that they rushed on, heedless of the rotten and treacherous nature of the ice, until an immersion in the cold water brought them to a sense of their danger and compelled them to seek refuge on board the ship, wet, cold, and uncomfortable. Many little rotges (*Alca alle*) were flitting about from the ice to the water, and the beautiful ivory gull (*Larus eburneus*) was also seen for the first time.

POLAR BEARS.

In thirty-four hours from first encountering the ice we reached the North Water, and our troubles were for a time at an end. It was an unprecedented passage. Only seventy hours from Upernivik to Cape York!

Melville Bay, with all its terrors, was behind us; a beautifully smooth unruffled sea, devoid of all ice, was in front; everything pointed to success, and the hearts of all in the expedition beat high with joy and delight at the speedy prospect of attaining the utmost realization of their hopes. Large icebergs were around us in every direction; but what cared we then for icebergs? We had continuous day; the North Water had been reached; our way lay northwards. In a few short days the entrance of Smith Sound would be reached, the threshold of the unknown region crossed, and then onwards to—where? We did not dare to anticipate, but we felt that the first step towards success had been gained, and that we had commenced our real work under most propitious circumstances. We would not predict, but we determined to deserve, success.

It was, for many reasons, a matter of congratulation that this "North Water" had been so speedily and so successfully reached. Instead of only two or three weeks of the navigable season being available for us to penetrate the hidden mysteries of Smith Sound, owing to our rapid passage, we could reckon upon a clear month or five weeks before being compelled to secure our ship in winter quarters; besides which, our fuel had been very materially saved by this quick run, and this in itself, to ships situated as we were, was no unimportant matter.

On reaching the neighbourhood of Cape York, the

"Discovery" was ordered to proceed shorewards for the purpose of communicating with the natives (the Arctic Highlanders of Sir John Ross), in the hope of inducing one of their number, a brother-in-law of Hans, to accompany the expedition; the "Alert" in the mean time shaping a course to the Cary Islands, at which latter place the "Discovery" was ordered to rejoin us.

The scenery, as we steamed along at a distance of about two miles from the shore, was most interesting. The hills along the coast were entirely clad with snow, whilst the long undulating ranges, as they receded far back to the horizon, appeared to be buried under the everlasting *mer de glace*. Numerous glaciers of various sizes, some of them being discharging ones, rolled down to the water's edge in one vast icy sheet. The width of one of these, the Petowik Glacier, is fully seven miles. Fragments from these lay scattered along the coast in every direction, whilst we had to thread our way through clusters of huge bergs of every form and size. Passing the crimson cliffs of Beverley, we were able to distinguish, in a few small patches, the so-called coloured snow whence the name originates; but not in the highly imaginative mass of bright colour depicted by Sir John Ross, in his interesting illustrated work describing his voyage to Baffin Bay. The question of the nature of this colouring matter on snow has now been definitely set at rest. It is an alga, the *Protococcus nivalis*.

We did not reach the Cary Islands so soon as we expected, in consequence of experiencing a strong S.E. current that had not been anticipated. A sudden rise of temperature of the surface water naturally led us to suppose that it must be due to the absence of ice, which, raising our spirits, made us regard with displeasure any hindrance to our progress.

Arriving off the Cary group early on the morning of the 27th, we were detained for a few hours landing a boat with a large depôt of provisions, sufficient to sustain 60 men for two months, or 120 men for one month. The depôt was placed on the easternmost island, and a large cairn was erected on the highest and most prominent point. Here also were deposited the last home letters which our friends were destined to received until after our own arrival in England.

The depôt was established as a safeguard for us to fall back upon in case of any accident happening to our vessels in Smith Sound. From this position it was expected that a party duly provisioned would have little difficulty in reaching the northern Greenland settlements, or at any rate the simple but hospitable natives of Cape York, who would, it was anticipated, afford us protection and assistance. This duty having been accomplished, and having been rejoined by our consort, the northward course was resumed.*

Crossing over to the eastward we steamed along on that beautifully clear sunny morning within a short distance of the western shores of Greenland. With the exception of icebergs, not a speck of ice was to be seen to disturb the smooth glassy surface of the sea. Passing the mouth of Whale Sound we made rapid

* The Cary Islands consist of a group of eight islands, besides small rocks or islets, and are situated in Baffin Bay, in lat. 76° 45′ N. They vary in size from two and a half miles in diameter downwards. They are composed of syenitic and porphyritic granite, overlaid in places with gneiss. They rise to a height of about 400 feet above the level of the sea, and possess a luxuriant vegetation, at least for these regions. They are much frequented as breeding places by the eider-ducks and looms.

progress northwards, steering between Northumberland and Hakluyt Islands, almost under their steep, precipitous, and in some places overhanging cliffs; on past Murchison Sound with the Crystal Palace glacier ahead, whilst on our port bow was easily discernible the opposite coast of Ellesmere Land, with the Prince of Wales Mountains, covered with snow or ice, rising above the western horizon.

It was indeed a glorious sight as we passed close to this little known land, opening out, as we proceeded, its many and large glaciers glittering white and radiant in the sunshine, growing, as it were, out of the clouds and rolling down grandly towards the sea, until the opaque masses plunged sullenly and silently into the deep blue water.

Animal life, so far as the feathered tribes were concerned, appeared in abundance. The lively little rotges or little auks (*Alca alle*) were seen in frequent clusters diving quickly under water as the ship approached. Looms (*Uria Brunnichii*), dovekies (*Uria grylle*), and king-ducks (*Somateria spectabilis*), alarmed at our appearance, rose in long flights, and circled around us uttering their discordant cries. The glaucous gull and the pretty kittiwake (*Larus tridactylus*) soared above our heads, whilst occasionally a graceful ivory gull (*Larus eburneus*) flapped its way leisurely along, its snowy wings contrasting with the background of clear blue sky. Here and there, on small fragments of floating ice, were seen huge walruses basking in the golden sunshine. Amid such scenes, which to be realized must be seen, the two vessels wended their way towards the entrance of Smith Sound, all elated with the fair prospect that was before them and hopeful for the future.

At half-past seven on the morning of the 28th of July both ships came to an anchor in Hartstene Bay, more commonly known as Port Foulke, the harbour in which Dr. Hayes wintered in 1860.

CHAPTER V.

SMITH SOUND.

> "Now far he sweeps, where scarce a summer smiles,
> On Behring's rocks, or Greenland's naked isles.
> Cold on his midnight watch the breezes blow,
> From wastes that slumber in eternal snow,
> And waft across the waves' tumultuous roar
> The wolf's long howl from Oonalaska's shore."
>
> CAMPBELL.

No sooner were the ships secured and breakfast discussed, than there was a regular rush for the shore. Some went for a scramble over the neighbouring glacier, named by Dr. Kane, "My brother John's glacier;" some went to collect specimens; others to take various scientific observations; and others to hunt and shoot — this spot having been found wonderfully prolific of game, more especially of reindeer, during Dr. Hayes's stay. No signs of any inhabitants were visible. This surprised us, as we were fully expecting to meet the natives of the village of Etah, situated only a couple of miles from the anchorage. A visit to the village during the course of the day proved the huts to be standing, but quite deserted. Traces of their having been recently inhabited were manifest, and portions of seal and walrus meat were discovered in *caches,* as if the migration was only temporary and a return was meditated. No other signs, however, of any living human being were found.

Leaving to others the exploration of the country in the immediate vicinity of the harbour, Captain Nares and myself started, in one of the whale-boats, with four men, for the purpose of visiting Life-boat Cove, where some of the officers and crew of the "Polaris" spent their second winter, 1872-3, and also to search for an iron boat on Littleton Island, said to have been left there by Dr. Hayes in 1860.

Sailing round Sunrise Point, we encountered a fresh northerly wind dead in our teeth, against which, under oars, we made but slow progress, whilst the cold spray flew aft into our faces where it almost froze. After about five hours' hard pulling Life-boat Cove was reached, and very glad we all were to get on shore and stretch our legs and restore the circulation of our blood.

Immediately on landing we met with traces of the late occupants. These consisted of a large cairn—which, however, had been demolished by others previous to our arrival, probably by the searching expedition sent out in the "Tigress" in 1873—a basket lined with tin, and a trunk, neither of which contained anything of importance; indeed, their contents and the strong odour prervading them convinced us that they were now the property of Eskimos. Strolling on a little further, a boat was seen, which, although somewhat of European shape, appeared to be of Eskimo construction, as it was simply a framework covered with skins; yet it was undoubtedly built under a white man's superintendence.

Continuing to advance until we reached the western

extreme of the spit of land on which we had landed, we conjectured, from the amount of *débris* by which we were surrounded, although no remains of a house were visible, that we were on the site of the Americans' winter quarters. Trunks, boxes, stoves, pieces of wood, gun-barrels, and odds and ends of all descriptions lay strewed about over an area of half a square mile—a desolate scene of ruin and misery!

Some of the boxes were marked with the names of their previous owners, and contained, amongst other things, books, principally relating to the Arctic regions. One trunk contained a few small articles of female apparel, such as a lace collar and black veil, and some faded ribbons; souvenirs from some fair damsel at home, which had probably, from the thoughts their presence created, beguiled many a long and lonely hour during the monotonous winter night. Numerous cairns and *caches*, under which were deposited lumps of seal blubber, led us to suppose that the natives intended returning, especially with such a mine of wealth to attract them as an abundance of wood and iron, so invaluable to an Eskimo.

Two other boats were also found, constructed in the same rude manner as the first. On one was painted, in good large letters, the word MAUMOKPO; though what it meant we were at a loss to conceive, but concluded it was an Icelandic name.

Two Casella thermometers, marked as low as 130° below zero, were also picked up in perfect order. It is to be regretted that these were not self-registering maximum and minimum thermometers, as it would have been most interesting to have ascertained the greatest amount of heat and cold at this spot during a period of more than two years.

Collecting everything that we considered of the least value, such as books and instruments, for the purpose of returning them to the United States Government, and taking possession of a couple of boats, which we thought would prove useful at some of our depôts, we embarked and proceeded towards Littleton Island, with our prizes in tow. Diligent search was made for the pendulum said to have been left by the "Polaris" people, but without success: also for the box chronometers and transit instrument, but with a like result. We could only come to the conclusion that, if these articles had been left there, somebody had been before us. Every cairn and *cache* was thoroughly examined, and so was every nook and crannie within a radius of half a mile from where we imagined the house had originally stood. A chronometer-box was picked up, but empty.

On landing at Littleton Island a careful search was instituted for Hayes's boat, but, although we made the complete circuit of the island, we failed to discover any traces of it whatever. At the south-west end we erected a cairn on the highest hill, about five or six hundred feet above the level of the sea, and obtained a round of angles with the theodolite. The view from the top of this hill was very cheering. Cape Sabine was distinctly visible; whilst farther to the northward could be seen the land about Cape Fraser, with *no signs of ice!* We were, however, too wary to indulge to excess in hopeful anticipations, knowing full well the vagaries of our capricious enemy, the ice; but still such a scene could not but tend to cheer and exhilarate, and send us back to our ship with light and buoyant hearts.

It was past midnight before we reached the

"Alert." Our sportsmen, we found, had been unsuccessful in their endeavours to shoot any reindeer; one, however, fell to the rifle of an officer of the "Discovery." Very few were seen, and those so wild as to render an approach within range no easy matter. Several ducks and a few hares, however, were obtained.

Leaving Port Foulke on the following morning, we crossed over to the west side, and erected a large cairn on the summit of Cape Isabella, about one thousand feet above the level of the sea. The ascent of this headland was both arduous and dangerous. The face of the cliff was very precipitous, and it was only by a zig-zag course that it could be effected. At one moment the way led over loose shingle, that gave way under the feet at every step; at another over a broad patch of frozen snow, one false step on whose slippery surface would precipitate one many hundred feet below; and at another we were clinging desperately with hands and feet to the hard, smooth, syenitic granite rocks, of which this cape is composed. Very thankful were we when the summit was reached; but much more so when we found ourselves again at its base, sound in wind and limb. To add to the difficulties, there was a high wind and dense snowstorm.

At a less high elevation, and in a secure niche amongst the rocks, were deposited an empty cask and about one hundred and fifty pounds of preserved beef. The cask was intended for the reception of any letters that might be brought up by a Government ship in the following year, or by any enterprising and adventurous whaling captain who should penetrate so far in order to bring us news. The provisions were left as a small depôt for any sledging party that might be dispatched to the southward. The site was marked by a small cairn. Records were left at each of these cairns detailing the movements and the prospects of the expedition, together with instructions regarding our letters, should any be brought thus far.

Some beautiful little yellow poppies were gathered on the slopes and crests of the hill, whilst the draba and saxifrage were found growing in profusion.

The navigation of these icy seas is most uncertain! Within twenty-four hours of the time that, from the summit of Littleton Island, we had been cheered by the view of an apparently open sea free of ice, and extending in our imagination for miles to the northward, we were battling with the pack, consisting of large floes and loose broken-up fields, that extended on both sides of us and as far north as we could see. From this period our troubles commenced; from this date our progress was one endless and unceasing struggle with the ice: ever on the watch, and never allowing a favourable opportunity to pass unheeded.

Shortly after leaving Cape Isabella the ice was observed stretching across Baird Inlet—the fixed land ice with loose detached streams. As we proceeded more ice was seen, which by degrees completely surrounded us, and we only succeeded, after much boring and charging, in forcing a way through, and into a well-protected little harbour to the southward of Cape Sabine. This bay was formed by a deep indentation in the land having a long jutting-out spit to the S.E. which acted as a famous breakwater, and was protected seawards by Brevoort Island. Here we were detained for five days, although several attempts were made to proceed, which resulted in one instance in a hopeless besetment in the ice for some hours. The pack was impenetrable; our only hope was to wait patiently for a strong wind to open out a passage. The place was in consequence called "Bide-a-wee" Harbour, subsequently changed to Payer Harbour, after the distinguished Austrian Arctic explorer of that name.

During our detention the time of the officers was not unprofitably spent. A rough survey of the place was made, its position was correctly ascertained, a series of magnetic observations were obtained, and long walks were taken in the neighbourhood, during which a large and rich collection was made in the interests of geology and botany. No game of any description was seen. Traces of Eskimo were discovered, but evidently of an ancient date. They consisted of the remains of igdlus or huts, also some bone spear-heads, and the runners and crossbars of a sledge.* Tidal observations were also taken in the harbour.

Here also, it may be said, we received our first lessons in the art of sledging; for, wishing to be initiated into its mysteries, a party, consisting of four officers and five men dragging one of our large twenty-feet ice boats on a sledge, started to travel over the pack. Our main object was of course to derive some practical experience in this all-important mode of Arctic exploration, and in this, I think, we succeeded.

We found the ice exceedingly hummocky, with narrow water spaces between, *just* too broad to admit

---

* The fact of one of these spear-heads being tipped with iron, although they all bear the semblance of great age, would lead one to suppose that the tribe by whom it was left must have had some intercourse with Europeans, unless meteoric iron was used. This would be a very interesting question to decide.

of our jumping over, yet not sufficiently wide to launch the boat into. So rough was the road that at one time the bows of the boat would be seen rising almost perpendicularly in the air, whilst all hands were engaged in long-standing pulls on the drag-ropes to the tune of "one, two, three, haul;" at another time the sledge would come down the side of a hummock with such rapidity as to give us hardly time to spring out of the way to avoid the sledge and boat coming over us, and many were the falls in consequence. It was, however, rare fun. Once while launching the boat into a pool of water she nearly capsized; as it was she half filled, and everything inside—provisions, clothes, instruments, guns, and ammunition—was thoroughly saturated. A gold watch that happened to be in a coat pocket was not improved by its immersion.

Another source of amusement during our stay in this harbour was chasing "unies," as narwhals are invariably called by the whalers; but, although a good deal of patience and perseverance was displayed in attempts to harpoon them, these qualities were never rewarded, and the boats always returned unsuccessful from their pursuit.

Our little check in this harbour produced a slight despondency in those who, for the previous few days, had been most sanguine of pushing on. This was always alluded to in the ward-room as the depression of the social barometer, and was for the future daily registered!

On the morning of the 4th of August, a southerly gale having blown all the previous night, a channel of open water was visible as far as Cape Sabine. This was an opportunity not to be lost. Accordingly, at 4 A.M., the anchors were weighed, and, before a fresh but bitter cold wind, both ships made sail, and succeeded, after having made so many futile attempts, in rounding the Cape. Bearing away to the westward we steered up Hayes Sound, keeping close in to the land, the grounded icebergs giving us timely notice of shoal water. At noon, opening a perfectly land-locked bay, and the ice being so closely packed ahead as to defy farther progress, the vessels were steered for the entrance, and we soon found ourselves in a beautiful inlet enclosed by high land, but bounded on one side by one of the grandest sights it is possible to behold: two enormous glaciers coming from different directions, but converging at their termination. They reminded us of two huge giants silently attempting to push and force each other away.

It was indeed a noble sight, and filled us with impatient curiosity for the moment when we could land and indulge in a closer inspection.

Accordingly, the anchors were no sooner let go than several started for the purpose of paying it a visit. Landing abreast of the ship, we had rather a rough and tumble sort of a scramble over loose masses of gneiss, until we emerged on the banks of the bed of the glacier—that is, the bed formed by the water running from the glacier during the summer thaws. The walking was most laborious, at one moment through a wet swampy bog, and at another over rough sharp-pointed stones.

The vegetation appeared luxuriant, and we found the traces of musk-oxen, reindeer, wolves, foxes, and hares in abundance; but, although we were provided with guns, we failed to secure any game, for the simple reason that we saw none. But the traces of musk-oxen were very fresh, and several horns of the reindeer were picked up. After a tedious walk of about four or five miles we arrived at the glacier—the stupendous and sublime work of ages. How insignificant and despicable did we appear in comparison to this gigantic creation of Nature! I can compare it to nothing except, perhaps, a frozen Niagara! The left-hand glacier was rounded off, like a huge icy wave to its end, whilst it receded from our view in long milky undulations until lost in the clouds. The right-hand one—the lateral and terminal sides of which were quite precipitous—was pressing against its neighbour until it had raised a slight ridge between the two. We were naturally desirous of ascending one or both of these glaciers, but time would not admit of such an undertaking, and we were therefore compelled to content ourselves by standing upon a small projection of each glacier, so as to be able to say that we had been on them.

That Eskimos had visited this locality was certain; for we discovered on our way out the site of an old settlement, and on the way back we observed two large cairns that had evidently been used as *caches*.

Alexandra Bay and Twin Glacier Valley, as they were henceforth designated, were the nearest approach to an Arctic paradise that we saw during our sojourn in the Polar Regions. A sheltered and well-protected harbour, with a locality abounding in game of various descriptions, are of such importance that it is impossible to prize them too highly. They should be the first and grand objects to be taken into consideration whilst selecting a spot for winter quarters.

Although we were not fortunate in obtaining game during our stay of only a few hours in this interesting neighbourhood, I have not the slightest doubt that, had we penetrated a little farther into the interior, or had we remained here a day or two longer, we should have been rewarded by an ample supply, the traces that we observed being both numerous and recent.

From tidal observations made during our brief stay in this harbour, we found that the flood tide in Hayes Sound came from the eastward, but that the ebb coming from the westward was the strongest. Whether Hayes Sound was a strait opening out to the westward or only a deep inlet was, and remains, a matter of uncertainty.

CHAPTER VI.

STRUGGLES WITH THE ICE.

" On those great waters now I am,
    Of which I have been told,
That whosoever hither came
    Should wonders there behold.

" Trim thou the sails, and let good speed
    Accompany our haste;
Sound thou the channels at our need,
    And anchor for us cast.

" A fit and favourable wind
    To further us provide,
And let it wait on us behind,
    Or lackey by our side."
                      GEORGE WITHER.

THE morning following our arrival in Alexandra Harbour saw us again battling with the ice in Hayes Sound, having been deluded into leaving our comfortable snug quarters by the report that the pack had drifted to the eastward, leaving a navigable channel extending to the north. The report was fallacious, but we succeeded in threading our way to the N.W. for about twenty miles, when both ships were helplessly beset, with but little hope of extrication without a shift of wind.

Many broad glaciers were in view, winding their

long white snaky lengths between the hills, some of which could be traced into the interior for ten or twelve miles, or until lost in illimitable space.

In twenty-four hours, the ice slackening enabled us to bore a way through, eventually emerging into a broad stream of water. How sudden and wonderful are the changes in these regions! From being closely beset, a couple of hours saw us in an apparently open sea with *no ice* in sight, and bowling along before a fresh southerly gale at the rate of seven knots. Social barometer very high! In the morning not a spoonful of water to be seen in any direction, in the evening not a vestige of ice!

Passing close to the western shore we were able to confirm our views regarding the Henry and Bache Islands of Hayes. They are undoubtedly connected, and therefore not islands; but whether they were also connected with the mainland we were not able to determine. In all probability the supposed islands are a peninsula, apparently of sandstone formation overlying trap, different to the granitic formation of the southern shore of the strait. The land appeared quite bare of vegetation, and bore a strong resemblance to the Silurian limestone formation of the land about Prince Regent Inlet, showing stratifications dipping to the northward at an angle of about 6°.

It does not do to indulge too freely in vain hopes in these regions. A period of eight hours was sufficient to cause our hopeful anticipations of a grand run to the northward to be "considerably eased down;" for in that time we were again stopped by the ice, and compelled to make fast to a floe, until the pack opened sufficiently to allow us to proceed. During the run we passed some very heavy floes—heavier than anything we had hitherto met, and quite sufficient in themselves to crush any unfortunate ship that should happen to get nipped between two of them.

Off Albert Head great excitement was caused by the floe, to which both ships were secured, being driven towards a large grounded iceberg. To be squeezed between the two would be fatal. Our destruction seemed inevitable. Yet we on board were helpless to avert the catastrophe. All that we could do was to prepare for a severe nip: unship the rudder, and lift the screw, and having taken every precaution to ensure the safety of the crew, in the event of the ship's demolition, we could only look on, and in silence witness, as we thought, the irresistible and destroying powers of the Ice-King.

The "Discovery" was at first in the most critical position, but a slight swerving of the floe relieved her from any immediate danger, whilst the same movement of the ice intensified our own.

Nearer and more swiftly were we hurried towards the grim and motionless berg, up whose sides the floe, as it came into contact with it, was seen to be literally walking and forcing its way, crumbling and falling into shapeless masses at its base.

Escape appeared impossible. It seemed hard at the very commencement of our voyage thus to lose our ship, and with it all hopes of success. Suddenly, when our fate seemed almost decided, the berg turned slightly, splitting up the floe to which we were secured and sending us clear. It was a narrow shave, and although we suffered a slight nip, no material damage was sustained.

Being myself too fully occupied with the work on

deck, one of my messmates kindly packed a few of my valuables together, ready to take away in case of having to abandon the ship. On going below after the ship had been secured, I found carefully packed in a haversack my journals, Bible and Prayer-Book, a few photographs, and three boxes of sardines!

It must not be supposed that we passed in idleness those days that we were beset in the ice and unable to advance. As a rule our time was more fully occupied then than when we had leads of water in which we could proceed. Steam had to be kept ready for any sudden emergency, and a constant watch had to be kept on every movement of the pack. Frequently had the ice anchors to be tripped and the vessel moved, in order to avoid bergs or floes closing in upon and nipping us. Occasionally, when the pack opened, or appeared what we called "slack," we would attempt to bore through; but as this invariably entailed a large consumption of fuel, and gave very little result, it was not resorted to more than was absolutely necessary. Every opening in the ice was taken advantage of, by which we slowly but surely made progress northwards.

The crow's-nest was never deserted. In it Captain Nares might almost be said to live, rarely coming on deck even for his meals; as for a night's rest, such a thing to him was quite unknown. From the "nest" the motions of the ice were closely scrutinized, the tides and currents were studied, and the influence of the wind on the pack ascertained. No opportunity was ever lost, and it was entirely due to this unceasing watchfulness that the expedition succeeded in advancing, although it was only inch by inch.

Victoria Head was reached on the morning of the 8th of August, but at the expense of damaged rudder-heads to both ships, caused by the constant backing into the ice whilst engaged in charging and breaking through slight streams that offered impediments to our advance. A detention here enabled us to pay the shore a visit. Great difficulty was experienced in landing on account of the ice-foot adhering to the land, which resembled a perpendicular frozen wall rising to the height of about twelve feet. Indeed it was more overhanging than perpendicular, as the action of the water had considerably undermined its base and therefore rendered it almost inacessible. By the aid of a long boat-hook staff and some rope we succeeded in clambering up, at the expense of bruised hands, the jagged surface of the ice cutting like penknives. This proceeding was not unattended by a certain amount of danger, for had the ice given way we should have been precipitated into the boat, in which case we should have been extremely lucky to have escaped without a fractured bone or limb.

The loose and rugged slabs of slaty limestone of which the hills were composed made the walking very arduous, added to which a thick fog and snowstorm that overtook us rendered our climb unprofitable so far as ascertaining the nature of the ice to seaward and the prospect of pushing on were concerned. The steep cliffs surrounding this prominent headland are wasted and worn by the combined effects of snow and weather, and present the same "battlemented" appearance so common to the Silurian limestone formation of the cliffs about Prince Regent Inlet and Lancaster Sound. A few fossils were collected, but, with the exception of some sprigs of the stunted willow and a single tuft of saxifrage, the land was devoid of all vegetation. Deep ravines stretched away into the interior, entirely free from both snow and ice. Traces of former inhabitants were discovered along the beach, consisting of the site of an Eskimo settlement and a few small cairns or fox-traps.

Hitherto the traces of these interesting tribes have been continuous along the western side of Smith Sound, and tend, in my opinion, to prove conclusively that the Eskimos were in former days far more numerous than they are at the present time. What has become of them? The solution of this important ethnological question would be of the greatest interest. Have they gradually died out? or have they migrated farther south, and are now represented by the "Arctic Highlanders," and by tribes settled on both sides of Lancaster Sound who are frequently visited by our whalers?

It is certain that at some remote time there was a movement of Eskimo tribes from Asia towards Greenland in these high latitudes, for traces of their encampments have been found along the shores of the Parry group from Melville Island to Lancaster Sound, where they are still living in Dundas Harbour and in Admiralty Inlet. The late Admiral Sherard Osborn and my cousin, Mr. Clements Markham, paid great attention to this subject during the Arctic Expedition of 1850–51, and prepared a descriptive list of all the Eskimo vestiges along the whole length of the Parry group.* We now traced similar remains

---

* See the "Selection of Papers on Arctic Geography and Ethnology," printed for the use of the Expedition by the Royal Geographical Society, p. 163.

up the western side of the channels leading north from Smith Sound, at Cape Sabine, on the shores of Buchanan Strait, on Norman Lockyer Island, on Capes Hilgard, Louis Napoleon, Hayes, and Fraser, at Radmore Harbour, and Bellot Island. The most northern point where human remains were discovered was at Cape Beechey, in 81° 54′ N. Here our naturalist found the framework of a large wooden sledge, a stone lamp, and a snow scraper made of walrus tusk. Beyond this point there was no sign of any human being having preceded us. This is the utmost northern known limit of Eskimo wandering, and here they appear to have crossed the strait, and to have made their way southward on the Greenland side. The most northern permanent human habitation in the world is now at Etah, near Port Foulke, and, under present climatic conditions, it would be impossible even for the Etah Eskimo to exist at Cape Beechey, in 81° 54′ N., whither their ancestors must have wandered in remote times. There is much yet to learn respecting these marvellous wanderings along the Arctic shores; and our expedition has certainly thrown considerable new light on the question. We have fixed the most northern limit of the Eskimo migrations, and have established the fact that they did not come from the north down Smith Sound, but merely wandered round its shores until the palæocrystic floes in Robeson Channel made them despair of finding there the means of supporting life. We have also proved that the people seen by Captain Clavering on the east coast of Greenland in 1823 could not have come round its northern extreme, but that they had found their way to the neighbourhood of the Pendulum Islands from Cape Farewell. They are useful contributions towards the final solution of a very important ethnological question, which, however, cannot be fully and conclusively settled until all the unknown parts of the Polar area have been explored.

CHAPTER VII.

WALRUS HUNT.—DOG DRIVING.

"So Zembla's rocks, the beauteous work of frost,
 Rise white in air, and glitter o'er the coast;
 Pale suns, unfelt, at distance roll away,
 And on the impassive ice the lightnings play;
 Eternal snows the growing mass supply,
 Till the bright mountains prop the incumbent sky:
 As Atlas fixed, each hoary pile appears,
 The gathered winter of a thousand years."
POPE.

DURING the remainder of the navigable season, I propose to present the narrative of the voyage in the form of a diary, giving the extracts as they were written down at the time, when the events they record were fresh in my memory.

Sunday, August 8th.—Snow fell very heavily during the forenoon, completely covering the surrounding hills, and lying several inches deep on our deck. Clearing up in the afternoon we found ourselves completely beset by the ice and drifting shorewards. Steam was resorted to and every effort made to reach a narrow lane of water, only a hundred yards distant, but without success. At four o'clock the ship experienced a slight nip, the ice piling up as high as our main chains, but fortunately for us it was of too soft a nature to do much damage. Half an hour afterwards the nip eased and the pack commenced to open, showing broad lanes of water. This sudden slackening of the ice was due to the total cessation of wind. We soon extricated ourselves from our unpleasant situation, and lay in eager readiness to take advantage of any opportunity of advancing that might offer itself.

11.30 P.M.—The ways of ice are indeed inscrutable! Five hours ago Grinnell Land loomed in the distance, and we had little prospect of reaching it for some time. Now we are actually made fast to the land-ice in Franklin Pierce Bay on the southern shore of Grinnell Land!

We esteem ourselves particularly fortunate in having reached thus far. Cape Fraser is not far distant, and this appears to be our Rubicon. Once passed, fewer difficulties are anticipated. We may very fairly reason that to the northward of this promontory will be found a "North Water" similar to the one north of Baffin Bay, the ice remaining in the broad part of Smith Sound like the middle pack in Baffin Bay and Davis Straits.

In the latitude of Cape Fraser Kane reported what he called an open Polar Sea, Hayes the same, whilst the "Polaris" actually navigated for some distance this "North Water." Why should we find it different?

The ice opened this afternoon in a miraculous manner, in one long lead from land to land, sufficiently wide for us to pass through; and then, as if it had opened expressly for us, closed again, and with such rapidity that our consort, who was following in our wake, having lagged a little behind, was caught and remained beset for some time; eventually, however, boring through and rejoining us.

August 9th.—We succeeded this morning in pushing on for three or four miles, when, being completely stopped by the ice, we were again compelled to make fast. In consequence of the heavy fall of snow yesterday, the surface of the water was coated with a soft sludgy substance, half ice and half snow, which greatly impeded our progress.

The statement made by Dr. Hayes in his interesting work, that "along the entire coast of Grinnell Land no glacier appears," is slightly inaccurate; for at the head of Franklin Pierce Bay two tolerably large glaciers are situated, whilst another was seen a few miles to the westward on the same coast. Doubtless Dr. Hayes intended to say *discharging* glaciers, in which case he would, I think, be nearly correct.

For three days were we detained, without the ice allowing us the slightest chance of moving, during which time a complete series of magnetic observations was obtained on the floe, the inclination of the needle being as much as 85° 34'. Both the dredge and trawl were also put into requisition and with good results. Amongst the many zoological curiosities brought to the surface, from a depth of fifteen fathoms, were some crinoids. These echinoderms are very rare, few specimens having been met with, until the deep-sea dredgings of the "Challenger" brought them more into notice.

A small island, since called Norman Lockyer Island after the distinguished astronomer of that name, was visited, and its highest eminence ascended for the purpose of watching the movements of the pack. Landing on the ice-foot that fringed the shore, we stepped on to a long shaly beach that rose in well-defined and regular terraces to at least two hundred feet above the level of the sea, showing the different tidal marks, and illustrating clearly the gradual upheaval of the land. Numerous traces of Eskimo were discovered on this small and remote island, consisting of the sites of several encampments, and a bone harpoon point, all apparently of very ancient date. The highest part of the island is from five to six hundred feet above the sea. It is of limestone formation, and on several of the rocks, especially those at its summit, distinct glacial marks were detected. Vegetation was scanty, although here and there the poppy, saxifrage, and willow could be seen cropping up between the stones.

Here too we succeeded in harpooning a couple of walruses. Three of these large animals were observed on a piece of ice, their large ungainly forms stretched out, lazily enjoying their *siesta*. Volunteers were not wanting for the purpose of attempting their capture; but as an indiscriminate attack would only lead to failure, it was determined to despatch one of the whale boats, specially fitted with a harpoon gun, and all the necessary implements and gear for securing these animals, in order to effect in a more organized and skilful manner the object we had in view.

Great difficulty was experienced in approaching our prey, as the boat had to be hauled over loose fragments of ice, and pushed through a sludgy consistency of soft ice, snow, and water, in which the oars were useless; so that it was feared the unavoidable noise would disturb and frighten them away. At length, after much trouble and no little exertion, we succeeded in getting within about eight yards, so sound was their repose, without exciting any suspicion in their minds that danger was lurking in their vicinity. At that distance, however, they evinced a

WALRUSES.

degree of restlessness, by lifting their shaggy heads and uttering jerky spasmodic snorts, that showed us only too plainly a retreat was meditated.

Selecting the largest of the three as his victim, our harpooner carefully laid his gun. A moment of breathless suspense followed, to be relieved by the report of the gun, a roar of pain and rage, and the disappearance in the water of the three walruses, while the piece of ice, on which a moment before they had been reposing, was covered with blood, convincing us that our shaft had taken effect. If any further proof was required in corroboration of this fact, a tugging at the line and the sudden moving of the boat was sufficient. Lances and rifles were quickly seized; for these animals, when wounded and maddened by pain, are ugly and dangerous customers, and have frequently been known to rip the planks out of a boat with their formidable tusks, and thus seriously endanger the lives of the crew. We had not long to wait; a disturbance in the water close alongside denoted that our victim was coming to the surface. An instant after, his bearded face with every expression of infuriated rage and demoniacal hate, his fiery eyes glaring with vengeance, appeared, and was immediately saluted with two or three rifle bullets. This warm reception served only to incense and irritate him, and he tried hard to wreak his vengeance on the boat; but his enemies were too powerful, and with the united aid of bullets and lance thrusts the unwieldy beast was forced to succumb to the superior power of his human antagonists. Towing the great carcase back to the ship, it was hauled up on the floe, and quickly *flinched*.* The blubber and flesh were packed in barrels, making a very welcome addition to the small amount of food that we had on board for our dogs.

Another walrus was harpooned on the following day, and these were the only two captured by the expedition during their stay in the Arctic regions. Walrus steaks, from this date, were for some time in great demand, whilst the liver was pronounced to be perfectly excellent, and even superior to pig's fry!

As a rule these animals are exceedingly difficult to kill, for in addition to their enormously thick skulls and coating of almost impenetrable skin and blubber, they are excessively tenacious of life. A rifle bullet, although a walrus may eventually die of the wound, is more than useless, as it will effectually scare him away, and thus all chance of securing him is lost.

---

* "Flinching" is a whaling term for cutting up a whale or walrus.

The only sure way of succeeding in their capture is by the use of the harpoon, and this weapon of course is only available at short distances.

During the temporary delays of the ships in the ice, amusement was not forgotten, and we often had rare fun. It is a very important point in an Arctic expedition to keep the men constantly employed and interested, otherwise they would, more especially when their onward progress was checked, be subject to gloomy moods and fits of despondency. Care, therefore, should be taken to guard against these feelings.

Amongst the numerous games purchased by the expedition before leaving England was a football, which, on occasions of this sort and when the ice would admit of it, would be produced, and a game kept up with great spirit, though with an utter disregard of all orthodox rules. So long as Jack got his kick, no matter in which direction the ball was propelled, he was satisfied! Officers and men would alike mingle in the game, every one determined to carry out the one grand object, namely, that of enjoying themselves. Skating and sliding on the ice were also accomplishments that afforded much pleasure and amusement, and were freely indulged in by all, irrespective of age or rank. Sometimes our Eskimo dogs would be taken out on the floe and harnessed to an empty sledge, whilst some would-be dog driver, anxious to attain proficiency as a whip, would make a start, and be seen tearing round the floe, regardless of weak ice and pools of water, at the rate of ten miles an hour, returning on board thoroughly drenched, but happy in the knowledge that he had succeeded as a dog driver.

Perhaps a few words here in connection with the dogs would not be out of place. As I have before stated, they lived almost entirely in the fore part of the vessel, and were consequently especial favourites with the men, by whom they were fed and greatly petted. Of course they were all named, their appellations being more characteristic than euphonious. They rejoiced in such names as Ginger, so called on account of his colour; Bruin, because he was minus a tail, having been deprived of this appendage in his youthful days; Boss-eye, on account of the obliquity of his vision, or as our men expressed it, because "his eyes were rove cross-jack brace fashion;" Soresides, in consequence of the unfortunate dog when it came on board suffering from an unhealed wound in its side. Sallie, Topsy, Sly-boots, Jessie, etc., were the names of others.

The only English dog in the expedition was my black retriever Nellie, an old shipmate and companion, who took no pains to conceal her displeasure and disgust at the introduction of such, in her estimation, a rough and rowdy pack; nor was she ever afterwards induced to cultivate their acquaintance. As she lived in the after part of the ship, she viewed with a jealous eye any attempts on the part of the Eskimo dogs to intrude on what she regarded as her own domain, and would invariably fly at and drive them forward.

Shortly after their appearance on board, and long before they had been used for sledging purposes, a species of rabies, or dog madness, broke out amongst them, which very quickly and alarmingly thinned their number. The first symptom of this disease would generally be the dog falling down in a fit, from which it would partially recover only to rush about in a frantic manner as if totally deprived of all sense and feeling. On some occasions they would rush into the water and be drowned, and at other times wander away from the ship to be no more seen; sometimes their sufferings would terminate in death, whilst at other times they would be shot in order to release the poor things from their pain.

All expeditions have experienced the same kind of disease and mortality amongst their dogs, for which there has hitherto been no remedy. It is a curious fact that hydrophobia is unknown among the Eskimo, and no man bitten by one of these dogs during a mad fit has ever suffered permanent injury from its effects. Frequently whilst employed sledging, they have been attacked by violent fits, resembling cramp, completely prostrating them, causing them to roll over on their sides and foam at the mouth. On these occasions they would be freed from the sledge, which after a time they would follow, when they would be re-harnessed and proceed as if nothing had occurred.

Dr. Colan devoted much of his time to the investigation of the nature and causes of this disease, and I have no doubt his researches will throw a flood of light over this matter that will prove of the greatest value to succeeding expeditions in the preservation of their dogs, and be the means of baffling the attacks of this insidious disease.

The dogs when employed in dragging a sledge are always harnessed in line abreast, and never, as generally supposed, ahead of each other in tandem fashion.

From six to ten or a dozen dogs form a team. They are capable of dragging as much as one hundred and fifty pounds per dog; but this is rather an excessive load and should not be exacted for any length of time. So strong and enduring are they that they will frequently perform a journey, over smooth ice, of twenty-five or thirty miles a day with this load; but with light loads and level ice they have been known to travel as much as seventy and even a hundred miles in one day.

There is something very exhilarating and exciting about dog sledging, so long as the weather is fine, temperature not too low, smooth level ice to travel over, and a light sledge to drag. But let all these various conditions be reversed, let the weather be thick and foggy, or a gale of wind blowing with a blinding snow-drift, a temperature of 50° below zero, rough hummocky ice to travel over, and a heavily laden sledge to be dragged by a tired and obstinate team, then dog sledging cannot be regarded as either a comfortable or desirable amusement.

The sensation of dashing along on a light sledge at the rate of ten miles an hour, the fine snow flying into one's face as the dogs tear through it pell-mell in their headlong career, or perhaps plunging down the side of a steep ravine when the utmost caution is required to prevent the sledge from capsizing and toppling over on the top of the dogs, is both novel and delightful. But when obstacles such as hummocks and deep snow-drifts have to be encountered, especially with a low temperature, the reverse is the case. Directly the sledge receives the slightest check from either of these causes, the dogs lie down, and look at you in the most provoking manner. It is no use having recourse to the whip, for not all the flogging in the world will make them advance until the obstacle has been removed, or the sledge carried over the difficulties that had retarded its progress.

The whip is the main feature in dog driving. To be a good driver it is therefore necessary to use this implement in a dexterous manner. The lash is a thong of sealskin about eighteen or twenty feet long, attached to a short handle of about twelve inches in length. It is, in the hands of an experienced driver, a formidable weapon, the punishment that the dogs receive from it being often very severe. They are guided solely by it, and it is amusing to witness the cunning and intelligence displayed by the outside dogs, who invariably get more than their fair share of the lash, in dodging under the lines of the others and emerging somewhere in the midst of the team in order to escape from its terrible infliction. Another very annoying and distressing piece of work connected with dog sledging is clearing the lines, which in a short time become in a grievously entangled state from the constant dodging about of the dogs, and this it must be remembered has to be done with hands encased in thick woollen mitts, for to bare them would ensure serious frost-bites. In consequence of the amount of provisions that have of necessity to be carried for the use of the dogs, it is almost impossible to use them for long journeys. None were employed during the expedition by any of the extended sledge parties; but for short journeys, or when dispatch was required, they were invaluable.

CHAPTER VIII.

SLOW PROGRESS THROUGH THE ICE.

> "He rose, the coast and country to survey,
> Anxious and eager to discover more.
> It looked a wild uncultivated shore,
> But whether human kind or beast alone
> Possessed the new-found region was unknown."
>
> VIRGIL.

THURSDAY, *August* 12*th*.—Early this morning, the floes opening slightly, an attempt was made to proceed; but it was a futile one, the ice remaining perfectly impenetrable. This delay is naturally causing anxiety, as our fuel is rapidly disappearing, from the constant demand for steam, and the navigable season is also as rapidly waning, young ice forming alongside the ship nearly an inch in thickness. Patience, combined with caution and perseverance, is an indispensable qualification for an Arctic navigator. At the same time he must be prepared, when occasion offers, to make a bold dash. Quick determination and an ever-ready eye to seize upon any available opportunity are also necessary attributes of the explorer who hopes to achieve success in ice navigation. Without them failure is inevitable.

In the forenoon both ships were slightly nipped. We succeeded in unshipping our rudder in time; but the "Discovery," receiving the squeeze more astern, had her rudder very severely injured. She was enabled, however, to patch it up sufficiently for temporary use and thus avoid the necessity of shifting it. In the afternoon the ice began to move to the eastward, enabling us once more to make a start. Hastily shipping our rudders we got under weigh, and having bored through a few streams of ice emerged into a fine lead of water extending between the land and the pack. Passing Cape D'Urville, we opened a large inlet. At its head was a deep ravine, containing two large glaciers which, running respectively from N.E. and N.W., met and formed one terminal face. At 9 P.M. the southern extreme of Dobbin Bay, called Cape Hawks, was passed. This is a magnificent promontory, which has, with some propriety, been compared, in appearance, to the Rock of Gibraltar.

It was a beautifully calm night as both ships silently rounded this bold headland, the water so still and unruffled that it was actually used as an artificial horizon for the purpose of taking an astronomical observation. The Cape itself towered over our heads as we steamed past, its reflection in the still quiet water being clearly visible, whilst deep ravines on either side stretched away apparently for miles into the interior, until lost amid the snow-shining mountains in the far distance. A large glacier at the head of the bay showed out prominently as it glistened in the light of a bright midnight sun, the bay itself being covered with an icy sheet, broken only by a few long low bergs, generated, in all probability, from the selfsame glacier. The few clouds that were visible in the almost cloudless sky presented an exquisite iridescence rarely witnessed, exhibiting clearly defined bright colours, extending in bands in a horizontal direction, the reflection of which in the clear pellucid water materially enhanced the beauties of the landscape. Such a scene, with all its surroundings, could scarcely be equalled in beauty, certainly not surpassed, even in sunny Italy.

Making the ships fast to an iceberg, preparations

CAPE HAWKS.

for landing a large depôt of provisions, similar to the one established at the Cary Islands, were immediately commenced. A jolly-boat, obtained from the "Valorous," was also deposited here. We have now two large depôts, besides boats, established in our rear, sufficient to sustain a large party for many days, should any untoward accident befall our ship.

Whilst engaged in these operations, an adjacent island—Washington Irving Island—was visited, and a large cairn erected on its summit. Our surprise may be imagined when, on reaching the top, the remains of an old cairn were discovered. At first its origin was attributed to Hayes, who visited the island in 1860, but on closer inspection evidences of a construction at a much earlier date were palpable, the stones of which it was composed being covered with lichen, denoting great age. Hayes, in the published account of his voyage, makes no mention either of having seen this cairn or of having built one on the island. It was, undoubtedly, the work of white men's hands; the object and necessity for building cairns is unknown, and therefore not practised, by the Eskimos. How then came this structure in such a remote and desolate part of the world? Can it be the work of some obscure navigator of years gone by, who erected this monument as a memento of his visit, but who never returned to relate the results of his adventurous voyage? This must for ever remain a mystery!

Of course it was quickly demolished and its site subjected to a very careful search, in the hopes of discovering some record or clue by which its history might be ascertained; but nothing was found, and we were forced to content ourselves with reconstructing it on a larger scale, and depositing a record at its base detailing the movements of the expedition.

The depôt having been landed, the ships were moved a little farther up the bay, although, to effect this, we were compelled to have recourse to powder, in order to "blast" a passage through the ice. The recent tracks of a bear were observed on the floe, being the only indications of the presence of these animals that we had observed since leaving Melville Bay. It naturally caused a little excitement amongst our sportsmen and would-be bear slayers.

The formation of the land around Dobbin Bay appeared curiously contorted; the stratifications dipping, in some places, to the westward at an angle of about 18°, whilst at others they assumed a perfectly horizontal direction. This irregularity of the strata may probably be accounted for by the trap, or other primary rock, forcing its way upwards through the limestone formation. Where these contortions appear the colour changes from the sombre grey of the surrounding limestone to a bright red and brownish hue.

In the afternoon, it being deemed expedient for the safety of the ships that they should be docked, the requisite instructions were given, and in four hours they were securely placed in two large commodious docks, cut out of the solid floe.

The process of docking is rendered necessary to prevent a ship from being crushed between two floes should she be so unfortunate as to be placed between them with the whole force of the pack driving against the outer one. This operation is frequently necessary whilst following the land-ice, although in these days of steam it is not so frequently practised as of old.

Our ice-saw crews had previously been organized, and, as it is absolutely necessary that the work of construction should be carried out with the utmost expedition, the whole of the officers and ship's company were stationed so as to take an active part in the proceedings. The instant the order was given for "all hands to cut dock" a most animated scene ensued. Triangles were quickly erected, saws placed in position, the dock measured and marked out by boarding-pikes placed at the several corners, and every one working as if their lives depended upon their own individual exertions. Three persons only were left on board the ship—namely, one officer in charge of the deck, the engineer at the engines, and a man at the helm—and, as it was necessary to keep the ship constantly moving so as to avoid pieces of ice, and also to place her in a good position for being docked, these three had no sinecure offices.

Occasionally a jet of water, followed by a loud report and a shower of fragmentary ice, showed that powder was used to shatter the larger pieces of ice that had been cut, but unless great care is taken in the use of this explosive, it is liable to damage the sides of the dock.

This was our first attempt at dock cutting, which will account for the time occupied in its construction. Ordinarily the work should be completed in about a couple of hours. When two or more ships are in company time is saved by employing all hands to cut one dock large enough to take in all the ships.

The diagram on next page will serve to illustrate the system employed by us whilst engaged in making one of these docks. The last triangular piece of ice that is taken out—namely, the portion marked on the plan by the letters C B F—is removed intact, and being placed across the entrance serves to close the dock and thus keep out all stray pieces of ice.

After four hours of such work as dock cutting entails, it was poor comfort for us to return on board wet, cold, and hungry, only to find that our fires had been allowed to burn out, and that we could neither get a cup of tea to refresh ourselves with, nor a chance of warming ourselves at the stove.* The Eskimo dogs, being turned out on the floe and tied to one of our anchor lines, made night hideous by their dreary and lamentable wailing.

For two days were the ships kept close prisoners; but on Sunday, August 15th, as soon as divine service was finished, a large party of men was actively engaged in cutting and blasting a passage between the floe in which we were imprisoned and the shore, for a lead of water had been observed in the channel which we were naturally desirous of reaching. Although Sunday was as much as possible observed as a day of rest, it was quite out of the question to a party situated as we were altogether to abstain from work on the Sabbath.

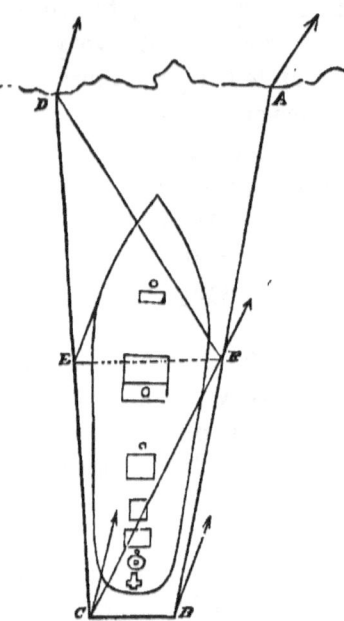

PLAN OF ICE DOCK.

No. 1 saw cuts from A to B 200 ft.
No. 2   „   „   D to C 200 ft.
No. 3   „   „   B to C 35 ft., and then on to F 115 ft.
No. 4 saw cuts from F to D 120 ft., and, if necessary, from E to F 48 ft.

DIMENSIONS OF DOCK.

Length . . . . 200 ft.
Breadth, at entrance . 65 „
Ditto, at head . . 35 „

* An amusing story is related of one of the officers. Whilst engaged in cutting the dock, he, without thinking, put his pipe in his trousers

WORK ON SUNDAY.

Our navigable season, we knew, was a short one; no opportunity could we afford to lose; and therefore we were compelled to work as much on Sunday as on week-days should circumstances arise which would make it necessary for us to do so. After about nine hours' hard work we succeeded in making a passage sufficiently broad for the ships to pass through. Our

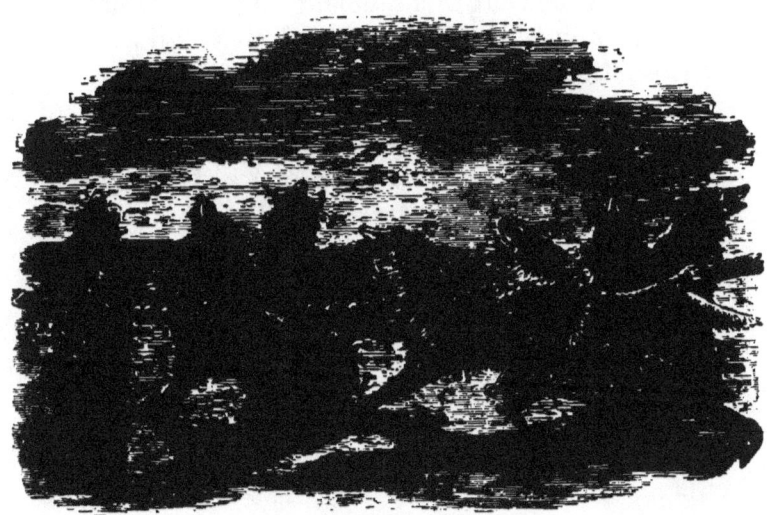

"THE MOANING OF THE TIED."

last explosion was a most effective one; no less than eight blasting charges, or torpedoes, were exploded simultaneously—these varied in size from five to twelve pound charges.

The result of this, designated by the men, "feu de

pocket, so as to enable him the more readily to work at his ice-saw. Feeling, after a time, a little warm about his legs, he attributed it to his exertions in working the saw, until a sharp and intolerable pain caused him to put his hand into his pocket. This speedily afforded an explanation: his pipe, being still alight, had burnt a hole through his trousers and shirt and was burning his leg!

joy" was wonderful; the floe split and cracked in all directions, enabling us with our long ice points and poles to clear a splendid channel. Hauling the ships out of dock, we steamed through the passage and into a fine stream of water round Cape Louis Napoleon. So narrow, however, was our channel that in rounding the point, to our great dismay, the "Discovery" grounded. A delay at this moment might have proved fatal to us, and it was therefore with no small amount of satisfaction, after a short detention, that we observed her again afloat. Our joy at being again on the move was short-lived. A few hours sufficed to bring us to the edge of a field of ice, to penetrate which seemed utterly impossible. To cut a dock in such ice, the floes being from ten to twenty feet in thickness, was also out of the question, even had we been provided with saws sufficiently long to do so. Blasting was resorted to, and by this means we were enabled to secure the ship in a small indentation in the ice that afforded some slight protection. So high was the ice that our boats, hanging from the midship davits on the outside of the ship, had to be turned inboard to prevent their being crushed. For three days were we kept in a state of feverish excitement without being able to make any progress, and yet constantly moving the ship to avoid destruction from drifting bergs and closing floes.

The shore was frequently visited, and the heights of Mount Joy and Cape Hayes ascended; but always the same scene met our view to northward—an impassable plain of ice.

Twice in one day were the ships nearly destroyed. A large iceberg that was aground close to us, and therefore protecting us from the pack, suddenly floated and drifted away. This released a large floe to which we were secured, and with which we drifted down rapidly towards another large berg that remained aground. It was an anxious time for us, for in five minutes, unless we could move out of the way, we must be inevitably crushed between the two. All hands were quickly summoned, a line laid out astern and made fast to some large hummocks, and by this we fortunately succeeded in hauling the ship clear; but only just in time, for as our bowsprit cleared the berg, the floe came into contact with it with such irresistible force that hummock was piled upon hummock in a truly alarming manner. Had we been caught, nothing short of a miracle could have saved us.

The noise of the ice as it squeezed against the berg was anything but pleasant to listen to; but still it was better than hearing our own timbers crashing to pieces in the same manner, and we all experienced a strong feeling of relief when the danger was past.

Little rest was enjoyed by any on these days during which we were subjected to the wayward will of the pack. Unshipping and replacing the rudder, and lifting and lowering the screw, were duties that had to be carried out several times during each day, and, although this sort of work is rather depressing and irksome, the spirits of the crew never flagged. They were always ready, cheerful, and willing. No matter what duty they were called upon to perform, it was invariably carried out in the same zealous, hearty manner that was so conspicuously manifested during the whole period of the absence of the expedition as to elicit the unbounded praise and confidence of their leader.

On the 19th of August the ice slackened sufficiently to enable us to proceed, and on that evening, to the intense delight of every one, we succeeded in rounding Cape Fraser.

During the last three weeks we had advanced exactly ninety miles, or at the rate of about four and a quarter miles a day. This cannot be considered a rapid rate of travelling, yet to accomplish even this necessitated a constant and vigilant look-out.

Cape Fraser is a bold promontory some thousand feet in height, terminating in a short projecting point of land about two hundred feet above the level of the sea. Above the talus appeared numerous caves in the cliffs, a peculiarity noticed for the first time, and the summit was studded with irregularities that, to an imaginative mind, might be perverted into gigantic beings, animals, or castellated towers. On one of these ridges was a heap of stones supposed to represent the "Twelve Apostles," and was so marked on the chart; but as we could never distinguish more than half the number at one time from any point of bearing, it was generally supposed on board that they adhered to true man-of-war regulations, and only appeared in their "watch on deck," half the number belonging of course to the watch below!

At 10 P.M., being again temporarily stopped, the ships were secured in a little harbour called Maury Bay. During our detention in the vicinity of Cape Fraser, we were able to confirm the observations made by Dr. Bessels of the "Polaris," relative to the meeting of two tides at or about this point. This fact materially strengthens the argument in favour of the insularity of Greenland, for it has been deduced from a series of tidal observations obtained by us that the tide to the northward of Cape Fraser—that is, the tide in Kennedy and Robeson Channels—is undoubtedly the same as the North Atlantic one, and therefore flows along the northern coast of Greenland.

Contrary to what might generally be expected, we did not encounter any very great accumulation of broken up ice in consequence of the meeting of these two tides : not more than would be caused by the fact of the channel decreasing in size to the northward at this point, and therefore offering greater obstruction to the ice whilst drifting northward, but facilitating its *general* drift, which is to the southward.

From the summit of Cape John Barrow, which forms one extreme of the little bay in which we were secured, we obtained a good view, and one which delighted and gladdened our hearts.

Northwards we could see as far as Cape L. von Buch; between us leads of water, although covered with much loose ice. To the eastward we could plainly distinguish Cape Constitution, with a large sheet of water along its base; but to get to it we should have had to penetrate a large expanse of pack. This pool of water was in all probability similar to one seen by Morton in the same place in 1855, and reported by him as an " open Polar sea," on which many imaginative theories have been based !

Our return to the ship was not accomplished without much difficulty, in consequence of our little harbour of refuge having filled with drifting ice, during the time we were on shore, which beset our boat. We were therefore compelled to haul and drag it over and through innumerable fragments of ice, reaching the ship wet and fatigued, but delighted with the intelligence we possessed and the prospect of pushing on.

Friday, August 20th.—At one o'clock this morning, being the top of high water, we made another start.

Taking advantage of the different broad lanes of water, we steamed rapidly past Cape Norton Shaw, and opened out Scoresby Bay—a grand harbour that would suit admirably for a ship's winter quarters, provided animal life existed. From the appearance of the land we imagined that game would be found in large quantities. A perfect cone-shaped hill on the north-west side is a very prominent feature of this bay. Indeed, the entire coast along which we are passing is composed of long ranges of hills more or less coniform, varing from one to two thousand feet in height. The coast line is very imperfectly delineated on our charts, the distance between the various bays and headlands are erroneous, and the positions are wrong; the error always being that they are placed too much to the northward.

Off Cape McClintock we had another narrow escape from being severely nipped, in consequence of attempting to pass through a channel between two closing floes. Although jammed for a short time, the pressure was not very great, and, the nip easing, the ship was released. Passing Cape Collinson we were again obliged to make fast to a large floe, as all the leads to the northward had closed up, thereby preventing farther progress.

The ice was moving rapidly to the southward—the whole pack drifting bodily—at the rate of from one and a half to two knots an hour. The floe to which we were secured was kept stationary by a couple of grounded icebergs that effectually resisted all its efforts to extricate itself. This rapid drift seemed to indicate the presence of a "North Water," or at any rate a very loose pack.

Advantage was taken of our temporary delay to establish a small depôt of provisions, consisting of two hundred and forty rations, near Cape Collinson, for the use of a travelling party which, according to existing arrangements, would be dispatched to the southward by the "Discovery" during the following year, for the purpose of visiting Cape Isabella, and bringing up any letters that might have been deposited there for us.

Saturday, August 21st.—Lanes of water appearing continuous to the northward, we got under weigh at half-past two this morning; but after two or three hours' boring and working under steam and sail we were forced to relinquish the attempt, being unable to penetrate the pack in the direction we wished to proceed. We therefore returned to our former anchorage, under the lea of a friendly berg, the ice continuing to drift south with marvellous rapidity.

Whilst detained here we were assailed by some furious squalls from the S.E., accompanied by a heavy fall of snow. During one of these the "Discovery" was blown away from her anchors, and it was with no little difficulty that she was again secured to the floe in safety. Thinking we should be able to reach some open water to the northward by the removal of the large floe to which we were fast, both ships' companies were employed in sawing off a large piece of it, which, impinging on one of the stranded icebergs, would, it was thought, release the floe if detached. The distance to cut through was one thousand feet. Notwithstanding the magnitude of the undertaking, every one set to work with a will and resolution that betokened confidence in being able to succeed in anything that was required of them.

Before the work was fairly commenced the ice appeared to slack to the eastward, and the captain, abandoning his former intention, determined to seek a passage through the pack instead of hugging the coast.

Getting under weigh at 9.30 P.M., we bored through a large extent of slack ice, into a fine piece of open water, which, when reached, we found possessed no outlet. It was a perfect salt-water lake surrounded by ice. In this we were obliged to dodge about under sail, waiting patiently for the ice to open and thus allow us a free passage.

As we proceed northwards the ice appears to be heavier and more formidable, and animal life seems to be getting more scarce. Few birds are seen. Occasionally the head of an inquisitive seal is protruded out of the water, but immediately withdrawn (if not killed) on being saluted by half a dozen bullets from the rifles of our keen and enthusiastic sportsmen, who are for ever on the watch to display their prowess in their endeavours to procure food for our dogs, by shooting these animals, who thus pay for their curiosity with their lives.

We appeared to be leaving the region of icebergs, for, although those met with lately were of great size, they were few in number. The one affording us protection this forenoon was no less than six hundred feet in length.

CHAPTER IX.

KENNEDY CHANNEL.

2nd Keeper.—" I'll stay above the hill so both may shoot."
1st Keeper.—" That cannot be: the noise of thy cross-bow will scare the herd, and so my shoot is lost. Here stand we both, and aim we at the best."—*Henry VI.*

> "Within a long recess there lies a bay,
> An island shades it from the rolling sea,
> And forms a port secure for ships to ride,
> Broke by the jutting land on either side."
> VIRGIL.

SUNDAY, *August 22nd.*—The rapidity of the changes that take place in these icy seas is almost inconceivable. In a few hours from being helplessly imprisoned by a dense pack of ice, we were actually plying, under steam and sail, in a vast expanse of water containing only a few loose streams of ice, through which we had no difficulty in penetrating. Our predictions were indeed realized, and to a greater extent than we had even anticipated. We had reached a " North Water," in which we were sensible of a very perceptible motion on board the ship. It is true that the pack, apparently as solid and as impenetrable as ever, extended along the west side of Kennedy Channel; but to the northward and along the east side was a clear and open sea, free of ice, with its surface agitated by the fresh northerly wind that was blowing, and rising and falling with true oceanic undulations.

Unfortunately for us, at least so far as making headway was concerned, the wind was not only very strong but directly ahead, compelling us to beat to windward under steam and fore and aft sails. We consoled ourselves, however, with the hope that the same wind would blow all the ice to the southward, and thus enable us to make good progress. The temperature being some six or seven degrees below freezing point caused us to feel the sharp wind in a very unpleasant manner, and made both the crow's-nest and bridge very disagreeable places of resort. The pleasure of feeling that we were really doing good work was, however, sufficient compensation for the discomfort that was felt.

Stretching over to the eastern side of the channel we passed close to Crozier Island, having Cape Constitution full in view. Its appearance coincides exactly with the description given by Morton.

This cape is the northern extreme of a bay called, by Kane, Lafayette Bay. It is steep and precipitous, and has no ice-foot adhering. Indeed, the base of the headland, as well as the adjacent one, Cape Independence, has the appearance of having been partially undermined by the action of the sea, thus forming an overhanging terrace, up which it would be impossible to ascend. Morton found its ascent totally impracticable, on account of the steep and rugged nature of the cliff. We were unable to detect any signs of a *mer de glace* over this land, although a light tinge along the summit to the southward of Lafayette Bay would lead one to suppose that it existed. This, however, was the only indication of an ice-cap that was perceived, and it was one on which little or no reliance was placed.

The positions of the various points along this coast are very fairly correct, being as nearly as possible in the latitudes ascribed to them by Dr. Bessels of the "Polaris," affording a striking contrast to the places on the opposite side of the channel, where the positions are so egregiously inaccurate. The deep inlet on the American chart called Carl Ritter Bay was not to be seen. The only indentation in the land in its assigned position was Richardson Bay, which we must naturally conclude was the one seen and named Carl Ritter by Dr. Hayes.

It was a curious fact that, whereas the land on the west side of the channel was completely covered with snow, the land on the east side was entirely free. This was not the only peculiar feature in which the two sides of the channel differed. Although apparently of the same geological formation, there was a great dissimilarity between the physical appearance of the land on either side. That on the east was flat and table-topped, rising to the height of about one thousand feet, separated into hills by broad valleys, whilst the stratification of the cliffs was regular and horizontal. That on the west side was, on the contrary, composed of conical-shaped hills, rising to an altitude of from two to four thousand feet, and intersected by deep ravines, whilst the stratifications were so distorted that the dip varied as much as from 10° to 45°.

Whilst the land on the east side appeared to have undergone a regular and steady upheaval, that on the west seemed to have been raised suddenly, the deep ravines between the numerous hills resembling the beds of ancient and extinct glaciers.

Monday, August 23rd.—A glorious run has been made during the last twenty-four hours, assisted, for a short time, as we have been, by a strong southerly wind; but alas! by 10 A.M. we arrived at the end of our tether!

Passing the entrance to Bessels Bay, we reached Cape Morton, from whence extended right across Hall Basin our implacable enemy, the ice—solid floes of immense area stretching to the northward as far as the eye could reach, with no opening, no outlet of any description, and no indications of water.

Polaris Bay was ahead of us, and we could plainly discern the position of the Americans' winter quarters; but with no hopes, for the present, of our reaching so far. We must again, as we have so often had to do before, exercise our patience, and wait for a more favourable opportunity for pushing on. The strong southerly wind now blowing will, in all probability, be succeeded by a calm or a breeze from the northward, either of which will have the effect of opening the ice. The "Discovery" having landed a small depôt of two hundred and forty rations at Cape Morton, for the use of travelling parties that will hereafter be dispatched for the purpose of exploring Petermann Fiord, both ships made sail and beat back to Bessels Bay, where we dropped anchor in seven fathoms, just inside, and under the protection of Hannah Island.

Bessels Bay is a long and narrow indentation in the land, extending in a N.W. and S.E. direction, having numerous small glaciers on either side, the majority of them discharging ones. The bay is in consequence nearly choked with small bergs.

This bay or fiord gives one the idea of having been

originally the bed of some large glacier, now extinct, whilst Hannah Island, which lies directly across its mouth, has every appearance of having been its terminal moraine, not only from its position, but also from its composition, for it consists of an immense heap of pebbles and drift, possessing apparently no determined basis, no underlying rock.

We were also able to observe here the undoubted *mer de glace* under which Greenland is supposed to be buried, and whose outpourings in this locality find their escape in Petermann Fiord and Bessels Bay.

A few eider-ducks, a seal, and some dovekies, with an ivory gull, were seen to-day.

Captain Feilden and Mr. Parr landed on the northern side of the bay, and, ascending a high hill, obtained a good and unobstructed view to the northward. Their report was very desponding—ice, nothing but ice, as far as they could see.

From what we can now observe, the land on the western side of Hall Basin appears to end abruptly somewhere about Cape Union, and does not continue to the northward, as represented in the last American Chart. I put no belief in the land reported to have been seen by some of the men of the "Polaris," and named President Land. Should the land terminate, as I anticipate, in about lat. 83° N. our chance of reaching a high latitude will of course be much reduced, although we shall have a grand field of exploration to the eastward and westward.

In the evening the captain and myself visited Hannah Island, and erected a cairn, in which a record detailing our movements was deposited, on its summit, in the most conspicuous place about the centre of the island. Here we had an uninterrupted view to the northward; but what we saw only confirmed the report brought on board in the earlier part of the day. The western side of the channel appeared free of ice as far as Cape Lieber, and a lane of water was visible extending from us as far as this cape. By this stream of water appears our only chance of getting on.

Tuesday, August 24*th*.—The captain left the ship early this morning to ascend the hill immediately above Cape Morton (two thousand feet in height), in order to ascertain from the nature of the ice what our prospects of pushing on were likely to be. During his absence a haul with the dredge was obtained, but with unimportant results: the continual movement of icebergs in the bay, all more or less aground, would hardly admit of much organic life at the bottom. Fossils abounded in the limestone on shore, and a large collection of specimens was made.

At noon the captain was observed, in his boat, off Cape Morton, with the signal flying for the ships "to weigh."

His orders were speedily executed; and, having picked him up, we were soon running quickly across to the western side. He gave us the very pleasing information that from the summit of Cape Morton he had observed a magnificent lead of water along the west coast, and extending in all probability as far as Cape Beechey. This was indeed delightful intelligence, and served to raise the social barometer many degrees.

Our coal was rapidly diminishing, and we knew that many more days of steaming such as those we had lately had would reduce our fuel to such an extent that we could hope to do little more; for without steam a vessel in these latitudes would indeed be helpless.

11 P.M.—Oh, the hopes and disappointments that we poor Arctic explorers have to endure! First of all a confiding anticipation in the future makes us joyous and expectant, and then we are plunged into the lowest depths of despondency.

Two hours ago we were steaming through a grand expanse of water, looking forward with confidence to reaching, in a few hours, Cape Beechey, or perhaps even Cape Union, both being distinctly visible ahead, whilst Capes Brevoort, Sumner, and Stanton were in sight on our starboard bow.

Passing Cape Baird, however, we were again met by our insatiable enemy, the ice, which defied all our efforts to penetrate it.

We are now slowly picking our way across Lady Franklin Strait towards Cape Bellot, in the hope of being able to reach some place of security where we can remain patiently until a northerly wind shall have cleared a passage for us. Whilst crossing Kennedy Channel we obtained a magnificent view up Petermann Fiord. It is an extensive opening, with no land visible at its head. This is a geographical problem which we hope we shall soon be able to solve. It is difficult to determine at present whether Lady Franklin Strait is really a strait or a deep inlet. We are inclined to the latter belief. This is another question we hope will soon be satisfactorily settled.

Wednesday, August 25th.—At one o'clock this morning, whilst threading our way amongst the ice-floes that bordered the coast, a herd of musk oxen was observed browsing quietly on an adjacent hill. Such an opportunity for obtaining fresh meat was not to be disregarded. A shooting party was quickly organized, and, whilst the boats were being prepared and the hunters getting ready their rifles, the ships were taken into a beautifully snug and land-locked harbour, protected at its mouth by a large island, situated on the northern coast of Lady Franklin Bay.

Here the anchors were let go, and the sportsmen despatched in quest of the game.

Separating into three distinct parties on landing, we advanced cautiously towards the spot where they were last seen grazing, hoping to be able to surround and capture the entire herd. Not only did we all enter keenly into the sport, but our mouths watered at the prospect of again indulging in fresh meat. We pictured to ourselves smoking-hot beef-steaks and savoury calf's liver, dainties that we had for some time been strangers to, being prepared for us after our return to the ship, never even dreaming of a chance of returning empty-handed.

The disposition of our force was well calculated, for the musk oxen being alarmed, in all probability by the blowing off of steam from one of the ships, started in full flight in the direction of a deep ravine. Here they were met by a couple of the hunters, who discharging their rifles dropped two of the herd. The remainder turned and dashed up the side of a steep hill, but only to be met by two more sportsmen, who made such good use of their time and weapons, that they succeeded in shooting the remainder, seven in number.

One of the first brought down was the bull of the herd, a noble fellow; but so tenacious of life that several shots had to be expended, at a very short range, before he bit the dust.

Elated with our success, and having sent back to the ship for assistance in conveying the meat on board, we commenced skinning, cleaning, and cutting up the animals, so as to guard against the possibility of any delay in doing so being the means of tainting the flesh

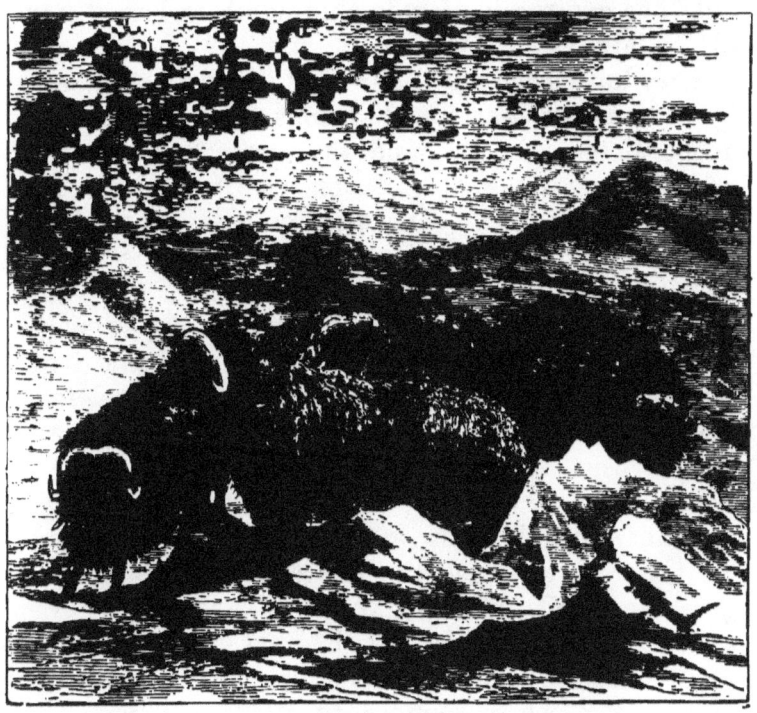

MUSK OXEN.

with the disagreeable musky odour. This, in consequence of the scarcity of knives amongst the party, was a long and tedious process; however, by nine o'clock we had the satisfaction of seeing our "morning's bag" safely on board, amounting altogether to 2,124 lbs. of good fresh meat. Not a bad morning's work!

These animals, from peculiarities they possess, are placed in a genus between the sheep and the ox, and are called *ovibos moschatus*. They are only met with in high latitudes, although traces of them, it is reported, have been seen as far south as 59° N. lat., but they are rarely seen in any numbers lower than 67° N. lat.

They have been seen, and shot, in large numbers, by the various search expeditions wintering at and about Melville Island, and they were also obtained on the opposite side of Kennedy Channel by the "Polaris" in 1872. The crew of this latter vessel succeeded in shooting twenty-six during the twelve months they passed in this latitude. They are gregarious, usually wandering in small herds, although occasionally single specimens are found. The herd just obtained by us consisted of one old bull and four old cows, and two young bulls and two young cows. They subsist on the scant vegetation of these regions—principally grasses and lichens—which they scrape up from under the snow, when the ground is covered. They hardly give one the impression of being very quick and agile, yet they ascend hills and climb over rocks and rough surfaces with great ease. They are reputed to be very irascible, and have frequently been known, when wounded, to attack a hunter and seriously endanger his life. The horns are very broad, covering the brow and crown of the head, and meeting at their base. Our bullets appeared to have no effect when fired at the head. From the bull we obtained no less than 385 lbs. of meat!

Finding that the harbour in which the ships were anchored possessed all the necessary qualifications for rendering the winter quarters of a vessel in the

Arctic Regions comfortable and secure, Captain Nares selected this spot as the place in which he would leave the "Discovery." It appeared in every way adapted for this purpose. A secure harbour, possessing two narrow entrances, with the water so shallow as to effectually prevent the larger and heavier pieces of ice from drifting into it, with a neighbourhood covered with a more luxuriant and richer vegetation than had hitherto been seen, and giving evidences of being well stocked with game—for, in addition to the musk oxen, numerous and recent traces of wolves, foxes, hares, and lemmings had been observed—the place seemed especially suited for passing the winter in; and its selection as the winter quarters of our consort was never regretted.

We all feel that the navigable season is rapidly drawing to a close, and that very few more days are left us. During the last week the temperature has never been above the freezing point; and the young ice has been forming to an alarming extent, even at midday. An advance, if farther advance is to be made, will be better and more speedily accomplished with one ship only, than by having two to look after. The responsibility is lessened, whilst the knowledge that there is another ship to fall back upon, in case of accidents, removes all anxiety.

When the decision that the two ships were to part company was promulgated, it was received with satisfaction, although we were all sorry to lose the companionship of our numerous friends. The evening was spent in an interchange of visits, and many a sincere and fervent "God speed," with a silent but expressive squeeze of the hand, was exchanged between the officers and the men of the two Arctic ships.

In order to strengthen our force on board the "Alert," and to have an extra sledge party for the purpose, if required, of communicating with our consort, an officer, Lieutenant Rawson, and seven men were received from the "Discovery;" the only thing that we were able to give in exchange being 900 lbs. of the musk oxen just procured—a by no means despicable offering!

Everything having been satisfactorily arranged, the "Alert" steamed away from Discovery Harbour on the morning of the 26th, exchanging hearty cheers with her consort as she passed; she hoisting the signal "May Providence prosper your efforts," to which we replied "Happy Winter;" and thus we separated, happy in the knowledge that a safe refuge was established in our rear, with the unknown before us, fervently praying for a successful issue to our undertaking.

CHAPTER X.

THE CROSSING OF THE THRESHOLD.

> " And now there came both mist and snow,
> And it grew wondrous cold.
> And ice, mast high, came floating by,
> As green as emerald.
> And through the drifts, the snowy cliffs
> Did send a dismal sheen ;
> Nor shapes of men, nor beasts we ken,
> The ice was all between.
>   * * * *
> With sloping masts and dripping prow,
> As who pursued with yell and blow,
> Still treads the shadow of his foe,
> And forwards bends his head,
> The ship drove fast, loud roared the blast,
> And *Northwards* aye we fled."
>   COLERIDGE.

Now that we are pursuing our solitary journey northwards, we can the more fully realize that our real work has commenced—the real work towards the achievement of that success which we all so ardently hope will crown our efforts.

Now that we are alone we shall be the more ready to avail ourselves of every opening in the ice that may present itself, every little chance that may occur, which we should be unable to do, if hampered with a second ship.

We had hardly advanced three miles, in fact were still just inside the entrance to the harbour, when the ice, closing in round the point, barred all egress. In endeavouring to steer clear of these fragments, the ship grounded on a projecting spit off a small island, but sustained no injury, floating again immediately she was lightened. As farther advance was out of the question, for the present, in consequence of the pack having drifted in, the vessel was secured under the lee of a natural breakwater at the entrance to Discovery Harbour, ready to take advantage of the first opportunity of making a start that should offer.

Accompanied by Feilden and Rawson, I made an expedition to Distant Cape, whence we obtained a good view of Robeson Channel; but it was anything but an inspiring one. There appeared to be a perfect block of heavy ice right across to the Greenland coast, although a few thin blue lines, denoting streams of water, could be discerned radiating in the pack to the eastward, but apparently leading to nothing.

Some terns, *Sterna Arctica*, were obtained on a small island, as also their young and eggs. The nests were simply little round holes, some in the snow, having a few small pebbles as a bed. Some knots, *Tringa Canutius*, were also obtained; but no amount of search was successful in discovering either the egg or the nest of this bird.

A fine sheet of water, situated on the breakwater, being frozen over, afforded our skaters an opportunity of indulging in their favourite pastime, and of practising both the inside and outside edges to their hearts' content.

The following day was also one of enforced idleness, and no movement could be made with the ship.

Snow fell heavily, much to our annoyance, as it prevented us from keeping a perfect watch on the ice in the channel, in consequence of its density. The ice was being set up Lady Franklin Bay at a great pace. Once during the day it appeared inclined

KNOTS.

to open and give us a chance of proceeding. The skaters and sportsmen were hurriedly called on board; but before steam could be raised the opportunity was lost. In navigating these waters it is necessary to be constantly on the alert, and prepared, at any moment, to take advantage of any chance that may occur; but with the small quantity of fuel we have remaining, it is also necessary to economize and husband that essential aid to advance as much as possible; our fires were therefore always kept low, except when the engines were actually working.

A small fragment of drift-wood was picked up on the island. It resembled some hard wood, but was so wasted and worn by attrition that it was impossible, without subjecting it to microscopic examination, to determine to what species it belonged.

The large island off which we were secured, and which forms the main protection to Discovery Harbour, was named Bellot Island, after the distinguished young French naval officer who lost his life whilst zealously prosecuting the search for Sir John Franklin and his ill-fated companions.

Saturday, August 28*th*.—A thick fog in the morning effectually frustrated all our hopes of advancing; but clearing up towards midday, we were rejoiced at seeing several leads through the ice in the direction of Cape Beechey.

Steam was quickly raised; but, in attempting to cant, the ship took the ground, and much to our chagrin and disappointment remained immovable. This was indeed tantalizing, as we knew by sad experience how capricious were the motions of the ice, and that every moment was of the utmost value to us.

Lightening the ship as much as possible, the rising tide floated her in about a couple of hours, and at 5 P.M., having hoisted up all our boats, we were again able to proceed.

As we rounded the point we hoisted the colours and dipped them three times as a parting farewell to our consort, who had just time to whip up the signal "Good luck" before we were finally shut out from each other's view.

Rounding Distant Cape, we found the channel full

of ice, some of the floes being very massive and of great extent; but between them existed narrow lanes of water, in some places choked by loose slack ice, through which we had little difficulty in penetrating, although at the expense of our rudder, which was so severely injured by the heavy nature of the ice as to be rendered almost useless.

At midnight, when within about a mile of Cape Beechey, ice was encountered stretching right across the channel and pressing so tightly in to the land as to form a dead block to our farther advance. We had then by estimation reached the 82° parallel of latitude. This check was a great damper to our hopes, especially as no bays, or protection of any description for the ship from the pack, could be found in our immediate vicinity.

Our only resource was to return a few miles to the southward and there, in a slight indentation of the land, affording little or no protection, secure the ship to an ice floe, and employ ourselves at once with the rather heavy operations connected with shifting the rudder. This work was performed in about three hours. In the mean time, a small herd of musk oxen having been observed on shore, our sportsmen were despatched in pursuit, and we soon had the satisfaction of hearing that they had succeeded in shooting three, the remainder of the herd having escaped over the hills. This was a very welcome addition to our stock of fresh meat. Our mizzen-rigging was now literally groaning with the amount of meat suspended there; for, in addition to the recent accumulation of musk-ox flesh, the remainder of our sheep, some seven or eight in number, had been slaughtered and added to the general stock. So hard were the portions frozen, that they were very truthfully compared to the legs of mutton and sides of sheep made of wood usually seen hanging in the front of a butcher's shop in a pantomime!

The bay in which we had taken refuge was, in consequence of the work there performed, named "Shift-Rudder Bay."

Sunday, August 29th.—At noon we were again under weigh, Captain Nares having ascended a high hill during the forenoon, from which he had observed an opening in the pack by which we might proceed. Cape Beechey was easily rounded; but, in consequence of the floes closing into the land, we had a very narrow escape of being caught whilst going round Cape Frederick VII., and it was only by pressing the ship at her utmost speed that we succeeded in rounding it in safety. Two minutes after we were round, the floe came into contact with the high steep side of the cape, crumbling against it and piling up hummock on hummock from the irresistible force of the outside pressure. What would have been the fate of our poor little frail ship had she been caught between these two stupendous works of nature?

The ice had now assumed a totally different character from any that we had hitherto seen, being infinitely more massive and heavy. The thickness was estimated at from eighty to one hundred feet, whilst the hummocks formed along the shore and round the edges of the floes were fully twenty-five and thirty feet in height.

These large hummocks received from us the name of "floe-bergs," the term being intended to convey the idea of masses of ice more bulky than ordinary hummocks, and formed in a different way. Some of these huge fragments that fringed the coast line were fully sixty feet in height, yet they were *aground* in some ten and twelve fathoms of water! This will give some idea of the massive nature of the ice with which we were contending. The region of icebergs, the creation of land glaciers, had been passed, and in their place were substituted these floe-bergs, the production of a floating glacier.

To contend with this massive ice required the greatest care and judgment, for little respect is shown to the unfortunate vessel that is exposed to the fatal embrace of what has been aptly termed by our old Arctic navigators "ye unmercifull yce." Before midnight the ship was secured to a large floe in Lincoln Bay, the pack having again closed in to the land, thereby obstructing our advance.

The positions of the different bays and headlands on the western side of Robeson Channel we found strangely at variance with the positions assigned to them on the latest American chart; indeed, the shore, as delineated, was quite unrecognizable. The land on the opposite side of the channel seemed, on the contrary, to be very accurately laid down.

With the exception of a little lemming (*Myodes torquatus*), captured by Captain Nares when he landed in the morning, a solitary dovekie (*Uria grylle*), fluttering about in the ice-encumbered waters, was the only living thing seen during the day. The first-named little animal was the first of its species caught alive, and excited considerable interest, every one being desirous of obtaining a peep at the diminutive little quadruped. One man, more fortunate than his messmates, was literally besieged, by those less lucky than himself in seeing the animal, with numerous questions regarding its appearance. When asked its colour the man hesitated, finding it difficult to describe; but suddenly brightening up he said, "Why, *lemon* colour, of course!" an answer that appeared quite satisfactory, agreeing, as it did, so well with its name!

These little mouse-like creatures are the smallest, yet the most numerous and common, of all quadrupeds in the Arctic regions. They are extremely pugnacious and fearless, and often attract attention, when they would otherwise be unobserved, by their shrill cries of rage at an approaching step. They hibernate in burrows under the snow, and live during the summer on the scant vegetation of these regions. When roasted and served up on toast, like sparrows, they were found to be excellent eating, although provokingly small.

On the same hill where the capture of this little animal was effected, our naturalist picked up a marine shell (*Astarte borealis*), about a mile from the beach, and at least a hundred and fifty feet above the level of the sea. This shell was in excellent preservation, the epidermis still adhering, and in a perfect state.

The apparent freshness of this specimen gave rise to many conjectures regarding the theory of the upheaval of the land, the evidence pointing conclusively to its being both recent and rapid. These regions offer a wide field for the geologist and student of natural history.

Monday, August 30*th*.—During the forenoon, there being no prospect of pushing forward, a large depôt of provisions, consisting of one thousand rations, was landed. This depôt was established for the use of travelling parties from the "Discovery," or from our own ship should it be determined to despatch any to the southward. It was not without some difficulty that the heavy casks were transported from the boats to a suitable position sufficiently removed from the encroachments of the pack. Their transit was only effected by a nautical process known as "parbuckling," by which casks and barrels are either hauled up or lowered down steep inclines.

On the brow of the hill immediately above the depôt a large cairn was erected, in which the usual records were deposited; the provisions themselves being so placed as to form a very conspicuous landmark to any ship passing to the northward, or to any sledge party travelling along the coast line. Whilst engaged in these operations, the pack was observed to slacken considerably, several leads of water opening to the northward, which we fondly hoped would afford us an easy passage towards the attainment of that object which was ever uppermost in our thoughts, and for which we were ready and willing to make any sacrifice—the object of exploring the unknown region, and of reaching a high northern latitude.

Steam was accordingly quickly raised, and another attempt made to proceed; but alas! having incautiously been tempted by promising lanes of water to stray farther from the land than had hitherto been our custom, we were soon hopelessly beset by very heavy ice, of at least eighty or one hundred feet in thickness, and fully ten feet above the surface of the water. So high was it that our boats, suspended at the davits, were seriously endangered, and had in consequence to be "turned in" to avoid being crushed altogether. We were, fortunately, surrounded by loose pieces of broken-off ice, which acting as cushions between the ship and the more massive floes, thereby saved the "Alert" from an unpleasant nip. As there was no saying when we might be deprived of the friendly aid of these "buffers," by any sudden movement of the pack, steam was kept ready in both boilers in order that we might take immediate advantage of any such motion for the purpose of extricating our vessel from her very unpleasant and perilous position.

An anxious night was spent by all on board, and many ineffectual attempts were made to push our way through cracks in the pack that appeared to be inclined to open. Sleep was out of the question—indeed, was hardly thought of—every one being prepared, with his little bag of necessaries, to abandon the ship when such an order, which seemed inevitable, should be given.

On the following day, by dint of much labour, a space was cleared round the stern of the vessel, which enabled us to ship our rudder, and, the ice having slackened a little, by constantly steaming ahead and astern we succeeded in clearing a larger space in which the ship could be worked, when, boldly attacking the pack, we forced our way through, and with relieved minds and thankful hearts extricated ourselves from our dangerous position, and once more secured the ship in Lincoln Bay. The time occupied in steaming through the pack, a distance of about a mile, was exactly five hours!

The ice was observed to be still tightly packed against Cape Union, and consequently hindered us from pushing on.

We had much reason to be grateful for our safe

deliverance from the pack, for, shortly after our extrication, a heavy gale sprang up from the S.W., the effect of which on the ship, beset in such ponderous ice, must have been disastrous in the extreme, and would in all probability have been fatal. Ice navigators, however, are not, as a rule, prone to indulge in ideas as to "what *might* have occurred had this or that happened:" their thoughts and minds must be directed entirely to the present and the future, only too happy and thankful, as the days go by, to find they still have their own good vessel to sustain them, and carry them through another day. To our engines we owed a deep debt of gratitude, for without the powerful aid of steam we should have been unable, before the gale burst upon us, to have effected our deliverance.

Towards midnight the gale freshened considerably, snow fell, and the weather altogether had a very ugly and threatening appearance. We, however, consoled ourselves with the hope that it would clear the ice out of the channel, and thus enable us to proceed. The noise of the pack grinding and squeezing as it was tossed about by a short turbulent sea was anything but pleasing to listen to, resembling in a measure the sound created by the dashing of the surf over a rock-bound coast. One can easily imagine the feelings of those old navigators, in their frail little barks, which gave rise to the expression that "the irksome noyse of the yce bred strange conceits among us." Very "irksome" indeed was that noise to us, and many were the "strange conceits" that we indulged in as we listened to the soughing of the wind and the crashing of the ice!

Wednesday, September 1st, must always be regarded,

at least by all those connected with, or interested in, Arctic research, as a red-letter day in the annals of naval enterprise, and indeed in English history, for on this day a British man-of-war reached a higher northern latitude than had ever yet been reached by any ship, and we had the extreme gratification of hoisting the colours at noon to celebrate the event.

Never was an ensign hoisted by such a number of eager and willing hands. All were desirous of participating in this act, and of sharing the honours of this important proceeding.

Our success in thus attaining a high position was due entirely to the S.W. gale, which blew with such fury, that by nine o'clock in the forenoon the pack was driven so far off the land that a narrow channel of water was left extending to the northward along the coast line. We were not long in availing ourselves of this grand opportunity. The ice anchors were quickly hauled on board, sail was made, and, with the steam ready in case it should be required, we were soon bowling along at the rate of ten knots an hour, " and *northwards* aye we fled." So far had the pack been blown off the shore, that the channel of water was fully three miles in breadth.

It would be impossible to describe the feelings of those on board the "Alert" at this unexpected piece of good fortune; for the lateness of the season, combined with the unprecedented solidity of the ice, had in a measure damped our ardour and forced us to realize the apparent hopelessness of attaining, this year, a high northern latitude. Eagerly and anxiously were the different reports from the crow's-nest listened to, and still to the delight of all came down the cheery words, "Water, plenty of water ahead, and no ice in sight."

Every one was joyous and elated as, at noon, they assembled round the ward-room table to inaugurate, in a glass of Madeira, generously supplied by our wine caterer, the auspicious event, and to wish success to their flag.

Unfortunately snow was falling heavily, and the weather was so thick that little could be seen. We could just make out that the land along which we were steering, and which trended to the N.E., was composed of high cliffs with numerous ravines and valleys running down to the water's edge; but, to our disappointment, we failed to observe either harbour or bay, or any place that would afford a refuge or protection of any description for the ship. Arctic navigation, like everything else, has its dark as well as its bright side!

After rounding Cape Union the coast trended away to the westward of north, and the wind, which had hitherto been blowing so fresh, suddenly subsided. So did our joyful anticipations, for one short hour after our ensign had fluttered out so gaily before the breeze, we were stopped by a barrier of ice of great thickness, through which there was no prospect of penetrating. The land also appeared to lose the bold rugged character that had been such a prominent feature between Lincoln Bay and Cape Union, and now assumed an undulating form as it trended away to the N.W., the coast being low and entirely covered with snow.

Having set our minds at rest that a farther advance, for the present, was perfectly impracticable, we reluctantly retraced our steps to the southward for about a mile, and secured the ship inside a fringe of grounded floe-bergs that lined the coast and which promised to afford us protection, in fact, the only protection, from the irresistible pressure of the pack. A depôt of provisions, consisting of two thousand rations, was immediately landed, in order to guard against all accidents that might happen to the ship, and also to be of use to our southern travelling parties, should we succeed in reaching a higher latitude in the ship. The weather still continued thick; but during a clear interval we succeeded in getting a good view to the northward from the summit of a hill about two hundred and fifty feet above the level of the sea. But it was a most cheerless scene that presented itself in that direction. Nothing but ice, tight and impassable, was to be seen—a solid impenetrable mass that no amount of imagination or theoretical belief could ever twist into an " open Polar Sea " !

We were reluctantly compelled to come to the conclusion that we had in reality arrived on the shore of the Polar Ocean; a frozen sea, of such a character as utterly to preclude the possibility of its being navigated by a ship; a wide expanse of ice and snow, whose impenetrable fastnesses seemed to defy the puny efforts of mortal men to invade and expose their hitherto sealed and hidden mysteries. Still we did not give up all hope of reaching a higher northern position in the ship. We knew the wonderful effect that a gale of wind would produce on the pack, and we hoped when the weather cleared, we should still be able to see, and reach, land to the northward.

For the present then we could only put our trust

in Providence, who had already guarded and favoured us almost beyond our most sanguine expectations, and pray that He might still continue to watch over and protect us, and grant us such a measure of success as would increase our knowledge of this world and thereby add to His glory.

CHAPTER XI.

FLOE-BERG BEACH.

> "The cold earth slept below,
> Above the cold sky shone,
> And all around
> With a chilling sound,
> From caves of ice and fields of snow
> The breath of night like death did flow
> Beneath the sinking moon."
>
> SHELLEY.

IN order more effectually to ensure the safety of the ship, the men were at once employed in removing a large quantity of loose ice, directly inside the line of friendly floe-bergs, so as to allow the vessel to be hauled farther in and thus obtain more complete protection from the encroachments of the pack. This was no easy work, for the wind had again sprung up and blew with terrific violence, whilst the temperature had fallen as much as ten degrees below the freezing point.

Before we had succeeded in completing our preparations a violent squall struck the ship, the lines by which she was temporarily held parted, and we were blown clean out from our harbour of refuge. Steam was instantly raised, and an anchor let go, which fortunately brought us up. During the succeeding hours the gale blew with increased fury, but being an off-shore wind, we were in a measure protected, whilst it had the effect of driving the pack off, so as to raise our hopes at the prospect of again proceeding northward.

Suddenly, without any warning, the wind shifted, and drove the whole body of the pack towards the land. Our danger now was imminent. To be caught between the fast closing ice and the grounded floe-bergs would be certain destruction, to escape to the southward before the pack impinged on Cape Union was quite out of the question, and to steam into the pack would be madness. Our only hope of safety was to endeavour to haul the ship inside the grounded floe-bergs, and again avail ourselves of their friendly protection. No time was to be lost; it was a case of almost life and death to us. The men, always to be depended upon in a crisis like the present, responded to the call with alacrity, and by dint of hard work we succeeded in hauling the ship into a safe position. We were not a moment too soon: it was a race between the ice and the ship, in which the latter was, fortunately for us, the victor. Scarcely had we reached our place of refuge when the pack came into contact with the bergs, scrunching and squeezing in a most unpleasant manner as it swept by, and serving to illustrate, in a very practical way, the dreadful fate to which we should have been subjected had we not been fortunate enough to escape in time.

It is difficult to imagine a more desolate position to pass a winter than the one in which we were placed. Our ship was on an exposed and, apparently, unsafe coast, without even the protection of a bay, within one hundred yards of a low undulating beach, on which, should any extraordinary pressure of the pack destroy our protecting bergs, we must inevitably be forced and wrecked, exposed to all the rigours of an Arctic winter; and yet, notwithstanding these unenviable drawbacks, the official announcement that this place had been decided upon as our winter quarters was received with a deep feeling of relief and thankfulness. This determination was not, however, arrived at for some days, when, from careful watching of the pack, it was decided that a farther advance was absolutely impossible.

Winter was advancing upon us with rapid strides, eager to seize us in its icy grasp; so quickly, indeed, that in two days we were able to *walk on shore* on the new and rapidly forming ice. The now steadily falling temperature was another and a sure indication that the navigable season was at an end.

Without a harbour or projecting headland of any description to protect our good ship from the furious gusts that we must naturally expect, the "Alert" lay, apparently, in a vast frozen ocean, having land on one side, but bounded on the other by the chaotic and illimitable polar pack.

The land had already assumed a wintry aspect, and the ship, to be in unison with her surroundings, had also put on a garb of snow and ice, each spar and each rope being double its ordinary thickness from the accumulation of frost rime. Everything was white, solemn, and motionless around us; no voice of bird or beast was heard to disturb the silence. All was as still and silent as the tomb—a silence that until then had never been broken by the presence of man.

> "No other noyse, nor people's troublous cries,
> As still are wont to annoy the walled towne,
> Might there be heard, but carelesse quiet lyes,
> Wrapt in eternal silence far from enemyes."

Night, to which we had long been strangers, gradually came upon us, the darkness increasing perceptibly as each day passed away. From the 3rd of September, on which day the sun set at midnight, the days decreased in length, and the stars were again seen to twinkle in the heavens.

From a neighbouring hill we obtained a clear and unobstructed view of our surroundings. The coast continued to the N.W. in a succession of large bays, terminating in an abrupt cape some forty miles distant. In order to assimilate the names of the various bays and headlands with those of the American chart, this extreme point was called Cape Joseph Henry. Beyond Cape Joseph Henry all was conjecture. It might be the southern extreme of a large bay or inlet, or it might be the northern termination of land. No land of any description could be seen to the northward—nothing but the rugged pack. So formidable and compact appeared this icy barrier that it seemed to stand out bold and resolute in its strength, effectually setting at defiance the puny efforts of man to penetrate its solidity, saying, as it were, "Thus far shalt thou go, and no farther." And, indeed, we had much cause to be thankful to Him who had hitherto watched over and protected us in many dangers, and who had allowed us to penetrate thus far into this remote and unknown portion of the globe.

A long range of high hills could be seen to the westward, whilst on the opposite side of the channel the distant land of Greenland was indistinctly observed, its most northern point bearing about N.E. (*true*).*

The positions of the northern extremes of land, on either side of the channel, were, for a time, a matter of some uncertainty, and it was really doubtful which was situated in the highest latitude. It was not until after the return of the autumn sledging parties that this important question was definitely decided, the land on the western side proving to be nearest the Pole.

It must not be imagined, because farther progress in the ship had ceased, that our labours had in any way diminished; on the contrary, we felt that our real work was about to commence: a work in which we should all share in a greater or less degree, and a work the achievement of which had been our sole engrossing thought since leaving England.

Before finally deciding upon the position of our winter quarters, Captain Nares was desirous of ascertaining whether a more protected spot could be found for the ship in the numerous bays to the N.W. than the exposed position she then occupied.

Accordingly, early on the 5th of September, Aldrich and myself started away with a couple of sledges, each drawn by a team of eight dogs, under the guidance of Frederic the Eskimo, and Petersen, the Danish dog-driver. Our route lay along the edge of the coast, where, at times, we were able to take advantage of the ice-foot on which to travel; but as a rule there was no continuity of this land-ice, and we were compelled to strike across an undulating country, deeply

* All compass bearings referred to are *true*, unless stated to be *magnetic*.

covered with snow, ascending hills frequently as high as two and three hundred feet above the level of the sea, whence we obtained good views of the surrounding country. The general direction in which we travelled was N.W., the coast line being a series of indentations in the land, some of such a size as to form fine harbours and bays; but, alas! they could not be utilized for our ship, for they were rendered unapproachable by a chain of high hummocks extending in every case across the entrances, whilst the water in the harbours appeared to be permanently frozen, and therefore inaccessible for a vessel.

It was a novel sensation to us to be thus dashing along on our light sledges, exploring a perfectly unknown country: a wild and barren tract of land, a snow-covered expanse, receding from our view in long undulations into the interior, until lost amongst the high conical-shaped hills of from one to two thousand feet in height, that invariably form the chief feature of Arctic scenery in these high latitudes. At noon we made a brief halt for luncheon, our appetites having been rendered doubly keen by the sharp cold air of a temperature some twenty degrees below freezing point; but which had, until the halt was called, been unheeded, the constant jumping on and off the sledge and assisting the dogs over difficulties having kept us in a perfect glow. Innocently pulling off our mitts, we commenced a vigorous onslaught upon the Australian beef with which we had supplied ourselves; but the first contact of our fingers with the handles of the knives proved the folly of such a proceeding, and compelled us again to resume our mitts. These, however, were now frozen so hard that they were with difficulty put on! Petersen using a tin cup to drink a little rum mixed with snow, and disregarding his mitts, burnt his hand rather severely, whilst we were all obliged to rub the edge of the cup well with our hands before putting it to our lips!

These little inconveniences were to us a source of great merriment; in fact, they must really be experienced before they can be properly and thoroughly appreciated!

The Eskimo dogs appear to me to be very differently constituted to their more civilized brethren. In England a halt for lunch whilst shooting is a signal for all the dogs to assemble and importune for fragments of the feast, which they greedily devour. My own dog "Nellie" would never be satisfied without obtaining a very large share of any impromptu meal. With the Eskimo dogs it is quite different. As soon as the sledges are halted they lie down and sleep, and rarely attempt to move until they are required to do so. Should a piece of meat be thrown to them they may condescend to swallow it; but they turn up their noses at a piece of biscuit, utterly despising it as an article of food. Yet these dogs are excessively voracious, and always hungry! Nothing in the shape of fresh meat, or even skin, is safe from their insatiable voracity; even the thongs that are used for lashing the different parts of a sledge together, unless they have been well rubbed over with tar, are unsafe, and will most assuredly be gnawed off. Notwithstanding this, they have little liking for cooked meat, positively refuse biscuit, and are not troublesome when they observe you eating.

We were *en route* again directly our luncheon was consumed, the dogs starting off with renewed vigour and speed after their short rest, when we came suddenly upon a precipitous ravine, almost too late to stop our team in their headlong career. By springing out of the sledge and holding on with might and main, we just succeeded in stopping them in time, pulling up almost on the very brink of the precipice. Retracing our steps for a short distance, we left the hills, and continued our course along the coast line,

DOG-SLEDGE IN DIFFICULTIES.

until our farther progress was checked by water, a channel connecting two large bays, which from their shape afterwards went by the name of Dumb-bell Bay.

Swimming about in this little sheet of water was a small flock of eider-ducks, eleven in number, that appeared to be as much surprised at beholding us as we were at seeing them. They did not, however, seem disposed to fly away. The only weapon we had was a rifle with twelve rounds of ammunition. With this we commenced hostilities, rejoicing in the anticipation of a fresh-meat meal when we returned to the ship. So utterly unconcerned did they appear that we actually succeeded in shooting five before the remainder took flight; but to our great chagrin we were unable to possess ourselves of any of our victims, as they had unfortunately all fallen into the water *just* out of our reach. This was very tantalizing, as neither of us felt inclined to risk being frozen for the sake even of roast duck by plunging in after them. We were reluctantly compelled to leave them. During the following week, however, they were recovered, having all been frozen together in the water. With the exception of these birds, no animal life was seen, although we observed numerous traces of ptarmigan and lemmings. Tufts of saxifrage and some grasses were seen, but so thickly was the land covered with snow that it was impossible to arrive at any conclusion regarding the vegetation of the country.

In consequence of the report that we brought back, Floe-berg Beach was decided upon as the position of the "Alert's" winter quarters, and preparations were immediately made for securing the ship, and for making as extensive an exploration of the land to the northward as the duration of light would admit.

The land in our immediate vicinity was also very naturally an object of special interest to us. Speculations were rife regarding its extent and formation. The possibility of obtaining game of any description was a matter of much importance to us who were doomed to pass so many months in these icy solitudes.

Alas! any hopes that we had cherished in this respect were soon found to be fallacious. The land, for the succeeding eight months, proved to be as devoid of life as its appearance was sterile and desolate.

On the 9th of September Aldrich went away with the dog-sledges, accompanied by two or three of his messmates, for three days, for the purpose of more thoroughly exploring the country in the hopes of obtaining game.

On the 11th I left the ship with Parr and Egerton and eighteen men, with the object of advancing a couple of boats to the northward along the proposed route of exploration. It was thought that they might prove useful during the future sledging operations of the expedition. We came back in four days, having successfully accomplished our mission.

On our return journey we encountered a furious gale of wind, which broke up the ice along the coast line, and forced us to drag our sledges over the hills, the summits of which were almost bare, the force of the gale having blown the snow completely off. Any one who has ever attempted to drag a sledge over a rough stony road will know the severe toil and labour that is required to be exerted in order to make any progress. Crossing a bay we made a short halt for luncheon on the ice, under the lee of a high hummock, and narrowly escaped destruction from having selected such a spot for a halt. Without our observing it, the ice began breaking up, and it was only by strenuous exertions that we succeeded in reaching the shore in safety, whence we observed the ice on which we had recently been encamped drifting in small fragments to seaward. If this disruption had not been observed in time, nothing short of a miracle could have saved us.

The violence of the gale was so terrific that pebbles and shingle were blown along by its force, mercilessly striking our faces and causing acute pain. Still we had to struggle onwards, for there was no possible lee under which we could pitch our tents and obtain shelter. An attempt to do so was unsuccessful, and had to be abandoned.

One of the men, failing from sheer exhaustion, had to be carried on the sledge. This seriously added to our difficulties, for it increased the load which the wearied sledgers had to drag, whilst it diminished the power of the draggers. But the indomitable spirit and pluck of the British sailor overcame all obstacles, and after an arduous march of eighteen hours in the face of a furious hurricane, we arrived, to our no small relief, alongside the "Alert." Never was a goal attained with more pleasure and satisfaction than was our Arctic home reached that night by the fatigued and half-blinded sledge travellers. Untrained as they were, this forced march had seriously overtaxed their strength and entailed much suffering. Some few were, on their return, placed under the doctor's hands.

Meanwhile those remaining on board the ship, but few in number, spent an anxious and trying time.

The young ice, by which the ship was surrounded, had been completely broken up by the fury of the gale, and had disappeared; and had it not been for the protecting grounded floe-bergs, small mercy would have been shown to the good ship "Alert," by "ye thick-ribbed ice."

Small fragments of the pack, large enough, however, to be unpleasant and disagreeable neighbours, would occasionally find their way between the floebergs, and drift about in our immediate vicinity. These it was our object to secure as speedily as possible, otherwise their incessant movement backwards and forwards with the tide would break up the young ice, or even prevent it from forming. The ominous grinding noise of the pack, as it swayed to and fro in the channel, and the terrible war that appeared to be raging between the floes as they came into furious contact with each other, pulverizing their sides or rending huge fragments from their edges, was a sound and sight that struck us with wonder and awe.

The grandeur and solemnity of the scene gave rise to thoughts of our own weakness and insignificance amidst these wonders of the far north.

On the morning after our return on board, the wind having subsided considerably, and a large channel of water existing between the land and the pack, Captain Nares determined upon seeking more secure and sheltered winter quarters in one of the numerous bays immediately to the northward of our present position, in the hope that the gale would have broken up the ice and so afforded us an entrance.

Steam was quickly raised and the rudder shipped; but from some, at that time, unknown cause we were unable to lower the screw into its place, or rather to enter the shaft. Our chance therefore of getting away was lost, as before midnight the gale was blowing as furiously as ever. The following day, however, the weather again cleared up, and renewed attempts were made to ship the screw, but always without success. Whilst so engaged a shift of wind occurred, and we had the mortification of seeing the whole body of the pack close the channel of water and resume its place along the coast, where it remained during the entire winter, effectually sealing us up. We had good reason to be thankful to our screw for causing our detention, for a subsequent examination of the coast proved only too plainly that the ice had not been broken up and blown out of any of the harbours that we should have sought, and that we should not have found any better sheltered position than the one we then occupied. In all probability we should have been caught by the fast closing ice—an occurrence rather unpleasant even to speculate upon. We afterwards discovered the reason for the failure of our attempts to ship the screw. On lowering it into the water, the ice formed so quickly in the "boss" that it effectually prevented the shaft from entering!

The ship was now secured by lines to the floebergs, and by anchors and cables to the shore, until she should be permanently frozen in.

We also busily engaged ourselves in making the necessary preparations for the autumn sledging operations. Travelling garments were issued, tents thoroughly overhauled, and sledges prepared.

On the 22nd of September Aldrich was despatched with three men and two dog-sledges, provisioned for fourteen days, as a sort of pioneering expedition; his orders being to proceed, if possible, as far as Cape Joseph Henry, there to erect a cairn and deposit a record with full information regarding the practicability of travelling, that would be of use to the main party which would follow him in a few days.

By the 25th the ice had again formed around the

ship, and was of sufficient thickness to bear heavy weights. This was the day selected for the departure of the sledging parties. The force consisted of three eight-men sledges, officered by Parr and May, the whole under my command. My sledge was named the "Marco Polo;" Parr's, the "Victoria;" and May's, the "Hercules." My orders were to advance as far to the northward, along the land, as possible, and at our extreme position to establish a large depôt of provisions in readiness for the use of the main exploring parties that would be despatched in that direction during the ensuing spring. Our provisions were all carefully weighed and packed; the maximum weight dragged by each man on leaving the ship was 201 lbs., decreasing at the rate of 3 lbs. per diem due to the consumption of provisions. The slight experience that we obtained during the previous few days' sledging stood us now in good stead; the men who had recently been so employed being regarded as veterans in sledge work by those who were for the first time being initiated into its mysteries. All started in the very best spirits, animated by the same desire to do their utmost, and to achieve, so far as in them lay, success and honour for the expedition.

The details connected with the sledging operations must have a chapter to themselves. I make no apology for not entering more fully into the journeys performed by Aldrich and others, as the description of one sledging expedition suffices for all, and I am, of course, best able to describe those in which I was myself personally engaged.

CHAPTER XII.

AUTUMN TRAVELLING.

> " When suddenly a grosse fog over spred,
>   With his dull vapour all that desert has,
> And heaven's cheerfull face enveloped ;
>   That all things one, and one as nothing was,
>   And this great universe seemed one confused mass.
>
> " Thereat they greatly were dismay'd, ne wist
>   How to direct theyr way in darknes wide ;
> But feared to wander in that wastefull miste,
>   For tombling into mischiefe unespyde :
>   Worse is the danger hidden than descride."
>
> SPENSER.

THERE are, I am sure, many among those "who stay at home at ease" who have little or no idea of what sledge travelling in the Arctic Regions is like, and who even fail to realize that it entails hard work of any description.

Their imaginations picture the travellers seated on sledges, comfortably wrapped up in shawls and furs, and drawn by a team of dogs or reindeer gaily caparisoned, with their bells jingling as they dash along at a rapid pace over a smooth plain of snow and ice. They imagine that after the toil of the day is over a large fire is built up, and, having obtained some salmon, venison, or other product of the chase, a sumptuous meal is cooked and discussed, after which the sledge travellers compose themselves to sleep in a nice warm snow-house or wooden hut constructed by their attendants. All this sounds very delightful, and is, to my personal knowledge, believed to be a fairly true picture of Arctic life by a large majority of people. Unfortunately it is the very reverse of sledge life on the shores of the Polar Ocean. Let us see what it is like in reality. There, great climatic hardships have to be endured, combined with physical labour of no ordinary description. No change or variety of any sort can be made in the fare, nor can more than a certain allowance be allotted to each individual. When that is consumed, hunger must be borne with patience until the time has arrived for the next meal, for until that is due nothing is obtainable.

For shelter at night time, a tent made of the very lightest material (for economy of weight is the most important point to be considered in sledge travelling) is all the covering to protect the travellers from the furious onslaughts of a biting wind, always accompanied by a blinding snowdrift. So searching is the latter that in spite of all efforts it will penetrate through every little orifice into the tent, covering everything inside with a layer of minute snow crystals, and rendering an uncomfortable night still more comfortless and disagreeable. Rolled up in their bags, with the hard frozen sea as their couch, affording little rest to their aching and frost-bitten limbs, the wearied sledgers vainly attempt in sleep to become oblivious to the present. As for a fire by which circulation might be restored in their numbed extremities, that is quite out of the question. A limited amount of spirits of wine, barely sufficient to cook the allowance of provisions, is all the fuel with which they are supplied. Even if the material for making a fire, such as driftwood, was available, it would be impossible to benefit by it, for it could not be lighted in the tent, whilst outside, under such circumstances as I have related, it would be impracticable.

This is a slight sketch of what has to be endured by the Polar sledge traveller; but a cheerful spirit, a contented mind, and an ardent desire to achieve success are quite sufficient to enable him to withstand the attendant hardships, and even to laugh at and treat them with contempt.

I cannot do better than quote the words of Sir George Nares, who, addressing our men before leaving England, whilst explaining to them the nature of the work that they were about to engage in, and speaking from his own personal previous experience of sledge life, said, "That if they could imagine the hardest work they had ever been called upon to perform in their lives intensified to the utmost degree, it would only be as child's play in comparison with the work they would have to perform whilst sledging!"

These prophetic words were fully realized, and were often recalled and commented on by the men during their initiation into the work of sledging.

The autumn sledge travelling has been alluded to by a very distinguished and successful explorer in the Arctic Regions, as "the very acme of discomfort." In the accuracy of this statement we, one and all, fully concurred.

The principal reasons that sledging at this period of the year is more disagreeable than in the spring are, first, because the rapidly decreasing light caused by the sun's altitude lessening day by day is decidedly opposed to either work or comfort. Before our return from sledging, the sun had illumined for the last time, until its reappearance the following year, the summits of the snow-covered hills in the vicinity of the "Alert's" winter quarters, and had sunk, slowly and majestically, beneath the southern horizon, bequeathing to us only for a short time a few bright rays until the long polar night wrapped us in its sombre mantle, and enveloped us in gloom and obscurity for many months.

> "'Tis gone, that bright and orbèd blaze,
> Fast fading from our wistful gaze;
> Yon mantling cloud has hid from sight
> The last faint pulse of quivering light."

A few hours of twilight, therefore, were all we had in which to work. Candles we had none. Our breakfast before we started in the morning and our supper after we halted in the evening had to be discussed in gloomy darkness. Our notes had to be written in our journals before entering the tent, even at the risk of frost-bitten fingers.

In the second place, at this time of the year the ice, over which the sledges have to be dragged, is of very recent formation, and is consequently weak and dangerous. The travellers are therefore more liable to immersion by breaking through the thin ice at this period of the season than they are during the spring, or indeed at any other time. Young, and therefore smooth and level ice, covered with a treacherous layer of snow, often entices the unwary to turn from the rougher but stronger floes to travel on its flat plain surface. An immersion is invariably the result. Sometimes the leading men on the drag-ropes break through this weak ice first, and, by so doing, time is given to stop and save the sledge; but very often the ice directly under the sledge gives way without previous warning, when every effort must be at once directed to save the sledge. Although this is always successful it is generally at the expense of the greater part of the biscuit, which is so saturated with salt water as to be uneatable, and the wetting, and the consequent freezing, of the tent with all its appurtenances. Nothing more wretched and miserable can be conceived than having to pass the night in a stiffly frozen sleeping bag, inside a tent, which at the best of times is barely large enough to accommodate the party of men for whom it is allotted, but which has been considerably shrunk by being frozen. Not the least unpleasant part is the process of pitching it, for having become as hard as a piece of board, it is with great difficulty unfolded; more especially as this operation has to be performed after the fatigues of a hard day's sledging, by wearied men, in such a temperature that it is impossible to expose the hands bare to the cold, and it must therefore be carried out with mittens on.

The constant wetting of the feet also renders the men more liable to frost-bites; whilst the heavy fall of snow, usually experienced in these regions during the autumn, renders the work ten times more arduous. For the air thus becomes so thick that it is impossible to see many yards ahead, and we have to trust solely to a compass as a guide. We might, in truth, fairly quote the lines from Spenser's "Faërie Queene," at the heading of the present chapter, as illustrating our difficulties in this respect—

> "That all things one, and one as nothing was,
> And this great universe seemed one confused mass."

And lastly this continual breaking through the ice of both men and sledge, combined with the heavy and incessant fall of snow, renders the task of walking and dragging a sledge one of extreme labour and anxiety. These were the little difficulties we had to

START OF THE AUTUMN SLEDGES.

experience during our novitiate in this autumn sledge travelling, and they must be generally expected by explorers who go away so late in the year.

In a future chapter I propose to give a full account of the routine of sledge life, of the equipment and scale of provisions, and of all other details connected with sledging operations in the Arctic Regions. I will now, therefore, proceed at once to give a brief account of our journey, for the purpose of laying out a depôt in the autumn, which occupied three weeks of very severe and harassing work.

At eight o'clock, on the 25th of September, the three officers commanding sledges, myself and Lieutenants Parr and May, assembled at breakfast in sledging costume, and a rattling good breakfast our caterer gave us. At 8.15 our standards were displayed on the sledges, the ship hoisting the ensign. At 8.30 the crews took up their stations alongside their respective sledges, and the order was given to march. Our men stepped out bravely, and as they did so three hearty cheers resounded from the ship. I called a halt and returned the salute with as much emphasis as twenty-four powerful pairs of lungs could give, and then continued the march. The young ice seemed strong enough to bear, so leaving the ice foot, on which the travelling was heavy, we ventured on the new ice. But we had not gone more than a mile when, to my horror, Parr's sledge, the "Victoria," went through! It was a case of all hands to the rescue, and after fifteen minutes of hard tugging and hauling we succeeded in dragging it upon a firm piece of ice. But everything was thoroughly saturated. There was nothing for it but to send back at once for another sledge and dry things. This being done, we again proceeded for about three miles, when suddenly I heard a crack, and looking round, there was my sledge through! We dragged it on shore, and unpacking at once, I was glad to find that we had suffered less than the "Victoria;" but it was bad enough. Our tent and gear at the top were of course saturated, and nearly all our biscuit spoilt. However, I did not think it advisable to return, so repacking we made another start, and shortly afterwards were rejoined by Parr. After marching for twelve miles I halted for the night with the temperature 3° below zero, the tent frozen hard and shrunk considerably. Next day we marched thirteen miles over ice whose blue uneven surface was as smooth as glass, making it very hard work for the men, who were sorely put to it to maintain their footing. They worked splendidly, trudging merrily along, making light of the heavy loads and the treacherous ice, thinking only of performing a good day's work, and of advancing the depôt as far north as possible.

On the third day, being unable to round a point of land owing to several lanes of water, we were obliged to unload the sledges and carry the things piecemeal across a neck of land about two miles in width and a hundred feet above the level of the sea. On the same evening snow began to fall, and from that time it fell incessantly until our return to the ship, increasing in depth day by day. This, combined with the softness of the snow as it fell, seriously impeded our advance, and we were frequently obliged to halt our sledges whilst the men were employed clearing a road with the shovels. So impervious was the air, owing to the heavy fall of snow, that it was only occasionally that we were able to obtain glimpses of the land as we journeyed onwards, rendering it most difficult to make out its conformation, or even the direction in which the coast line trended.

From the unaccustomed work of dragging, the shoulders of the men began to evince symptoms of rawness, although they constantly shifted their drag belts from one shoulder to the other. In spite of these little drawbacks, and the dull overcast weather that generally prevailed, the spirits of the men never flagged, and every night the labour of the day would be forgotten, and singing and laughter would be the only sounds heard issuing from our little camp, long after we had comfortably settled ourselves in our sleeping bags.

It was amusing to listen to the quaint remarks and witty conversation of the men, as, reclining in their bags and smoking their pipes, they would, regardless of the generally dreaded presence of the commander, broach lower deck topics, and freely discuss and criticize them. I was much surprised at the extensive Arctic knowledge which they possessed, showing that they had read largely on this subject, and were anxious to learn yet more.

I must own that the subject of eating and drinking monopolized a very large share of the conversation; nor did they only occupy our minds whilst awake, for they frequently formed the subject of our dreams. On one occasion when I aroused the men in the morning one of them said, "Oh! I am sorry you called me so soon, sir, for I was dreaming that I was eating plum pudding, and if you had let me finish it would have been as good as a breakfast to me!" Gales of wind were, of course, serious impediments to our advance, and were of not unfrequent occurrence. They invariably necessitated a halt, as, irrespective of the cold wind being productive of frost-bites, it was almost impossible to make way through the blinding snow-drift, which did not admit of anything being seen even at the distance of a yard or two!

On the 4th of October, half our provisions being consumed, and there being the prospect of very heavy travelling before us on our homeward journey, it was decided to return. The depôt was therefore established, on the brow of a ridge just above our encampment. It consisted of 870 lbs. of pemmican and 240 lbs. of bacon. May and myself pushed on, with the object of reaching Cape Joseph Henry; but the weather was too thick to obtain any view, and, for the same reason, it was impossible to ascertain the trend of the coast or the nature of the travelling to the northward. The floes seemed to be composed of very heavy ice, and the hummocks were piled up to a great height along the coast, especially off any projecting points of land. Lieutenant Aldrich had, however, ascended a hill some two thousand feet in height, and was fortunate in having a fine clear day. From Cape Joseph Henry the land, he saw, trended away to the westward, but there was no indication of anything but the impenetrable polar pack to the north. We reached a latitude of about 82° 50′ N. before turning our steps homewards.

On the return journey the dragging became infinitely more irksome and laborious. The snow had accumulated to such a depth as to render some of the ravines and promontories almost impassable, being above the men's knees nearly all the time. On one occasion we were compelled to take our sledges up a range of hills two hundred and fifty feet above the level of the sea, in order to pass a precipitous cliff, off which was a stream of water, and then to lower them down a steep incline on the opposite side. To add to our difficulties, a sudden fall of temperature produced many severe frost-bites, principally on the feet and toes. Circulation was always restored as speedily as possible by the application of the warm hand, and the injured part was then dressed with glycerine ointment and lint.

The hills, over which we were obliged to take our sledges, subsequently went by the name of the "Frost-bite Range," in consequence of the many casualties sustained during the time we were on them.

On the 9th the temperature was 15° below zero, and the boots, stockings, and foot wrappers were frozen to the men's feet. On coming down the hills the sledges had literally to be lowered to the ice-foot from a height of two hundred and fifty feet, at a very steep angle. Thence it was necessary to follow the shore, where enormous hummocks of ice were piled up, having huge cracks and fissures, into which we sunk to our necks in snow. In crossing some sludgy ice between the hummocks, on the 11th, Lieutenant May unfortunately went through, and was so severely frost-bitten that he eventually had to suffer amputation of one of his great toes.

The sun set at about one in the afternoon. A glorious sight: the colours of the sunrise and sunset seeming to be blended together. This was on Tuesday, and at breakfast on the following Friday all the provisions would be expended. The 13th was the last day of the sun's appearance.

On the 14th the temperature was down to 25° below zero, and the travelling very heavy; but our sufferings were nearly over. At seven we sighted the ship, and hoisted our sledge standards. All the officers and ship's company came out to meet and help us, and by 8.50 P.M. we were on board.

Some of the frost-bites were so severe as to render amputation necessary. This arose from the difficulty of finding out the injury in time. A frost-bite steals upon one like a thief in the night, and before the victim is aware it often happens that mortification has set in. No less than half the party were placed on the sick list from being more or less severely frost-bitten.

It was a very great relief and comfort to us to be again on board, and extremely gratifying to receive such a welcome as that extended to us by our mess-mates. They were already feeling a little anxious at our prolonged absence, knowing that we were only provisioned for twenty days, and fearing that our return journey would be greatly delayed by the late excessive fall of snow.

How comfortable the ward-room looked, with the lamps burning brightly, a cheerful fire blazing in the stove, and, what delighted us almost still more, a clean white cloth spread upon the table, and on it a sumptuous repast, made doubly inviting by a couple of decanters of madeira and port! These little comforts and luxuries, though they may appear to casual readers unimportant and insignificant, are thoroughly enjoyed and appreciated by wearied and foot-sore travellers who have been strangers to light, comfort, and a good meal, though only for three short weeks. The pleasure of a warm bath and the enjoyment of brushing one's hair are beyond all description! We were all a little thinner when we returned; but, with the exception of the frost-bites, none the worse for our expedition.

So far as the results were concerned we were quite satisfied, considering them perfectly successful.

We had established a depôt of provisions some forty miles to the northward of the ship, which would very materially assist the sledging campaign of the ensuing spring. A large amount of thorough practical experience had been gained, which we hoped would bear good fruit in the coming year. And we had succeeded in reaching and passing the highest latitude attained, to the northward of Spitzbergen, by that distinguished Arctic navigator, Sir Edward Parry, forty-eight years before, during his memorable journey over the frozen sea towards the North Pole.

These were the most important results gained by the autumn sledging.

The disappearance of the sun before our return necessarily prevented a more protracted exploration being made. As it was we only had sufficient light during midday for a very few hours' work.

Perhaps, as it was our first experience in sledging, it was as well we were not able to remain absent for a greater length of time. As an instance of the manner in which the different articles increased in weight during the autumn travelling, we found on our return to the ship that the tent which had previously weighed 32 lbs. had increased to 55 lbs., the coverlet from 21 lbs. to 48 lbs., the lower robe from 18 lbs. to 40 lbs., the floor-cloth from 11 lbs. to 29 lbs., and everything else in proportion! This increase is due to the absorption of all moisture, which instantly freezes. In the spring, although the temperature is far lower, this moisture, even when frozen, is extracted by exposure to the sun. In the autumn this is impossible, as the sun has disappeared.

WINTER QUARTERS, H.M.S. "ALERT."

CHAPTER XIII.

WINTER QUARTERS.

> "Let winter come! let polar spirits sweep
> The dark'ning world and tempest-troubled deep.
> Though boundless snows the withered heath deform,
> And the dim sun *ne'er* wanders through the storm,
> Yet shall the smile of social love repay
> With mental light the melancholy day."
> CAMPBELL.

THE sledge travellers having all returned, the necessary preparations for passing the winter were immediately taken in hand.

Notwithstanding the loss of the sun, which took its final departure on the 11th of October, we had for many days sufficient light, during five or six hours of the day, to enable us to carry out the manifold duties connected with the preparations for a winter in the Arctic Regions.

Although the ship was completely frozen in, and the ice in which she was imprisoned was increasing in thickness day by day, additional precautions for her safety were taken by burying a couple of the largest anchors on shore, and freezing them into their holes by pouring water over them; to these were attached the chain cables. These we felt would be a perfect security for us against any off-shore gale.

Provisions in large quantities were landed as a precaution, in case any unforeseen event should, during the winter, cause the destruction of our ship, and so at one fell swoop deprive us both of home and supplies. Out of the casks and cases so landed a spacious house was constructed, capable, if necessary, of affording accommodation to our entire party. This house, which went by the name of "Markham Hall," was used as a receptacle for sails, rope, sledge gear, and all articles that could not be conveniently stowed under hatches on board. Its dimensions were forty-nine feet long, by twelve feet wide, and ten feet high. The mainsail was used to roof it over. It was altogether a very grand edifice, and we were, and I think with some reason, very proud at the result of our architectural skill.

The building mania seemed to be very prevalent amongst the officers, the majority of whom employed themselves in constructing snow-houses for various purposes near the ship. One officer went so far as to commence a *colonnade*, reaching from the shore to the ship, the pillars to be made of frozen blocks of snow, but the undertaking was of too gigantic a nature to be carried out with any hope of success, and was abandoned after a few days' work.

A wooden observatory, brought out from England for the express purpose, was set up for the transit instrument, and this with a house adjoining, in which was placed the alt-azimuth instrument, being the head-quarters of our astronomical observers, Parr and May, went by the name of "Greenwich."

Snow-houses were constructed on shore for the several magnetic instruments, and these latter were securely fixed by being firmly frozen on snow pedestals. The three houses in which the instruments were placed were connected, one with the other, by sub-glacial passages, one being no less than a hundred

DIAGRAM ILLUSTRATING THE MAGNETIC OBSERVATORY AT "KEW."

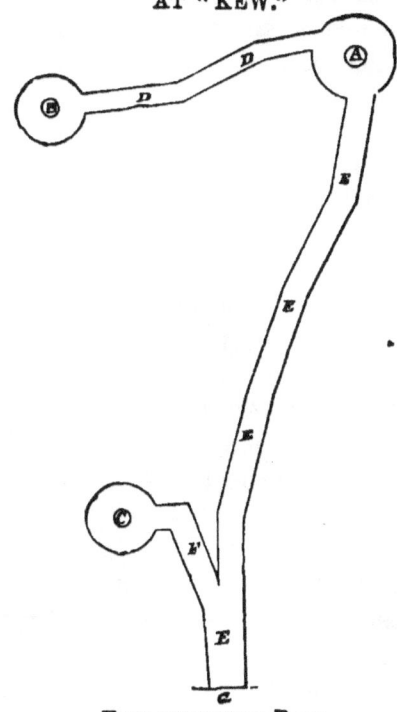

Explanation of Plan.

A   The Unifilar House.
B   The Barrow Dip Circle House.
C   The Declinometer House.
D D   Passage connecting A and B, 37¼ ft. in length.
E E E   The main passage, 120 ft. long.
F   Passage leading to Declinometer House, 44 ft. from entrance.
G   The main, and only, entrance. Distant from the *Alert* 504 ft. All houses and passages were "sub-glacial."

and twenty feet in length. The whole establishment, which was most complete and reflected great credit on its architect, was called "Kew." Giffard and myself were the two officers entrusted with the charge of the magnetic observations, and many a cold and comfortless hour had we to spend, in our endeavours to add to the slight knowledge we possess in this interesting branch of science.

Several other snow-houses were built for various purposes. One was for the reception of our powder, as it is most important that such a dangerous and combustible article should be removed from the ship, where of necessity so many fires have to be kept up. The place in which the powder was stored was called "Woolwich." Others were constructed in which were deposited all our salt beef for present use, and these buildings, of course, went by the name of "Deptford," after our great naval victualling depôt in England.

Altogether the neighbourhood of our winter quarters had the appearance of a young thriving settlement rapidly springing into maturity, rendering what would otherwise have been a barren and desolate scene, one of cheerful life and activity.

The salt beef, which was exceptionally tough and salt, more so indeed than the ordinary salt "junk" used in the navy, was kept in a snow-house; because we found, by experiment, that it was rendered more palatable by so doing. In all probability the process of congelation tended to extract, or precipitate, a very large portion of the saline matter with which it was impregnated, and thus deprived it, to some extent, of its hardness and saltness.

By the 26th of October the ship was completely "housed" in by a set of awnings, extending from the after part of the top-gallant forecastle to the mizzen-mast. This "housing" was made of a material called tilt cloth, similar to that used to cover waggons in England. It was spread on spars lashed between the masts, having curtains on each side so fitted that they could readily and easily be triced up when required for purposes of ventilation. Hanging lamps

FLAG-STAFF POINT.

were suspended from the spars over the centre of the deck, which were kept alight night and day. The funnel, which was provided with a hinge, was lowered down, and formed a famous and convenient stow-hole for rope. The number of coils that were deposited in it was truly marvellous.

Two gangways were cut in the ship's side: the one on the port side being used as the general one for entrance and exit; the one on the starboard for carrying out all slops and dirt to a large dirt-heap established between the hummocks, some hundred yards from the ship. A smaller dirt-heap was temporarily used nearer the ship, the accumulations being removed to the larger one once or twice a week.

Although, as a rule, the snow was not well adapted for building purposes on account of its consistency, we were able to supply ourselves with blocks from certain places where the snow had drifted in large quantities and hardened by pressure.

A snow wall, constructed from solid blocks obtained from these quarries, was formed round the ship at about six feet distance, and at the height of about four feet. When this was completed the space between the ship's side and this wall was filled in with snow, reaching as high as the fore and main channels, forming a perfectly solid and impervious embankment that would effectually aid in preserving the warmth of the ship. The upper deck was cleared of all superfluous articles, and was covered with snow about twelve inches deep. A layer of gravel and ashes was strewn over the surface; but I am not sure that we benefited much by this measure, for it was rendered so slippery by being frozen that it was by no means an easy matter to walk on it.

All skylights and hatchways were carefully covered up, two only of the latter being kept open as a means of ingress and egress. These were so constructed with porches and double doors as to prevent the admission of the outside air. The doors, being fitted with weights, were made self-shutting, so that the closing of one door was insured before the opening of the other. Snow walls were also built up round the porches, and in fact round the hatchways and skylights not in use, so as to render them all the more impervious to the cold air.

Round the funnel of the galley fire there was a large space, inclosed by a wall of snow, in which was deposited every morning a supply of ice or frozen snow, to be converted into water sufficient to last twenty-four hours. The ice for this purpose was procured from a large floe about one hundred and fifty yards from the ship, which in all probability was formed by the thawing and subsequent re-freezing of the snow on its surface. When it was difficult to find work for the men to do outside the ship during the winter, they were employed in conveying this ice to a large depôt that was formed close to the vessel, protected from the Eskimo dogs by a snow wall, from which during gales of wind or other bad weather we were able to supply ourselves.

Our boats were all hauled up in a safe position on shore. Sails were left bent, but securely furled and covered. Ropes that were not unrove were carefully hauled taut, so as to prevent our being kept awake during a gale of wind by an uninterrupted "devil's tattoo"—that is, the continual flapping of a rope against a spar, which produces a very aggravating and monotonous sound.

Former expeditions were supplied with Sylvester's warming apparatus, which, by means of pipes leading along the whole length of the ship, warmed the "between decks" with hot air. The only means for heating the vessel at our disposal were by stoves. These were placed in various parts of the ship, and put under the charge of men who were periodically selected for this service. Stringent regulations were issued regarding the economical consumption of fuel, and also to guard against all accidents from fire.

As it is necessary in all ships wintering in the Arctic Regions to devote a certain place to the washing and drying of clothes in which a high temperature can be constantly kept, we appointed for this purpose a compartment on the fore part of the lower deck, commonly called the fore-peak. The men had certain days during the week allotted to them for the use of this place, and it was found that clothes washed and hung up one afternoon would be invariably dry on the following morning.

The vapour arising in this room did not reach the deck on which the men lived, but was conveyed through a trap hatch leading into the fore-peak to a large space under the top-gallant forecastle, inclosed by a snow wall and made its exit through an up-take formed of a piece of funnelling. The compartment was heated by a stove, the fire in which was kept burning night and day.

The very difficult question of ventilation below was carefully considered. It is one of the most important and serious matters that can come under the consideration of the commander of an Arctic expedition. Nothing is so essential to the preservation of health as the pure and free circulation of air on the living deck.

In this respect we were not so well off as our predecessors, for they, being supplied with the Sylvester heating apparatus, were able to admit a more constant current of air, and thus keep their habitable deck in a better state and more free from condensation than ours. We found it a very difficult matter to prevent in the slightest degree the accumulation of moisture on the beams overhead, caused by the condensation formed by the number of people living on the deck, and by the vapour arising from the galley fire. Several up-takes and down-takes were fitted in holes cut through the upper deck in our attempts to remedy this serious defect, but as a rule they had little effect in counteracting it. Men were incessantly employed during the winter in wiping the moisture off the beams with cloths. If the hatchway doors were kept open, even for a short time, this moisture was at once converted into ice, which, of course, thawed and dripped immediately the temperature was raised. This drip was a constant source of annoyance to us during the whole winter, and it was one to which we had, in part, to submit.

Whilst all these necessary preparations for the safety and warmth of the ship were being carried out, the comforts of those who were about to brave the rigours of an Arctic winter were not forgotten. Warm garments were issued, consisting principally of a complete suit of seal-skins and warm woollen guernseys. It must not be supposed that our seal-skins were of the same material as those soft fur jackets so much in vogue with the fair ones at home. Ours were obtained from the ordinary Greenland seals, whose skins are covered with coarse bristly hairs. They were, nevertheless, quite as warm, and were indeed our favourite articles of clothing after the unpleasant aroma, which seems inseparable from clothing of this description, had worn off, or until we had become so accustomed to it as to fail to notice it!

Carpet boots, or moccasins made of moose-skin, were worn on the feet. The former were furnished with tops, made of duffel, reaching as high as the knees, and with cork soles over an inch thick. With any temperature below zero leather boots and shoes must be discontinued, as they freeze so hard that the material loses its flexibility, and renders the foot in consequence more liable to frost-bite. Moccasins, worn over a couple of pairs of blanket wrappers, and a pair of thick woollen stockings reaching above the knee, are undoubtedly the most comfortable foot-gear, and the best adapted for low temperatures. Blanket wrappers are, as their name indicates, strips of blanket, generally about sixteen inches square, worn folded round the feet in lieu of socks and stockings, than which they are infinitely warmer.

As a rule, officers and men were dressed alike. Occasionally some of the former would make their appearance in long fur coats with hoods that they had obtained from the Hudson's Bay Company's store and other places in London, but the majority adhered to the clothing supplied to them by Government.

A special winter routine was made out, and commenced shortly after the return of the sledge parties. It was strictly adhered to through the long winter night that ensued.

I must not omit to mention the duty of keeping open the "fire hole"—a very necessary and important precaution, that must be taken, in order to be able to obtain a supply of water in case of fire breaking out on board. As a rule, in all ships that have wintered in the Arctic Regions, the water has frozen below the suction valves of the pumps, thus rendering them totally useless. In order, therefore, to obtain water, a hole was invariably cut through the ice near the ship, which was generally placed in charge of the quarter-master of the watch, whose duty it was from time to time to clear off the young ice from its surface, so that at any moment water might be obtained in buckets. In the "Alert," in consequence of our valves being much lower, our pumps were never incapacitated from this cause; still they were liable to be rendered useless by the water in the pipes becoming frozen. We therefore always kept our fire-hole in working order. It was close to the bow of the vessel, and was inclosed by a snow hut, so as to guard against the danger of anybody falling in whilst walking about in the dark. By fixing a tide-pole in the hole, and by devising a self-registering apparatus with a line leading from the tide-pole to the forecastle of the "Alert," we were able to obtain a very complete and valuable series of tidal observations. From having the registering-guage on board the ship, these observations were continued uninterruptedly, and were unaffected by gales of wind or bad weather, that would otherwise have prevented any one from going outside the vessel in order to note them.

Thermometric observations were, as may be imagined, very carefully attended to, and the temperatures both inside and outside the ship duly registered. Maximum and minimum thermometers, by which the greatest heat and the greatest cold for each consecutive twenty-four hours were recorded, were established in different places, and were noted every day at noon by an officer especially appointed for that duty.

Each compartment in the ship was supplied with one of these thermometers, and on the living deck the temperatures at three different heights—namely, at the deck, about half-way up, and at the beams—were daily registered. For the outside air one of the ice-saw triangles was erected on the floe, sufficiently distant from the ship to neutralize any influence that might be derived from her presence, and on this, at the height of about twelve feet, were placed several thermometers. In addition to these, there were other thermometers on the hill about a quarter of a mile from the ship, and about one hundred yards above the level of the sea, so that we were able to obtain a correct mean of the true temperature of the air. We were also able to ascertain the temperature of the snow, and the ground at different depths; and also, by means of solar radiation thermometers, we succeeded, on the return of the sun, in getting the temperature due to its rays at various altitudes.

CHAPTER XIV.

THE ROYAL ARCTIC THEATRE.

> "Haste thee, Nymph, and bring with thee
> Jest and youthful jollity,
> Quips, and cranks, and wanton wiles,
> Nods, and becks, and wreathed smiles,
> Sport that wrinkled Care derides,
> And Laughter holding both his sides."
> MILTON.

Sir Edward Parry, during his first and subsequent winters in the Arctic Regions, fully recognized the importance of not only exercising and improving the minds of those under his command, during the long period of enforced inaction, but also of amusing them, and letting them feel that they also were assisting in the amusement of their shipmates. To do this he instituted an evening school on the lower deck, the officers acting as teachers; and he established periodicals, dramatic and other entertainments, in which he himself joined and took a conspicuous part.

His wise example has been generally followed by the different expeditions that subsequently wintered in the Arctic Regions.

It is, in fact, very necessary to exercise both the physical and mental powers of the men during the dark months, for when once the ship has been safely established in winter quarters little work remains to be done. The officers are constantly employed in taking and working up observations in various branches of science; but the seaman has little to do but reflect on, and possibly brood over, his situation. It is, therefore, absolutely essential that some means should be devised to drive from him all unpleasant thoughts, and to make him feel that it is in his power to relieve the tedium of what would otherwise be a long and monotonous winter.

Each ship had been provided, before leaving England, with a printing-press, and an officer and seaman* had been instructed in its use.

As soon as it was set up and in working order, the following prospectus was issued by the " firm."

"THE ARCTIC PRINTING OFFICE.

"Messrs. Giffard and Symons beg to inform the public that they have obtained—at an immense cost and with infinite trouble—possession of the extensive premises, lately occupied by Mr. Clements Markham, situated in Trap Lane, within half a minute's walk of the foremost Quarter Deck Ladder, and easily accessible to all parts of the city.

"They have fitted up their new establishment—*regardless of expense*—with all the *latest inventions* and *newest machinery*, to enable them to carry on the noble art of printing in a style and with a rapidity hitherto quite unattainable.

"They therefore expect from the public that support and assistance which it always gives to the *truly deserving*.

"Charges moderate. No credit given. All work required to be executed to be paid for in advance.

"N.B. Everything undertaken promptly and correctly executed.

"H.M.S. 'Alert,'
"July 28, 1875."

The "cost" and "trouble" alluded to in this production, that were expended in obtaining a convenient place in which to carry out the "noble art of printing,"

* Lieutenant Giffard and Robert Symons, A.B.

were caused by the fact that our photographers were equally anxious, with our printers, to possess themselves of the small cabin lately occupied by my cousin, and which is so grandiloquently alluded to as "extensive premises." In fact, for some little time it was a very sore and vexed question between those two celebrated and energetic firms. Trap Lane was so called in consequence of the after-hold being immediately outside the door of the cabin; and it occasionally served as a very disagreeable kind of man-trap when, through inadvertence, the hatch had not been replaced. As this part of the ship was, during the early part of her commission, in total darkness, owing to the piles of stores that were stowed in every available corner, it is no wonder that unsuspecting individuals should occasionally have fallen into the trap!

Our printing-press was, it is almost needless to say, of great use to us during the winter; for, although it never printed very much for the public service, it was constantly called into requisition for the purpose of striking off programmes for our dramatic and other entertainments; and on such important events as birthdays and Christmas-day we indulged in the extravagance of printed bills of fare. On the whole the printing establishment on board the "Alert" tended very materially to beguile the tedium of our long nights, and must therefore be regarded as a decided success.

Our school was opened on the 1st of November; from which date, until the reappearance of the sun, the attendance was regular and constant. It was composed of nearly the whole ship's company, and was divided into classes under the direct superintendence of the officers. Reading, writing, history, arithmetic, and navigation were the principal subjects in which the pupils were instructed.

The school was held on the lower deck between eight and nine o'clock in the evening, the classes occupying the different mess-tables. Only two men out of the entire ship's company were unable to read and write, and these two men were placed in a class with two others, who were unable to read and write English.* This class was presided over by the doctor, who kindly volunteered to devote himself to the instruction of the "cripples," as they were facetiously called.

As an illustration of the improvement which has taken place in the education of the men belonging to the Royal Navy during the last half-century, it may be mentioned that, whereas in Parry's time it was quite the exception to find a man that could read or write, with us the exception was entirely the other way, only two men out of fifty-five being ignorant of those accomplishments.

Never were seen such painstaking and willing scholars as our men showed themselves to be. It is impossible to conceive a more orderly or well-conducted school, and it was a pleasure to the masters to devote their time to classes that evinced such an earnest desire of acquiring knowledge as did those on board the "Alert."

Here might be observed a staid old seaman, whose great brawny hand appeared more suited to grasp the marline-spike than the pen, vainly endeavouring, with his elbows squared, his weather-beaten face close down over his work, and his tongue thrust

* Petersen, the Danish interpreter, and the ship's cook Dominick a native of Gibraltar.

out, to arrive at some satisfactory result in a simple addition sum. As a contrast to this, at the opposite table might be seen a smart young sailor, who had distanced all his competitors in arithmetic, asking abstruse questions in mensuration of such a nature as to make even his tutor feel uncomfortable!

After the classes were dismissed, the men enjoyed an uninterrupted evening to themselves. Games of various descriptions, such as chess, bagatelle, draughts, and cribbage, had been purchased for their amusement before leaving England, and were in constant requisition during the winter. A large space on the starboard side of the deck, abaft the living deck, was allotted to the smokers, and here were held our dramatic and weekly entertainments on Thursdays. On Sundays Divine service was performed in the same place.

Books were also a source of great amusement and interest to many of the men who were studiously inclined, as the well-thumbed volumes in our library soon testified. Several men wrote regular journals, which were even kept up by a few whilst they were sledging. Amongst the officers, chess, backgammon, and a rubber in the captain's cabin, formed the chief amusements. Although gambling is discountenanced (or ought to be) on board every well-regulated man of war, we so far forgot ourselves as to indulge largely in this vice. Seldom was a game played without a stake on the result! The stakes, too, were exorbitant, frequently as much as one lucifer match per game! It must be remembered that matches were very scarce and precious articles with us, and it was therefore a very high and valuable stake. On one occasion, one of my messmates was so rash as to wager a tallow-candle on the result of a game; but this was an offer of such magnitude that no one was sufficiently brave or sporting to accept it.

Among the many valuable gifts showered upon us by kind and generous friends at home was an excellent piano, and fortunately amongst the officers there was a very talented musician, to whose good nature and willing efforts to please must be attributed many a pleasant hour, when our hearts were warmed by well-known airs bringing back happy home memories.

Thursday evenings were always devoted to dramatic entertainments, magic-lantern exhibitions, instructive lectures, reading, and music both vocal and instrumental. These entertainments were kept up with the same spirit, and without a break, during the whole winter. They went by the name of our "Thursday Pops," and afforded much pleasure and amusement. They were announced to the general Arctic public by the following printed notice, which was widely circulated.

H.M.S. "ALERT."
THURSDAY POPULAR ENTERTAINMENTS.

On Thursday, the 11th of November, 1875, will commence a series of popular entertainments, that will consist of lectures, readings, recitations, and music, both vocal and instrumental, etc. No trouble or expense have been spared in obtaining the services of a great number of the most talented men of the day. The entertainment will be given in the airy and commodious hall situated in Funnel Row.

PROGRAMME:

Astronomical Lecture (with discussion)	. . .	apt. NARES.
Song . . "I knew that I was dreaming"	. .	Mr. GOOD.
Song . . "Watercresses" . . .	. .	Mr. SHIRLEY.
Reading . "The Jumping Frog" . .	. .	Dr. MOSS.

Song .	. "An Englishman am I" . . .	. Mr. Cane.
Song .	. "Broken down"	. Mr. Bryant.
Glee .	. "The Wreath" Messrs. Aldrich, Pullen, and Rawson.	
Song .	. "The White Squall" . . .	. Mr. Maskell.

God save the Queen.

No encores. Doors open at 7.30. Sledges may be ordered at 9 o'clock

Messrs. Giffard and Symons, Printing Office, Trap Lane.

This was the first notification issued regarding our weekly entertainments, and, coming out a day or two before the performance, it naturally caused considerable excitement and flutter amongst the Arctic playgoing world!

Except on the evenings exclusively devoted to the legitimate drama, these entertainments were always preceded by a lecture delivered by one of the officers, on some interesting and at the same time instructive subject, adapted to the knowledge and intelligence of the audience. A list of the lectures so delivered cannot fail to be of interest.

1. On astronomy . . . . . . Capt. Nares.
2. A few words on magnetism . . Lieut. Giffard.
3. On geology . . . . . . Capt. Feilden.
4. A few words on meteorology . . Lieut. Aldrich.
5. A few words on steam . . . Mr. Wootton.
6. Mock moons under the microscope . Dr. Moss.
7. On light . . . . . . Lieut. Parr.
8. An historical lecture . . . . Mr. White.
9. A few words on astronomy . . Com. Markham.
10. Our food in the arctic regions . . Dr. Colan.
11. A few words on arctic plants . . Rev. H. W. Pullen.
12. On hydrostatics . . . . . Lieut. May.
13. Sledging experiences . . . . Capt. Nares.

Nearly all the officers took part in these lectures, and I have not the slightest doubt that all would have done so had there been any more Thursdays to spare. They were eagerly listened to by the ship's company, and afforded quite as much pleasure as the readings and songs that followed, in the performance of which they all, with only one or two exceptions, took part.

The first real dramatic entertainment came off on the following Thursday. Our plan was for the men

ROYAL ARCTIC THEATRE—SCENE FROM "ALADDIN AND THE WONDERFUL SCAMP."

to act one piece and the officers another, and this was found to work very well. But the rehearsals were a difficulty, and we were frequently compelled to shut ourselves up in our own cabins in order to secure the necessary quiet and privacy to enable us to become perfect in our different parts.

The costumes were, of course, a subject of much

discussion and deep interest. The making up of dresses, and the manufacture of wigs from musk-ox skins and oakum, sorely taxed our ingenuity and employed minds and fingers that had hitherto been strangers to such occupations. Many were the needles broken, and many were the fingers pricked, before our ideal costumes were realized. Eiderdown quilts had to be converted into the robes of a lovely oriental princess; old uniform coats were beautified with spangles and tinsel, and appeared as the fashionable habiliments of a dandy of the seventeenth century; whilst a wicked magician, of the Hebrew persuasion, appeared in a coat of unmistakeable clerical cut.

Egerton was an indefatigable stage manager, and the scenic arrangements under the direction of Moss, who was also the artist, could not be excelled. Aldrich at the piano (as our orchestra) was a host in himself, adding materially to the success of the entertainments. In fact, officers and men vied with each other in their endeavours to promote amusement and hilarity, and if their histrionic abilities were not of the highest order, the zeal and energy of the actors fully compensated for this deficiency.

We enjoyed a rare freedom from harsh ill-natured critics. These pests do not venture across the Arctic Circle. All who visited the Royal Arctic Theatre (re-opened after a lapse of twenty-one years) came with a firm resolve to please or be pleased. Acting upon this determination, our entertainments were bound to be successful. The following prologue, composed for the occasion by Pullen, was spoken at the opening of our theatre, on Thursday, the 18th of November, 1875.

"Kind friends, with kindly greetings met to-day,
We bid you welcome to our opening play:
You, whose indulgent smile forbids the fear
Of scornful wit or captious critic here.
To-day we welcome you, and not to-night,
For all is noon with us—all summer bright;
And though the southern sun has ceased to pour
His glittering rays upon our ice-bound shore—
Has ceased awhile to touch with drops of gold
The crystal corners of our hummocks bold;
We bear a warm soft light that never fades—
A lustrous light amid these Greenland shades;
All trustful of each other's love, we learn
With steady flame our lamp of Hope to burn;
And suns may set, and twilights disappear—
They shall not rob us of our Christmas cheer;
Nor blinding drift, nor frozen wave, shall chill
Our laughter glad—for laugh, brave boys, we will;
Kindling yet once again the genial glow
Of happy English homes on Arctic floe.

"Yet once again; for none would here forget
We are but sons of fathers living yet;
In work and play alike, we but renew
The deeds of men who taught us what to do.
And though, more favoured than the rest, we soar
To loftier flights than theirs who went before;
Though ours the boast, by skilful guidance led,
In virgin climes our shifting scene to spread;
We love to read on history's faithful page,
Of ancient triumphs on our Northern stage,
And boldly for our brave forerunners claim
An Arctic 'cast' already known to fame.

"Now let the tell-tale curtain rise, and say
What we have done to while your hours away.
Such as we have, we bring you of our best,
And to your kind forbearance leave the rest.
One only grief is ours, and you shall share
With us the burden of that gentle care.
One cherished form we miss—one touch alone—
One glance of love—one tender, thrilling tone.
Ah! in the sweet homes of our native isle
The dear ones move, and minister, and smile.

We would not wish them here, but this we know,
Their thoughts are with us every step we go:
Their life sets northward o'er the cold, grey sea:
They live in wondering what our life may be;
And heart draws near to heart, and soul to soul,
Till each has found its true magnetic pole.

"God bless and keep them in His mighty hand—
Our wives and sweethearts, and the dear old land!"

The prologue was warmly applauded. At its conclusion the curtain rose, and the following programme, showing the plays that were acted and the cast of characters, was proceeded with.

THE ROYAL ARCTIC THEATRE

Will be re-opened on Thursday next, the 18th instant, by the powerful dramatic company of

HYPERBOREANS!

Under the distinguished patronage of Capt. Nares, the members of the Arctic Exploring Expedition, and all the nobility and gentry of the neighbourhood.

The world-wide reputation of this company is quite unrivalled. The manager has spared neither trouble nor expense in forming this company, and has selected none but the very best *artistes*—the ladies being from England—who, having numerous other engagements, can remain for a short time only.

The scenic arrangements, under the control and manipulation of that celebrated artist, Professor Moss, *must* be acknowledged to be unparalleled in the experience of ages and of the highest order.

The orchestra, under the management of Signore Aldrichi (lately from Milan) cannot fail to be appreciated by the audience.

At 7.30 will commence the celebrated nautical farce

THE CHOPS OF THE CHANNEL.

CHARACTERS:

Leander Hellespont	Mr. Stuckberry.
Mr. Counter Balance	Mr. Woolley.
Gratings (Steward)	Mr. Burroughs.

Mrs. Hellespont . . . . . Mdlle. Francombi.
Mrs. Veneer . . . . . . Mdme. Maskelli.
  Time . . The present day.
  Scene . . Saloon of a Boulogne steamer.
    Interval of ten minutes.

During the interval the renowned vocalist, Mr. Stone, will sing THE IRISH BARBER.

After which will be performed the screaming tragico-comico burlesque entitled

   VILIKINS AND HIS DINAH.
    CHARACTERS:

Master Grumbleton Gruffin, a rich (soap) merchant of London,
 the original parient . . . . . . Com. Markham.
Baron Boski Bumble, ancestor of the celebrated beadle, the
 original lovier so gallant and gay . . . Mr. Egerton.
William Wilkins, socially and convivially known as Vilikins,
 a young apprentice, in desperate love with . . Mr. Rawson.
Dinah Gruffin, the sole feminine offspring of the above-
 mentioned soap-merchant, in love with the aforesaid
 Vilikins . . . . Mdlle. Blanc.
  Scene 1. . . Lawn of Gruffin's house.
  Scene 2. . . Interior of Gruffin's house.
  Scene 3. . . Lawn of Gruffin's house.
    God save the Queen.

This, the first appearance of the "Hyperboreans," was eminently successful, and elicited both laughter and applause from our very appreciative and demonstrative audience. Mademoiselle Blanc (Mr. White) made a fascinating little Dinah of six feet high, dressed in a Dolly Varden costume, whilst the other ladies were all that could be desired, and looked charming in their gorgeous silk and muslin dresses.

In this respect we had a decided advantage over our consort, the "Discovery;" for her space on board being somewhat limited, the building of an ice theatre on the floe became necessary. Here, though the building was spacious and elegant, the temperature was rarely above zero! The ladies were therefore unable to indulge in low dresses, and a close observer might have detected underclothing composed of seal-skins beneath their otherwise gay and brilliant costumes.

Occasionally, as the two following bills will show, we were agreeably surprised by the announcement of an entire change of programme.

H.M.S. "ALERT."

THURSDAY POPS.

December 16th, 1875.

Great attraction! The latest novelty of the season!!
THE WIZARD OF THE NORTH!!!　☞ For one night only!!!!

PROGRAMME:
The entertainment will commence with
A FEW WORDS ON STEAM . . Mr. Wootton.
After which the only and veritable
WIZARD OF THE NORTH,
en route to his hyperborean domicile,
will exhibit and expound some of his original and inimitable illusions and feats of prestidigitation, consisting of the following wonderful and startling tricks:—

The vanishing egg.
The magic die.
The mysterious sixpence.
The magic shawl.
A startling surgical operation.
The marvellous watch trick.
Tricks with cards.
The magic bag trick.
The wonderful generating hat.
The astounding prestidigitorial metamorphosis, performed with
an egg and silk handkerchief.
The inexhaustible bottle.
Our very able and renowed pianist, Lieut. Aldrich, will, as usual,
preside at the orchestra.
To commence at 7.30 precisely.
God save the Queen.

Messrs. Giffard and Symons, Printing Office, Trap Lane.

THURSDAY POPS.
H.M.S. "ALERT."
January 20th, 1876.
GRAND PHANTASMAGORIAL EXHIBITION
and
MUSICAL ENTERTAINMENT.

To commence with
A FEW WORDS ON ASTRONOMY, by Com. Markham,
Illustrated by the aid of a magic lantern.
To be followed by a series of
DISSOLVING VIEWS,
Consisting of coloured representations of
Remarkable places in England,
Photographic sketches of foreign countries, etc.
After which, the wonderful and startling adventures of
SINDBAD THE SAILOR
Will be related by the Rev. H. W. Pullen.
In the next place Com. Markham will give a life-like and
entertaining display of various specimens in
NATURAL HISTORY;
and
Lieut. Aldrich will recite the true and touching
TALE OF A TUB.
To conclude with some highly amusing
COMIC SCENES.
To commence at 7.30 precisely.
God save the Queen.

Messrs. Giffard and Symons, Printing Office, Trap Lane.

These amusements may be considered light and frivolous, for men engaged in such a serious undertaking as that upon which we were embarked; still they all tended to one point—namely, the successful issue of the enterprise. For they kept the minds of the men employed with pleasant and agreeable thoughts, drove away all feelings of tedium and dulness, and thus assisted largely in promoting the general well-being and satisfactory sanitary condition of the expedition during the long night of nearly one hundred and fifty days. They effectually banished despondency, and assisted in making all hands cheerful, happy, and contented.

CHAPTER XV.

WINTER OCCUPATIONS AND AMUSEMENTS.

"Darkness, Light's eldest brother, his birthright
Claimed o'er this world, and to heaven chased light."
DONNE.

"Behold the wandering moon
Riding near her highest noon,
Like one that hath been led astray
Through the heavens' wide pathless way;
And oft as if her head she bowed,
Stooping through a fleecy cloud."
MILTON.

THE sun, as has been mentioned in a previous chapter, took its final departure on the 11th of October. From this date darkness gradually settled upon us, reaching its greatest intensity on the 21st of December. The type of a leading article in the *Times* newspaper was taken by us as a test of the darkness. This was last read in the open air at mid-day on the 6th of November, and then only by a few with a great deal of difficulty. Many unsuccessful attempts were made on subsequent days. For a fortnight on either side of the 21st of December, the difference in the light between noon and midnight, on a clear day, was almost imperceptible, on a dull day it was quite inappreciable. Occasionally, at other times, at midday a faint luminous band might be observed along the southern horizon, but this was all the indication we had of the difference between day and night.

We did not forget to celebrate on the 21st of October the Battle of Trafalgar, remembering that our great naval hero, Nelson,* was himself an old Arctic navigator. Our caterers provided us with a good dinner, and we were regaled, as a great indulgence on such an auspicious occasion, with an extra glass of wine! Two elaborate bills of fare were placed on the table, on one of which was very creditably sketched the "Alert" in winter quarters, and on the other was depicted the Battle of Trafalgar, with the motto on each, "England expects every man *this* day to do his duty!" As there was a good dinner on the table, and the cold weather had made us wondrous hungry, we all responded nobly to the call!

The 5th of November was another anniversary that could not pass unnoticed. On that evening the effigy of Guy Fawkes, ingeniously stuffed with squibs and seated on a cask well smeared with tar, was duly paraded round the upper deck, accompanied by the drums and fifes playing the "Rogue's March." It was then dragged, on a sledge, to the summit of a neighbouring hummock, and there solemnly burnt in presence of the whole ship's company. The band continued to play until the lips and fingers of the fifers became so frost-bitten that they were compelled to desist. It was a novel sight to see the dusky forms of the men, clad in seal-skins, dancing round a blazing fire on the top of an enormous mass of ice, whilst in the background was the ship with her masts and yards thickly coated with snow, and all her ropes

---

* Nelson served as a midshipman on board the "Carcass," in Captain Phipps' North Polar Expedition in 1773.

clearly defined in the bright "bonfire light." A beautiful balloon, manufactured by Moss out of various coloured tissue-papers, also formed a prominent feature in the evening's display. Unfortunately, shortly after it was released, and before it had ascended to any very great height, it caught fire and was quickly consumed.

It must not be supposed, because I enumerate all the little incidents connected with the amusements of the men, that other and more important work was neglected. On the contrary, the officers were unceasingly engaged during the winter in taking scientific observations in their respective departments; each officer being awarded some special subject. These included observations in astronomy, magnetism, electricity, meteorology, tides, spectrum analysis, observations for the detection of the polarization of light, chlorine, and specific gravity estimations. The pursuit of these investigations was at times a matter of great difficulty and extreme personal discomfort. It necessitated attendance in, and consequent exposure to, a temperature many degrees below zero, for several hours at a time. Under these circumstances it is no easy matter to handle delicate instruments, the manipulation of which, even in a temperate climate, requires the utmost care and caution. Made extremely brittle by the intense cold, a fall to any of the small metal movable parts of an instrument, such as the needles, would be fatal, yet it is almost impossible to touch them with the uncovered hand. The breath freezing on the arcs and verniers of the instruments during the time of observation, and on the glasses of the telescopes and mirrors, adds seriously to the difficulty; whilst the unequal contraction of different metals during intensely cold weather renders some of the instruments totally useless.

Paraselenæ, or mock moons, and auroras were of frequent occurrence, but none of the latter were sufficiently bright to call for special mention. These phenomena were always carefully examined, and the results recorded. As a rule the auroras consisted of faint coruscations darting across the heavens through the zenith, frequently in the form of an irregular arch terminating at each end on the horizon, and generally accompanied by various small luminous patches.

The lunations of the moon were periods that were always looked forward to, and gladly welcomed, affording as they did, on clear bright days, a marked contrast to the gruesome darkness that generally prevailed. These clear days were not inappropriately termed "moony" ones, and were taken advantage of to perform all work that was considered necessary outside the ship.

> "Rising in clouded majesty, at length
> The moon unveiled her peerless light
> And o'er the dark her silver mantle threw."

Even on these bright silvery "moony" days it was unsafe to venture to any distance from the ship, as the sudden "veiling of her peerless light" by fog or clouds would produce total darkness, and so prevent the unfortunate wanderer from finding his way back.

Great attention was paid to the important duty of seeing that a proper amount of exercise was taken by every soul on board. Open-air exercise was the more essential to health, because the air we breathed on board was not as pure as might be desired. This was inevitable, and the evil could only be partially counteracted by strict attention to the enforcing of outdoor exercise. A walk was constructed along the floe near the ship, for a distance of half a mile, marked at every two or three yards by small heaps of empty preserved meat tins, placed there by our industrious doctor. We were thus able to take our exercise along this promenade even on the darkest day, and the number of times that each individual walked up and down during the day was proudly recounted at the dinner-table. The darkness prevented walks to any greater distance for a considerable time. This then was our fashionable lounge, and was called the "Ladies' Mile" after the drive of the same name in Hyde Park.

Our greatest annoyance was undoubtedly caused by the incessant drip in our cabins and elsewhere on board. So bad was it that all books had to be removed from the shelves, or from any position where they were in contact with the ship's side or the beams overhead. Especially over our beds did we suffer, and could only make certain of a dry night's rest by taking the precaution of nailing a blanket over the bed, or sloping one as an awning! No means that we could devise, although many experiments were tried on the living deck of the men as well as by the officers in their cabins, lessened the condensation from which we suffered, and which increased with any rise of temperature. One officer went so far as to light, and keep burning for a whole day, no less than fifty-two candles and one lamp in his cabin, hoping by these means to dry it thoroughly; but although it answered the purpose for a day or two, at an enormous cost, it was soon as bad as ever. During the time of his *illumination* he succeeded in raising the temperature of his cabin from 40° to 75°! It is decidedly unpleasant, whilst writing, to have a continual stream of water pouring down upon your head and upon your paper; yet it is impossible to prevent this disagreeable drip.

One of my messmates, more fortunate than his brother officers, had brought an umbrella with him, and this being spread over his chair protected him from the wet, and thus enabled him to read or write in comparative comfort, and, what was perhaps of greater consequence, with the perfect preservation of his temper.

It may appear like affectation on my part when I say that any rise of temperature, during the winter, was viewed by us with dissatisfaction. Clad as we were to resist a cold of many degrees below zero, we were made absolutely uncomfortable by the *heat* when the thermometer indicated any degree with a + sign. The only real good that we derived from such a rise of temperature was that we were able more freely to throw open the doors leading down to the lower deck, and thus admit a thorough circulation of fresh air; on one occasion during the month of November the temperature rose as high as 23°, and in December it reached the unprecedented height (for that season of the year) of 35°! These, of course, were only occasional jumps, never of long duration, and were apparently produced by gales of wind from the S.W. Our experience at the "Alert's" winter quarters was that a breeze of wind raised the temperature, and that our coldest weather was always registered on perfectly still and clear days! During boisterous tempestuous weather the pack, although stationary, moaned and groaned weirdly, as if unhappy gnomes, imprisoned in the cold grasp of the frozen sea, were bewailing their hard fate, and pleading for release from their icy fetters. The young ice, too, in the vicinity of the ship cracked in a most alarming manner, each crack being accompanied by a sharp and loud report, and formed great fissures, leaving the surface, which had hitherto been smooth and level, rugged and uneven. Well might the "Ancient Mariner," describing such a scene, say—

> "It cracked and growled, and roared and howled,
> Like noises in a swound."

This movement of the ice, slight as it was, exposed the "Alert" to great pressure, and although it did not amount to an actual "nip," nor did it in any way cause injury to the ship, it made her list over several degrees. Now, as we in the ward-room were on a limited allowance of wine, namely two glasses a day, this heeling over of the vessel caused us great annoyance, as it prevented our glasses from being filled to the brim, a custom that had been rigidly followed out since leaving England. This curtailment of our "rights," as we were pleased to call them, was very naturally regarded with a certain amount of disfavour. In order to lessen, if we could not entirely rectify this evil, we supplied ourselves with ingeniously made little wedges, which, being placed under the *lee* side of the wine-glass, brought it so nearly upright that we succeeded in very nearly getting our full allowance.

The birthdays of the officers were invariably celebrated by the best dinners that our indefatigable and energetic caterers could provide, always having in view the chance of the ship spending three winters in the Arctic Regions. As a special indulgence we were also allowed on these occasions a glass of port wine after dinner, a treat that we ordinarily had only twice a week. The composition of the *menus* for these sumptuous feasts was always a subject of anxious

MENU.
POTAGES.
Mulligatawny.
POISSONS.
Pégouse à la Couverture de Laine.*
ENTRÉES.
Petits Pâtés d'Homard à la Chasse.†
Rognons à la Pain rôti.
RELEVÉS.
Mouton rôti à l'Anglais. Tongues on Gimbals.
ENTREMETS.
Poudin aux Raisins.
Blanc-manger à la Hummock.
Petits pâtés d'Hahis à la place d'Eccleston.
DESSERT.
Poudin glacé à la Hyperborean.
Figues. Noce.
Gâteau à l'Irlandais.
Café et Liqueur á la Jesson.

November 11th, 1875.

---

* Blanket wrappers were articles of wearing apparel.
† The name of the cook was Hunt.

care and forethought on the part of those who were entrusted with this important duty. Long and earnest were the consultations that were held, before one of them was satisfactorily composed and placed in the printer's hands.

As we were living in a land in which little could be obtained in the way of change, the object was to diversify as much as possible the names of the same viands, so as to make the guests believe that the dinners were entirely different. The names given to some of the dishes were decidedly original. On the previous page is the first *printed* bill of fare that was placed on the table.

Shortly after the ship had been established in winter quarters, a careful calculation was made of the amount of fresh meat we possessed.

By fresh meat, I mean meat of the musk-oxen and sheep that we had killed, and not the fresh *preserved* meat, of which we had an ample supply. It was found we had sufficient to yield fourteen meals, at the rate of one pound per man per meal. It was, therefore, determined to issue a fresh meat meal twice every three weeks, and, at the doctor's recommendation, this was done on two consecutive days. In his opinion this method of apportioning it was the most conducive to health.

Beer, of which we had been provided with ten hogsheads specially brewed for us by Allsopp, was issued, so long as a cask was "on tap," twice a week. On these days half the allowance of spirits only was served out.

On Sundays Divine service was regularly performed between decks; the morning and evening services being read on alternate Sundays.

Prayers were read daily on the upper deck. The Holy Communion was celebrated on the first Sunday in every month. Considering the small number of men from among whom the choir was selected, and the necessarily slight amount of practice they could have, the singing at church was very creditable. Aldrich played the accompaniment on a harmonium that we had obtained from the ward-room officers of the "Valorous," before parting company with that ship at Disco. The credit of originating and instructing the choir was, of course, due to Pullen and Aldrich.

Medical inspections were held regularly on the first day of each month, when every officer and man was minutely questioned and examined. Nothing could be more satisfactory than the medical report of the sanitary condition of the men at the conclusion of these examinations.

The amount of compulsory open-air exercise that had to be taken by each man was two hours a day; but most of the men, that is to say all the working hands exclusive of cooks, stewards, and servants, were invariably at work, *outside* the ship, for at least five hours a day. A very favourite and at the same time healthy pastime of the men in their leisure hours, when the moon was up, was that of "tabogganing." This consisted in dragging one of our small satellites or dog-sledges to the summit of a neighbouring hill, and then coming down, two or three on the sledge, at the rate of about sixty or seventy miles an hour! The men enjoyed this amazingly, and used to race one sledge against another. As they were not very expert in the management of these "taboggans," and had little confidence in their own steering, they would, when they saw there was a chance of their sledge coming to grief, tumble out and roll for some distance after it. Fortunately the snow was soft and they never came to harm.

Rawson, who had acquired a knowledge of this sport in Canada, was the first to introduce it in the far north. The dexterity with which he managed his "taboggan" was marvellous, and he would frequently, accompanied by one of his messmates, come down the steep side of one of the highest floebergs in the vicinity of the ship. Poor "Nellie" could never understand whence the motive power of these machines was derived, and used to rush round barking at us in a frantic manner when we first started, until left far behind plunging in the soft snow and struggling to keep pace with us.

It was wonderful how this dog withstood the cold. The colder the day the more she appeared to enjoy it, dashing about in the soft fine snow and picking up pieces of ice in her mouth for the purpose of having them thrown for her. It must be remembered that for any one of us to touch a piece of ice with the uncovered hand in a temperature 50° below zero would have been a very serious matter; yet Nellie was able, in the same temperature, to carry pieces of ice, or bits of metal or stone, in her mouth for hours together. The only cause of annoyance to the poor old doggie was the caking or balling of the snow between her toes, which used to trouble her a good deal. To obviate this, four little flannel moccasins were made for her feet; but, although she enjoyed wearing them and seemed to be proud of her appearance in them, they had to be discontinued, as we were afraid that the tying them on sufficiently tight to prevent their coming off might stop the circulation of the blood and thus produce frost-bite. On the whole, however, Nellie throve wonderfully well, and until the following summer enjoyed perfect health. She was my constant companion wherever I went, attending me during my walks, and lying curled up at my feet in the observatory during the long hours that I was employed

NELLIE.

taking magnetic observations. She always slept in an arm-chair in my cabin, being provided with her own little blanket, on which her name was embroidered.

Before concluding this chapter it will be as well to relate an interesting and rather curious incident connected with one of our Eskimo dogs.

In Aldrich's sledge journey to Cape Joseph Henry, one of his dogs (Sallie), being attacked with a fit, had to be cast off from the team and was no more seen by him during that journey.

On crossing the floe with my sledge party about a week after, we were suddenly joined, to our great surprise, by an Eskimo dog which the men readily recognized as Sallie; all our attempts to make her approach were unsuccessful, although she followed us at a distance during the day and hovered round our camp, picking up scraps of pemmican that had been purposely left out for her during the night. She eluded all attempts at being caught, running away on the ice and disappearing amongst the hummocks. She followed us faithfully, at a distance, until the day we returned to the ship, when she vanished altogether. She was last seen on the floe about four miles from the "Alert."

Amid the many preparations for the winter, poor Sallie was forgotten and had almost passed out of recollection altogether, when one day in December, more than *two* months after she had been last seen, a strange dog was observed hovering round the ship. This strange dog proved to be the long-lost Sallie!

No amount of coaxing would persuade her to come near us, and she was eventually driven off by the other Eskimo dogs, and took refuge on the pack. On the following day she again made her appearance, and this time we succeeded in getting her on board and into a place of safety. She was terribly thin and emaciated; but being well cared for and attended to, she rapidly picked up, and was eventually the strongest and best dog in our whole team.

The question as to how she had existed during her

long absence from the ship was a difficult one to solve. At first it was surmised that she had attached herself to a pack of wolves; but this idea was scouted, as no tracks had been seen to lead us to believe that these animals existed in our neighbourhood. It is not probable that she obtained anything from the ship during the time she was missing, or that she picked up scraps from the other dogs, for on her appearance she was at once driven away by her old companions. The only probable conclusion that we could arrive at was that she had supported life by hunting and feasting on lemmings, for the traces of these little animals were the only indications that we had of the existence, outside our own circle, of animal life.

CHAPTER XVI.

AN ARCTIC CHRISTMAS.

"So now is come our joyful'st feast,
  Let every man be jolly,
Eache roome with yvie leaves is drest,
  And every post with holly;
Now all our neighbours' chimneys smoke,
  And Christmas blocks are burning;
Their ovens they with baked meats choke,
  And all their spits are turning.
Without the door let sorrow lie,
  And if, for cold, it hap to die,
We'll bury't in a Christmas pye,
  And ever more be merry."
                                    WITHER.

ON the 21st of December the sun reached its greatest southern declination. We felt on that day that we had cause for rejoicing. The sun had arrived at the limit of its southern journey, and now it would, every day, be travelling to the northward, and therefore in our direction. So rapidly had the time passed that Christmas stole upon us unawares, and we were only reminded of its approach by the strong odour of good things being cooked that pervaded the whole ship, bringing to our minds the fact that preparations for its celebration had actually commenced. Nothing was omitted that could possibly add to the comfort and enjoyment of the men on this day. The ship's stores were thrown open and they were allowed to provide themselves with an unlimited amount, so long as there was no waste, of flour, raisins, sugar, and preserved fruits, and in addition to the regular daily allowance of meat, a pound of musk-ox beef and a pound of mutton were issued to each man. For the two previous days, during which they had been disturbed as little as possible, the men were engaged in making the necessary preparations for spending their Christmas as happily and as socially as if they were in a more genial climate. It must be remembered that this was a day looked forward to by all, not only in the light of a festival, but because it was also regarded as the turning-point of the winter. After Christmas every day would bring us nearer to the sun, whose bright face we all so ardently wished to welcome once more. Moreover, Christmas-day, to a community situated as we were, "away from the busy haunts of men," must always be regarded as an epoch, a day looked forward to, and when passed, a day from which many events are dated.

In addition to the supplies afforded by the stores of the ship, we were largely indebted to kind, and in several instances unknown, friends and well-wishers to the expedition in England for many little articles that assisted to amuse our men during this festive season. Amongst these the kind and generous ladies of Queenstown must not be forgotten. These ladies had, previous to our departure from England, formed themselves into a Committee, and had sent to each ship a large Christmas-box containing many useful, and indeed valuable, articles. Each officer received some little package, personally directed to himself, and every man was presented with some pretty little

Christmas-box. Nothing could have been more happily thought of, and it would have done the fair donors good could they but have witnessed the pleasure testified by the recipients at the distribution of the contents of their case.

I must not omit to mention another Christmas-box, kindly sent by Mr. Mason, the inventor, I believe, of "Somebody's Luggage," and containing all sorts of amusing little articles suitable either for decorating a table or a Christmas-tree.

Another act of kindness on the part of our friends in England was also much appreciated by both officers and men. A young lady, a relative of one of the officers, had taken the trouble to direct a letter to each individual on board, containing a beautiful Christmas card. To make it appear as if they had been actually delivered through the post, a second-hand postage-stamp had been affixed to each envelope. Her kind forethought afforded a great deal of pleasure to the recipients of those letters.

Christmas eve was spent very merrily by all on board the "Alert." The piano was carried out from the ward-room to the main deck, where dancing was kept up with great animation until eleven o'clock! It is wonderful how fond the English man-of-war's man is of dancing. So long as he can obtain music and a partner to dance with, without regard to sex, he will continue to fling his legs about with great vigour until compelled by heat and exhaustion to desist! The men on board the "Alert" were no exception to this rule; one and all joined in the dance, and seemed thoroughly to enjoy it. Poor Aldrich did not get a moment's peace. As soon as one tune was finished, he was called upon for another. Polka, waltz, and galop followed each other in rapid succession, officers and men joining alike in the general hilarity of the evening.

Christmas morning broke cold and clear; its stillness occasionally interrupted by light puffs of wind from the S.W. Divine service was performed in the forenoon, the pulpit being decorated with branches of artificial holly. When church was over, a little exercise was taken on the "ladies' mile." On my return I found my cabin brightened up by small twigs of variegated holly, a delicate and touching attention on the part of some of my messmates, who had provided themselves with artificial branches of this plant before leaving England. At one o'clock, everything being in readiness, the officers were invited to inspect the lower deck. Preceded by our drum and fife band playing the "Roast Beef of Old England," we paid a formal visit to the men's quarters. The lower deck was beautifully and tastefully decorated with flags, coloured tinsel paper, and artificial flowers, whilst the different mess tables were literally groaning under the weight of the good cheer that adorned them. Everything had a cheerful and comfortable appearance, and, above all, the radiant healthy-looking faces, beaming with pleasure, that so cordially and heartily greeted us with the compliments of the season. Of course, dancing was the prominent feature of the afternoon, Aldrich, with his usual good nature, being again victimized at the piano. At six o'clock, for on such an important occasion we departed from our usual dinner hour of half-past two, we all assembled in the ward-room for dinner, and great was our astonishment and delight at seeing in the centre of our table a magnificent bouquet of artificial flowers. This was, I believe, the happy thought of a lady who had recently been admitted into the circle of "Arctic relations." The bright-coloured flowers, reminding us of home associations, were more thoroughly appreciated than even the good dinner which was provided for us, for which reference must be made to the following *menu*, composed by Pullen :—

H.M.S. "ALERT."

À la Juliènne soup is the *potage* we favour,
   And soles fried *au naturel* serve us for fish;
We have cutlets and green peas of elegant flavour—
   Beef garnished with mushrooms—a true English dish.

Then a mountain of beef from our cold Greenland valleys,
   Overshadowing proudly boiled mutton hard by,
Till our appetite, waning, just playfully dallies
   With a small slice of ham—then gives in with a sigh.

For lo! a real English plum-pudding doth greet us,
   And a crest of bright holly adorns its bold brow;
While the choicest mince pies are yet waiting to meet us:
   Alas! are we equal to meeting them now?

So we drink to our Queen, and we drink to the maiden,
   The wife, or the mother, that holds us most dear;
And may we and our consort sail home richly laden
   With the spoils of success, ere December next year!

In addition to the bill of fare, the annexed poem by the same accomplished author was printed and placed in front of each member of the mess.

On this glad Christmas Day,
   While happy bells are flinging
O'er bright lands far away
   Their burst of joyous singing,
We love to think that each sweet lay,
   That sets those echoes ringing,
Hushed music from our icy bay
   To loving hearts is bringing.

> Hushed music that shall tell
> How He has left us never,
> In whose dear sight we dwell,
> Who aids our high endeavour;
> Who, from the hearts that love us well,
> Our short lives will not sever,
> . For whose good gifts our breasts shall swell
> With grateful praise for ever!

Our drum and fife band, of their own accord, played several airs very creditably during our dinner, which was brought to a conclusion by a few short speeches. In the evening dancing was again kept up with great animation; every one appeared cheerful and happy. In no region of the world could this Christmas-day have been spent with more mirth and more genuine fellowship than it was by the little band of explorers, so far removed from all home ties and associations, who were celebrating it that day, in a latitude farther north than man had ever before penetrated.

On reviewing the events of the year we felt we had much to be thankful for. We had succeeded, in spite of many dangers and difficulties, in establishing our ship in winter quarters in a position farther north than even some of the most sanguine had, at one time, dared to hope. The English flag had been displayed, both by sea and by land, in a higher northern latitude than any flag had ever before been seen, and although our prospects of further exploration in a northerly direction were somewhat damped, owing to the land trending west, we knew that there was much to be done during the ensuing year in defining and exploring the coasts to the east and to the west. A wide field of exploration was still before us, and there was much useful work to be done during the ensuing spring in a hitherto unknown region.

Half our winter had passed, and although the long dark night of one hundred and fifty days might, by some unacquainted with the many resources we possessed to while away the time, be considered dull and monotonous, monotony and despondency were unknown on board the good ship "Alert." We all looked forward with eager hope to the return of the sun, strong in our determination to do our best, and with our appetites for sledging considerably whetted by the initiation we had received during the autumn.

Hitherto we had, with one exception, enjoyed perfect immunity from sickness, and we all thought that if there was no cold weather in the Arctic Regions to produce frost-bites, the appointments of medical officers to the expedition, so far as their professional qualifications were concerned, were undoubted sinecures. The frost-bites had, however, been very severe, and at the end of the year there still remained on the sick list four of the poor fellows who had been attacked during the autumn sledging, three of whom had suffered amputation of the big toe.

Compelled to keep to their beds, the winter to them must have, indeed, been wearisome; but no word of complaint was ever uttered by them, and they appeared as cheerful and in as good spirits as the best of us. Their only distress was the idea of not being allowed, in consequence of their misfortune, to participate in the spring campaign. The sequel, however, proved, although they took no part in the *extended* sledging operations, how well and how nobly they worked in their brave endeavours to assist and succour their poor, weak, and stricken comrades; but we must not anticipate.

We had hitherto experienced, in comparison with

what we had been led to expect, tolerably mild weather, as Arctic winter weather goes; and the cold had not been so severe as we anticipated; $-46\cdot5°$ or $78\frac{1}{2}°$ below freezing-point being, up to the end of the year, the minimum temperature registered. This was by no means an uncomfortable temperature, although superficial frost-bites, especially on the noses and cheek-bones, were of constant occurrence. Solitary walks were, of course, prohibited; and it was particularly impressed upon every one that, when they were absent from the ship, they were carefully to watch their companions' faces in order to detect a frost-bite at once, and so be able to restore circulation before permanent injury could be sustained. Face-covers were occasionally worn, but were not in very great favour. They have the disadvantage of freezing to the face, which they also conceal, and so prevent a comrade from seeing and reporting a frost-bite.

In the neighbourhood of our winter quarters there had, up to this time, been a remarkable absence of all animal life. Occasionally the quarter-masters would report that during the night they heard the howling of wolves in the distance, and one night the Eskimo dogs, who were lying curled up in the snow outside the ship, made a sudden rush for the gangway, and evinced great eagerness to get on board. This stampede was attributed to the presence of wolves, but no tracks of these animals had been seen to justify our arriving at such a conclusion. With the exception sometimes of a peculiar, whistling, moaning sound, caused by the rise and fall of the ice with the tide, the stillness of the nights was undisturbed.

We had long been aware that the ice of which this part of the polar sea was composed consisted of huge massive floes, not of a few seasons' formation, but the creation of ages, real thick-ribbed ice. Except along the west coasts of Banks and Prince Patrick Islands, no such ice had ever before been met with in the Arctic Regions. It therefore became desirable to apply to it a special name by which it might be provisionally known. After some discussion, Captain Nares decided upon calling the frozen sea, on the southern border of which we were wintering, the "Palæocrystic Sea," the name being derived from the two Greek words παλαιος ancient, and κρυσταλλος ice. This term was used for the great frozen polar sea during the remaining period of our detention on its borders.*

Atmospheric phenomena, such as halos and paraselenæ, were by no means uncommon, and occasionally we were astonished by the heavenly bodies behaving, as it appeared to us, in a very eccentric manner. On one occasion the star Aldebaran was reported to be jumping about in a strange way. Such unusual behaviour on the part of a star brought us all up in the cold, and there, sure enough, was Aldebaran doing exactly what was reported, and altogether conducting itself in a very erratic and unstarlike manner. The illusion was caused by the fall of minute, and imperceptible, frozen particles; but it was some time before we could satisfy ourselves that the star was not actually in motion, many of the men remaining to this day unconvinced. One of our Scotch quartermasters informed me, some time afterwards, that it

---

* The word may not be formed on strictly accurate principles, but it is sufficiently expressive of the fact it is intended to represent, and it is now endeared to us by association and by common usage while serving in the far north.

was a "vara curious star;" and although the laws of refraction were explained to him, he still persisted in his belief that the movement of the star was due to itself, and would not believe in any other explanation.

At the beginning of the winter, shortly after the return of the sledge parties, the doctor and myself being busily engaged in the construction of a snow house on shore, observed a most brilliant meteor fall, apparently about a quarter of a mile from us, its course being from S.E. to N.W. It was of a bright emerald-green colour, and was falling so quietly and slowly that we at first thought it was a rocket, or Roman candle, let off by some one astern of the ship, it being distinctly visible for many seconds. When it arrived, in our estimation, at about forty feet from the ground, it suddenly burst, displaying bright red and green colours. It was seen by others, from different points of observation; all being unanimous in their opinion that it was one of the most beautiful sights, of the kind, they had ever witnessed.

CHAPTER XVII.

A HAPPY NEW YEAR.

The old year dies on southern skies,
   And leafless woods that moan and quiver;
The shadows creep o'er ocean deep,
   And silent lake and rustling river;
And all is gloom around the tomb
   Of wasted moments, lost for ever.

The new year gleams on silver streams,
   Where meadows smile in sunlit glances;
The dark shades flee across the sea,
   And the wild wavelet laughs and dances;
And all is bright where new-born light
   Brings hope to man and golden chances.

O happy year! that tells us here
   The same sweet, ever-welcome story,
That soon, so soon! one radiant noon
   Shall plunge in light yon summits hoary,
That point our way through endless day
   To joyous triumphs, home, and glory.

H.M.S. "Alert,"   H. W. PULLEN.
January 1st, 1876.

THE above lines, composed by the poet laureate of the expedition, greeted us at the breakfast table on the morning of the 1st of January, 1876.

The New Year was ushered in with every demonstration of joy, gratitude, and hope by our little party assembled together, so far removed from the civilized world. We were joyful because a new year had dawned upon us in undiminished numbers; grateful for the many mercies that had been vouchsafed to us, and hopeful concerning our future prospects. We could not look back with regret upon the past year, for to us it had indeed been eventful; but officers and men looked forward to the coming year with feelings of confidence, resolutely determined faithfully to perform their duties, placing their trust in Him who had hitherto so well watched over and protected them, and firm in their reliance on His continued aid and support.

It is generally the custom in the navy to strike the bell sixteen times at midnight on New Year's eve— eight bells for the old year and eight bells for the new! Of course with us this custom was rigidly adhered to; but not only did we strike sixteen bells at *our* midnight, but we also struck the same number at six minutes to eight, which, allowing for the exact difference in time, would be midnight in England, so that we had at least the satisfaction of knowing that our bell was being employed in the same way as many others in the navy at the same time.

Perhaps it may be interesting to my readers to know exactly how we received the New Year! I will, therefore, quote my remarks as they appear, word for word, in my journal.

"At five minutes to twelve, we all congregated round the ward-room table, on which was spread a sumptuous cold collation, consisting of a *real* English ham, Bologna sausages, brawn, and sardines. Strong whiskey punch, in the brewing of which all had a share, was ladled out to each, and from the encomiums which were passed on its flavour and strength, the old proverb that 'too many cooks spoil the broth' was completely upset. As the bell struck, a neat little speech was made by our orator the doctor, the compliments of the season were wished to all, nor were those at home forgotten, our glasses were emptied, and then in true Highland fashion, with one foot on the table, the other on our chair, and with hands joined, we all sang 'Auld lang syne,' the drum and fife band accompanying us outside, the song being taken up by the men on the lower deck, who, true to their tastes, had been '*dancing* out the old year.' Such was the manner in which the year 1876 was inaugurated in latitude 82° 27′ N., where no human being had ever welcomed a new year before."

A more cheerful, happy, and contented party it would be difficult to imagine anywhere; utterly oblivious of the solemn darkness and desolate sterility that prevailed without, they thought only of the "joyous triumph" that they hoped to achieve, and then of their return to old England. Everything wore a cheerful aspect. No leader could have more reason to be satisfied with the health and spirits of those under his command, than Captain Nares on the 1st of January, 1876.

On that morning, at the usual monthly medical inspection, he had the satisfaction of receiving the report that the men were in a better state of health than they were at the last examination. Appetites, which during mid-winter had been waning, had gradually returned. So contented were we, that many were actually pitying our friends in England, because they were unable to enjoy such delicious musk-ox beef as was put on our table for dinner on New Year's day!

Our first crop of mustard and cress was gathered on the 2nd of January. It was not an abundant one, but there was sufficient to give a mouthful to each person, and what little we had was certainly very refreshing. It had grown up devoid of all colour, and had a very *washed-out* appearance. The garden was a small shallow box kept close to the ward-room stove. In consequence of the success attending this—our first—attempt at agriculture, several gardens were started, and we were enabled to issue, at different times, small quantities of this excellent antiscorbutic; though how far the loss of colour detracts from its medicinal qualities is a difficult problem to solve. Although the colour was absent, the fresh *taste* appeared to remain, there being no perceptible difference between that grown on board the "Alert," and the same reared in the heat of the sun in more favoured climes. As a rule, the best crops were those grown on a blanket.

On the 8th and 9th of January we experienced a heavy gale of wind from the southward. It was impossible, whilst it lasted, to venture outside the ship, even to take the thermometric observations, although they could be registered only a few yards from the gangway: they had therefore to be discontinued during the time the gale lasted. It blew for forty-eight hours with relentless fury, when it exhausted itself in fitful gusts, more or less strong, until it abated altogether. The housing over the ship suffered sadly from this storm, several tons weight of snow having collected on it from the tremendous drift, in some places breaking it through, and in others "bagging" it down so as to render walking underneath an impossibility.

All our out-door establishments were completely

buried with snow, and we were compelled to send parties of men to excavate them, in order to effect an entrance at all. In fact, our men were for some time engaged in repairing the ravages of the storm. The accumulation of drift on the weather side of the ship was enormous, and took the form of a perfectly solid snow-wreath. This was caused by the eddying wind driving the snow from the side of the vessel to a distance of about four or five feet, where it settled, resembling a great frozen wave, whose curling crest was fully seven feet in height.

On the opposite, or lee, side of the ship the ice had cracked, leaving several large fissures, through which the water oozed and flowed over. The spring tides had also caused the ship to rise in her icy cradle, the greater part of the banking having, in consequence, slipped through between the edge of our dock and the ship's side and disappeared. This also had to be rectified. Our gale of wind had undoubtedly been productive of much extra work, irrespective of the anxiety and the by no means pleasant time spent, during its duration: for as yet our protecting bergs had not inspired us with absolute confidence regarding the shelter they might afford in such tempestuous weather as we had recently experienced. So well, however, did they answer our purpose during this gale, that all cause for anxiety was from that time removed, and for the future we felt as safe and as secure as if we had been frozen up in a well-sheltered and land-locked harbour.

When the wind was at its height, a piece of musk-ox meat, suspended in the mizzen-rigging, was blown down, and was, of course, at once assailed by the Eskimo dogs who had been admitted into the ship during the gale. Fortunately it was frozen so hard that they were unable to get their teeth through it, and although it had been some time in their clutches before it was rescued, little loss was sustained.

At noon on the 17th of January, a faint tinge of crimson, blended with a slight silvery streak of twilight, could be observed in the southern horizon, and although it was only of short duration, it became more decided and lasted for a longer time on each successive day. These bright harbingers of returning light were anxiously watched, and gladly were they welcomed as they assumed a more decided appearance.

Although there was no despondency or depression of spirits on board the "Alert," the monotony of the long dark nights could not but be felt, and we all eagerly looked forward to the time when the glorious rays from our bright, though long-absent, sun should again crown the summits of the distant hills with their sparkling and joyous light. All on board were interested for different reasons in the return of the sun: the sledge travellers, because it would bring light and heat to cheer and sustain them on their lonesome and arduous journeys, which they knew would be commenced as soon after its return as possible : the sportsmen regarded it as the precursor of game ; and all hailed with delight the symbol of returning day and the assurance of the approaching termination of their long dark night. By the 1st of February, those gifted with sharp eyesight were just able to decipher a leading article in the *Times* on the floe at noon. It was remarked that one of our officers afflicted with short-sightedness was able, by the dim twilight, to read not only with greater ease and accuracy than others, but also some days before them, and therefore by a dimmer light.

We had hitherto had no exceptionally severe weather; but during the latter part of January we experienced a foretaste of the intense cold that we were a month later destined to endure. With a temperature 50° below zero, it is necessary, when exposed to it, to keep the body in constant motion, otherwise a frost-bite will imperceptibly seize hold of one. On first emerging into this temperature a slight difficulty of breathing would be experienced, and tears would be involuntarily brought to the eyes, which immediately became small nodules of ice, and as such had to be extracted. This is hardly to be wondered at when it is remembered that we had to undergo a transition of temperature from our living-deck to the open air of over 100°! In spite of this cold, however, we were not much troubled with frost-bites, except on the face. Our dearly bought experience, during the autumn sledging, will account for our comparative immunity from these very troublesome and painful attacks.

Apropos of frost-bites it is related, that one of the members of the expedition, on getting up in the morning, during the cold weather, found, to his horror, that one of his toes and a part of his foot were quite black. Thinking he was severely frost-bitten, and wishing at once to assure himself of the fact by the only practical method that suggested itself at the time, he seized a pin, and made a furious dig at the supposed injured part. He very quickly found that, although discoloured, it was not totally devoid of all sensation, nor was the circulation of blood in any way impeded. The fact was, that his servant, on the previous day, had patched up his sock with a piece of fearnought, and, in order to assimilate the colour, had inked it over—which fully accounted for his terrible frost-bite!

It was our invariable custom to keep the hair, especially that growing on the face, as close as possible. In spite, however, of this precaution, it was impossible to prevent the breath from freezing on the short stubbly beard and moustache, which would soon be converted into a perfect mass of ice—a decidedly uncomfortable appendage. On returning from our short walks, we frequently found our cap, comforter, and collar of the coat frozen into one solid and compact mass.

Occasionally an amusing incident occurred to vary the sameness of our daily life, as the following story will show. During the darkest part of the winter one of the magnetic observers had occasion to visit the observatory. Taking his lantern, and accompanied by Nellie, he reached the door, which to his surprise was open. Supposing it to have been blown open by the wind, for it had been blowing very hard the previous night, he entered the long tunnel leading up to the Unifilar House. Before he had gone far a strong animal smell assailed his olfactory organs; this, with the fact of Nellie exhibiting great restlessness, induced him to examine the ground, when he clearly detected the traces of some animal, but of what description he was unable to decide.

He was now placed in rather an unpleasant position, for to advance head-foremost through a narrow passage into a small house in which a great Polar bear might have established himself, was to say the least a rash act; yet he was unwilling to return on board, and probably be for ever after chaffed by his messmates for being frightened at nothing. Putting on a bold front, he determined at all hazards to push on, and ascertain what the animal was that had

P

dared to violate the sacred precincts of the observatory. As he advanced the peculiar odour became stronger, and he was sorely tempted to retreat, thinking discretion was the better part of valour. Arriving at the entrance to the house, however, he plucked up courage, and with the lantern well in front of him, and Nellie close at his heels, he dashed in, and there, lying down and looking almost as frightened as himself, was, not the great white bear that he expected to meet, but "Bruin," the largest of our Eskimo dogs, who, during the boisterous weather of the preceding night, had sought shelter in our observatory, and had no doubt found it a very snug and comfortable place, infinitely preferable to the bleak and exposed floe. It was a long time before the place was rid of the unpleasant smell peculiar to Eskimo dogs.

As the light increased day by day, the men were employed in re-embarking the stores and provisions landed, and in demolishing "Markham Hall." It was necessary to accomplish as much as possible, as Captain Nares well knew, before the departure of the sledging parties, for so few men would be left on board that little could be done during their absence, and there was no saying how soon after their return the ship would be able to break out of winter quarters. The Eskimo dogs were also now regularly fed and attended to. Hitherto they had been left to do pretty much as they liked, and their regular meals during the winter had been few, and served at uncertain times. Notwithstanding the small amount of food that was issued to them, they were all in capital condition, in fact a little too "fleshy" for dragging purposes, as they always received the scraps and surplus food from the allowance of the ship's company, and this was more than enough to keep a much larger pack of dogs than we possessed. They were also regularly exercised in dragging a light sledge, their day's work increasing as the days lengthened.

We could not but notice the sallowness of complexion which the returning light revealed, only too palpably, in the faces of our companions, caused by the long absence of the sun, and which had hitherto been unnoticed by the light of lamps and candles. Like our mustard and cress, we were devoid of all colour, yet apparently in good and sound health. There is something essentially health-preserving and life-giving in the rays of the sun, without which everything must wither and eventually die. This was, in the sequel, but too fully exemplified in our case. For although we were all in excellent spirits and supposed ourselves to be in perfect health, yet the seeds of that terrible disease, which subsequently crippled us so disastrously, must have already germinated unknown to ourselves.

But little did we suspect, at that time, the approach of the evil that eventually overtook us.

Many of the large floebergs near the ship were observed to be literally rent in twain, owing in all probability to the contraction of the ice by the intense cold—the outer part of the floeberg being exposed to a greater cold than the interior. These rents will also account for the loud sharp reports that were frequently heard during the winter, and which were for some time wrapped in mystery.

Towards the end of February a few hares were seen, and two or three were shot; but they were very timid and shy, and seldom gave our sportsmen opportunities of exhibiting their prowess. Lemming tracks were abundant, and occasionally these little animals would be seen running along the snow. Nellie regarded them as being created for her especial enjoyment in hunting, and would vainly endeavour to unsnow them after they had taken refuge in their holes. Woe betide the unfortunate little lemming observed by Nellie at any distance from its habitation. A dash, a gobble, and all was over! In vain did we try to break her of these murderous propensities, not only for the sake of the victims but also for herself, as

LEMMINGS.

the swallowing of little balls of fur cannot be conducive to health. All was futile! Nellie considered the chase of these little creatures as an undoubted privilege with which no one should interfere.

The long twilight enabled us to extend our rambles, and we visited the snow hut built by Rawson last autumn when attempting to get south, about five or six miles from the ship, and in which he had deposited a small quantity of provisions. To our surprise we discovered that, with the exception of the pemmican which was in a tin, and the tobacco, all had disappeared! Biscuit, bacon, tea, sugar, and cocoa, all had gone. A hole through the roof of the house pointed at once to the means of ingress; but who were the thieves? Foxes or wolves had not been seen, nor had any traces of them been observed!

Even supposing these animals to be the depredators, how did they effect their escape from the house after once they had got in? It was simple enough to scrape a hole through the roof and jump down; but it was not so easy to jump straight up a height of six or seven feet through a small hole! Suspicion fell for some time on our long-missing dog Sallie; but it was never satisfactorily ascertained whether dog, wolf, or fox was the culprit. Of one thing there could be no doubt. The robbery had been committed by a very cunning and intelligent beast. Spots of blood on the pemmican tin showed unmistakeably that this also had been attempted, but had proved too hard and strong. The tracks, which were always to and from the floe, were too indistinct to enable us to make out the nature of the animal, but the general idea was that it was a fox.

Of course, with returning daylight, the serious work of sledging and the preparations for the spring campaign occupied our attention to the exclusion of almost everything else. On Saturday, the 26th of February, our school assembled for the last time, the classes being dismissed in the evening only to reassemble again if the ship spent another winter away from England. It would not be fair to dismiss our pupils without a word of commendation. Their attendance was most regular, and their efforts to learn beyond all praise. Nothing could exceed their diligence, nor excel their desire to please and reflect credit upon their masters, and I do hope that many will have benefited by the instruction they received in their Arctic school.

On Thursday, the 24th of February, was performed our last dramatic entertainment. The following was the programme.

ROYAL ARCTIC THEATRE.

H.M.S. "Alert."

Thursday, 24th February, 1876.

☞ Last performance of the season.

GRAND REPRESENTATION

of the

Original pathetico-comico-burlesque operetta entitled the

LITTLE VULGAR BOY,

or

WEEPING BILL.

Founded on the celebrated Ingoldsby Legend, "Misadventures at Margate."

Written expressly for the occasion by the

Rev. H. W. PULLEN.

Scenery by Professor Moss, M.D.   Music by Lieut. Aldrich.

Manager: Lieut. May.

Preceded by

Reading .	. "The Blessed Babies" .	. Mr. Hunt.
Song .	. "Fie, for shame" . .	. Mr. Symons.

CHARACTERS:

Mr. Brown, an old buffer, slightly green . . Commander Markham.
Mrs. Jones, a landlady, slightly cross, but with a keen
   eye to business . . . . . . G. Le C. Egerton, Esq.
Jack Robinson; a seafaring man, slightly figurative
   in his language, and violently in love with Mrs.
   Jones . . . . Lieut. Giffard.
Weeping Bill, a little vulgar boy, slightly out at
   elbows, and fairly sharp for his age . . Lieut. Rawson.

K´55, the irrepressible Bobby, slightly self-important,
and the natural enemy of Weeping Bill . . Rev. H. W. Pullen.

   Scenes 1 and 3 . . The Jetty at Margate.
   Scenes 2 and 4 . . Mrs. Jones's lodgings.
    To commence at 7.30 precisely.
     God save the Queen.
Messrs. Giffard and Symons, Printing office, Trap Lane.

This piece, as set forth in the bill, was written expressly for the occasion by Pullen, and not only did he compose it, but he also assisted in its performance. It was a very successful hit, and was most deservedly applauded, loud cries of "Author" following the fall of the curtain.

The ensuing Thursday witnessed the last of our "Thursday Pops," and this terminated our season's festivities. At it Captain Nares delivered a very able and instructive lecture on his sledging experiences, bringing a few "facts" home to the men, as to the sort of work they were about to perform, and the kind of life they would have to lead. His announcement that we should, in all probability, spend another winter in the Arctic Regions was hailed with delight. He also announced his intention of returning to England before the third winter, provided no unforeseen event happened to detain the expedition.

The following was the programme for the evening's entertainment.

    THURSDAY POPS.
     H.M.S. "Alert."
 Positively the last entertainment this winter.
     March 2, 1876.
 The season's festivities will terminate with the following
     programme:—

1. The Palæocrystic Sea and Sledging Experiences. Capt. Nares.
2. Ballad . . "The *Shannon* and the *Chesapeake*" . Mr. Cane.

3. Song	"Susan's Sunday out"		Mr. Stuckberry.
4. Reading	"Two Bab Ballads"		Rev. H. W. Pullen.
5. Ballad	"Over the Sea"		Mr. Maskell.
6. Song	"Rummy old Codger"		Mr. Pearce.
7. Ballad	"Seeing Nelly home" ;		Mr. Self.
8. Recitation	"On the Arctic Expedition, by J. D."		Sergt. Wood.
9. Song	"Billy Woods the grocer"		Mr. Gore.
10. Ballad	"Beating of my own heart"		Mr. Ayles.
11. Part Song	"O who will o'er the downs so free"		
	Messrs. Aldrich, Pullen, May, and Wootton.		

To conclude with the grand Palæocrystic Sledging Chorus, by the entire strength of the house.

To commence at 7.30 precisely.

God save the Queen.

Messrs. Giffard and Symons, Printing office, Trap Lane.

This chapter would be incomplete without the words of the "Grand Palæocrystic Sledging Chorus."

This was also composed by our talented poet laureate, and was most enthusiastically received by the whole ship's company, who vociferously joined in singing it on all appropriate, and other, occasions.

It brought in the names of all the sledges that were employed in the early part of the spring campaign, and became henceforth, as it were, the "Arctic National Anthem."

Chorus.

Not very long ago,
On the six-foot floe
  Of the palæocrystic sea,
Two ships did ride,
Mid the crashing of the tide—
  The *Alert* and the *Discovery*.

The sun never shone
The gallant crews upon
  For a hundred and forty-two days;
But no darkness and no hummocks
Their merry hearts could flummox:
  So they set to work and acted plays.

> There was music and song
> To help the hours along,
>   Brought forth from the good ship's store;
> And each man did his best
> To amuse and cheer the rest:
>   And "nobody can't do more."

Air—"*The Shannon and the Chesapeake.*"

Here's a health to *Marco Polo* *—
May he reach his northern goal, oh!
    And advance the flag of England into realms unknown!
May the *Challenger* † be there,
All comers bold to dare,
    And *Victoria* ‡ be victorious in the frozen zone!

May our *Poppie* § be in sight,
With her colours streaming bright,
    And the *Bulldog* ∥ tug on merrily from strand to strand!
And the *Alexandra* ¶ brave
See our banner proudly wave
    O'er the highest cliffs and summits of the northernmost land!

Here's a health to *Hercules*,**
Whom the autumn blast did freeze,
    And all our gallant fellows whom the frost laid low!
Just wait a little longer,
Till they get a trifle stronger,
    And they'll never pull the worse because they've lost a toe.

Here's a health, with three times three,
To the brave *Discovery*,††
    And our merry, merry guests, so truly welcome here!
And a brimming bumper yet
To our valiant little pet—
    The lively *Clements Markham*,‡‡ with its bold charioteer!

---

* Commander Markham's sledge.
† Lieut. Aldrich's sledge.
‡ Lieut. Parr's sledge.
§ Lieut. Giffard's sledge.
∥ Dr. Moss's sledge.
¶ Mr. White's sledge.
** Lieu. May's sledge.
†† Lieut. Rawson's sledge.
‡‡ Mr. Egerton's sledge.

Here's a health to all true blue,
To the officers and crew
   Who man this Expedition neat and handy, oh!
And may they ever prove,
Both in sledging and in love,
   That the tars of old Britannia are the dandy, oh!

CHAPTER XVIII.

RETURN OF THE SUN.

> "Most glorious orb! that were a worship, ere
> The mystery of thy making was revealed!
> Thou earliest minister of the Almighty
> Which gladdened on their mountain tops the hearts
> Of the Chaldean shepherds, till they poured
> Themselves in orisons."
>
> BYRON.

THE 29th of February was the day on which, according to astronomical rules, the reappearance of the sun was to rejoice the hearts and gladden the eyes of our little party. On the previous day, a general holiday had been proclaimed to give the men a chance, by ascending some of the hills in our neighbourhood, of welcoming the sun a day earlier. In this, however, they were doomed to disappointment. The glorious orb would not come out to be welcomed; for the simple reason that it was still just below the horizon. We were, however, rewarded by seeing its rays reflected in the northern sky, which was beautifully illumined with the most brilliant prismatic colours. Cairn Hill, and the hills to the southward by Cape Rawson, were the chief points of observation. The former was abreast of the ship, and about a mile distant; its height being about four hundred and fifty feet above the level of the sea. On the summit was built a large cairn, hence its name. On the cairn was reared a long staff, to which was hoisted an iron oil cask, so as to form a

CAIRN HILL.

conspicuous landmark to guide wanderers back to their ship.

By ten o'clock on the forenoon of the 29th, the ship was nearly deserted, and officers and men could be seen dotting the floe and snow-covered ranges as they wended their way to the most prominent adjacent hills, on which little knots of men could already be seen assembled, in order to catch a glimpse of the rising sun. We feared, however, on starting, that we should be again disappointed, as there was no clear sea horizon to the southward, and the sun would hardly have sufficient altitude to show itself above the distant land. These fears were not without foundation, as the result proved.

Shortly before noon our excitement was intense as a bright ray shot up vertically from the sun's position and illumined the summits of the surrounding ranges, whilst a radiant light was shed around.

> "As rays around the source of light
> Stream upward ere he glow in sight,
> And watching by his future flight
> Set the clear heavens on fire."

Our hopes grew high as noon drew near, but again were we disappointed, and again were we compelled to return to the ship, defeated in our object of welcoming back the "Prodigal Sun.!"

The next day was cloudy, but on the following one, by going aloft about ten o'clock, we had the satisfaction of announcing that about one-third of the sun's disc was visible, as it crept slowly along the southern horizon. Instantly the rigging swarmed with men, scrambling up with elephantine agility to greet the fiery orb after its long absence, and looking more like animated bales of furs than human beings. It appeared of a deep reddish orange colour, but was so distorted by refraction that its shape was more that of a truncated cone than a spherical body.

By noon Cairn Hill was covered with expectant visitors, and well were they repaid for the trouble of the ascent. Although little of the sun could be seen above the distant land, we knew that it was there, and what we did see was bright, and *appeared* with a slight stretch of the imagination to be warm!

Romeo's words—

> "Night's candles are burnt out,
> And jocund day stands
> Tip-toe on the misty mountain tops,"

were on our lips as we beheld the beautiful colours in the northern sky. The roseate tints blending with the violet seemed to belong more to southern climes than to the sterile inclement regions that we were inhabiting. The summits of the hills, the "misty mountain tops," were bathed in its glorious rays, whilst its luminous beams danced and glimmered along the distant ice-floes. It was a bright and glorious sight, and we remained long admiring it, and revelling in its rays—in fact, until warned by a peculiar sensation in our feet that the temperature was actually 100° below freezing-point; and however ecstatic we might feel at the re-appearance of the sun, Jack Frost still reigned supreme, exacting implicit obedience to his will, and making those who disregarded his injunctions suffer for their heedlessness.

Undoubtedly the Arctic Regions, and the farther north the better, would be a good place for Parsees; for none of the followers of Zoroaster could have exhibited more anxiety for the return, and more delight at the appearance, of their deity, than we did before and after the bright rays of the sun first fell upon us! Their god Fire would also receive, during the long cold Polar winter, the utmost homage and attention. Sun and Fire worshippers would require in these regions little to stimulate them to devotion.

Strange to say, our extreme cold came with the

returning sun. During the latter end of February the temperature had been gradually getting lower and lower, until on the 4th of March it had fallen to $-74°$, or $106°$ below freezing-point. This was the lowest recorded by the expedition, obtained from the mean of several thermometers, and, so far as we could ascertain, the lowest really authentic corrected observation that has ever been registered in any part of the globe. From noon of the 3rd until noon of the 4th the mean temperature was $-69°·68$, whilst the lowest mean temperature registered for any twenty-four consecutive hours was from four A.M. of the former until four A.M. of the last-mentioned day $-70°·31$. From six P.M. on March 2nd until six A.M. of March 4th, namely thirty-six consecutive hours, the mean temperature was as low as $-69°·93'$, and for the week ending March 4th the mean temperature was $-60°$!

It was amusing to observe the eager excitement with which every one received the latest intelligence regarding the state of the thermometer, and when it was announced that the "lowest on record" had been registered, there was a general shout of exultation. During the intense cold several experiments were tried by exposing various substances to its influence, and with the following results. Glycerine, on which a temperature of $-50°$ had little effect, became, at $-70°$, perfectly solid and quite transparent. Rectified spirits of wine became of the consistency of hair-oil. Concentrated rum, $40°$ over-proof, froze hard when exposed in a shallow vessel like a saucer, but when in a large quantity it resembled honey or molasses in consistency. Whiskey froze hard, and we actually broke off bits and ate it! In consequence of this latter proceeding we have since our return to

England been, not without reason, accused of "hard drinking," an accusation we are, of course, unable to refute! Chloroform was the only substance on which the low temperature had no apparent effect. Our temperatures were obtained by taking the mean of ten thermometers that were exposed, to which result was applied the corrections from Kew for each instrument. These had been ascertained when the instruments were tested at the Kew observatory before leaving England. The corrections and errors of the instruments could, of course, only be approximately ascertained after the freezing-point of mercury had been passed, as there was nothing beyond that with which the spirit could be compared. The slightest impurity of the spirit used, or the presence of even the most minute portions of extraneous matter in it, would no doubt seriously affect the accuracy of the observation. As an instance of the range exhibited by these instruments, it may be interesting to know that one thermometer indicated as low a temperature as $-82°$, while, *at the same time*, another showed only $-60°$; but by applying the errors deduced at Kew, the result was as nearly as possible the same. I think that the minimum temperature recorded by us was, if not absolutely correct, as nearly so as it was possible to arrive at.

Although we never again experienced such a severe burst of cold as we did during the first few days of March, the temperature remained extraordinarily low, and mercury was in a frozen state during nearly the whole of that month. The presence of the sun appeared to have little effect on the temperature, but thermometers exposed to its rays would frequently rise as high as zero, and sometimes above that point.

The difference of temperature at the summit and at the base of Cairn Hill, whose height, as has been stated, was four hundred and fifty feet, was 5½°, the thermometer rising as the hill was ascended, and falling again as it was brought down.

Traces of ptarmigan had frequently been observed in the snow, but it was not until the 22nd of March that the first bird was seen, although our sportsmen had been most diligent in their search for them. On that day two of our pedestrians succeeding in flushing one solitary ptarmigan, but, as is usual in such cases, they were without guns. Very few of these birds were afterwards seen in the neighbourhood of the "Alert." Their appearance caused some little excitement, for we looked upon them as the harbingers of spring, and as a token that our long winter had well-nigh terminated.

On the 25th of March, there was a partial eclipse of the sun, which was clearly visible to all those who took the trouble to go on deck and, with a piece of smoked or coloured glass, examine it in spite of a very low temperature. The first contact was observed at six minutes past four in the afternoon, and the egress at six o'clock. About ·65, or little more than half the sun, was obscured.

During the middle of March the quarter-deck housing was removed, and we were again able to enjoy daylight on the upper deck. Although the low temperature did not yet admit of our removing the snow from the hatchways and skylights, yet we were able to clear the tops of our cabin illuminators, and thus obtain below a slight amount of daylight, sufficient at any rate to obviate the necessity of incessant candle-light during the day. It was not until the middle of May, whilst the sledge travellers were absent, that the skylights were cleared and the snow removed from the upper deck.

Fire is the most disastrous accident that can possibly happen to a ship wintering in the Arctic Regions, and it should be most carefully guarded against. It may result in having your house, together with all your provisions, consumed, and yourselves, perhaps not burnt, but destined for even a more terrible fate, namely, turned out on the ice without food and without shelter, exposed to a pitiless temperature, with no covering or protection of any description. Such a situation would prove fatal in a few hours. Men so placed would realize the dreadful fate so vividly and graphically described by Jules Verne as having befallen Captain Hatteras and his companions when their ship was destroyed and they were deserted by their shipmates.

In the "Alert" we had one alarm from fire, which, although it might have ended disastrously, did very little injury. It originated in our "drying-room," where, through the carelessness of the man in charge, some of the clothes had been allowed to hang in dangerous proximity to the stove. These igniting quickly communicated the fire to the surrounding objects, and for a little time it was doubtful whether the conflagration might not assume a very serious aspect. In spite of the occurrence happening at nightime, the men exerted themselves with such good will that the fire was speedily extinguished, with no further damage done than the destruction of a few clothes, although it was some time before we could rid ourselves of the smoke, which unpleasantly permeated the whole ship. The temperature at the time was 58°

below zero, which would have rendered the work of supplying water from the fire-hole not only a difficult, but also a dangerous task, and one which must have resulted in many severe frost-bites.

During the latter part of the month of March the officers were employed in dismounting the various instruments in the observatories, carefully packing and putting them away, as most of them would not be required again until the following winter. This was a very necessary proceeding, as before the return of the officers from sledge travelling the observatories with all their "fixings," such as pedestals, etc., being composed of snow, would have melted away during the summer thaw. By the end of the month the observatories were entirely stripped and left bare, when they gradually fell into decay. "Woolwich" was also "unsnowed," and the powder brought off to the ship and stowed in the magazine.

In addition to all this work, the crews of the different sledges destined to take part in the spring campaign were, in this month of March, specially exercised, under their respective officers, for several hours during the day. Their regular daily exercise had also been carefully attended to throughout the winter.

Occasionally they were employed laying out depôts of provisions to the southward, to be used by the sledge parties proceeding northwards from the "Discovery," or sometimes dragging their laden sledges over the pack in the immediate vicinity of the ship, with the object of gaining experience in crossing ridges of hummocks, and of realizing the kind of travelling with which they were so soon to become more intimately acquainted. These little journeys gave us an insight into the endless difficulties that we were hereafter called upon to contend with, and the obstacles we were destined to surmount. We foresaw that we should have "stiffish" work before us, but we did not doubt that we should render a good and satisfactory account of the duty entrusted to us.

After several cries of "wolf," one actually did make its appearance on the 1st of April. Early in the morning of that day an animal had been observed, by the quarter-master of the watch, stealthily prowling round the ship. Supposing it to be a bear, the alarm was given and one or two of our hunters went in chase. More would undoubtedly have followed their example, but recollecting the day, they preferred remaining in their warm beds for an hour longer to the risk of being informed, when they came on deck fully equipped for the chase, that it was the 1st of April!

The traces left in the snow showed unmistakeably the character of our visitor. Instead of being a bear, it proved to be a wolf, but so alarmed was it at the disturbance made on board that it scampered over the hills and eluded our pursuit. That same afternoon, however, accompanied by my usual companion Nellie, I took a long walk to the southward, following the trail of the wolf for some distance. On my return, and when about two miles and a half from the ship, I happened to look round, and there, about a hundred yards off, and following in my track, was a tall, gaunt, raw-boned and famished-looking wolf. He was of a yellowish colour, and in size larger than our biggest Eskimo dog. Of course, as is generally the way in cases of this sort, I was totally unprovided with arms of any description, and was therefore unable to add his skin to our natural history collection. I cannot say whether Nellie or her master offered the greatest attraction to this animal; but whichever it might be, he followed us, sometimes at not more than ten yards distance, stopping if we stopped, and advancing when we advanced, until we were within about half a mile from the ship, when some of my messmates coming out to meet me, he bolted over the hills and made his escape. My great anxiety at the time was for my poor old Nellie, who showed a great inclination to become better acquainted with the wolf, and I had the utmost difficulty in restraining her. Whenever she strayed a little from my heel, the brute would make a bolt at her, and I have little doubt that she would have been killed if he had once succeeded in his endeavours. On the same evening we discovered the tracks of four musk-oxen, but although we followed them up for many miles we did not succeed in seeing them. The fact of the latter being in our neighbourhood fully accounted for the presence of the wolf, who was no doubt following their tracks.

CHAPTER XIX.

DETAILS OF SLEDGE TRAVELLING.

> " Give me some ink and paper in my tent,
> I'll draw the form and model of our battle :
> Limit each leader to his several charge,
> And put in just proportions our small force."
>
> *Richard III.*

HITHERTO I have purposely abstained from alluding to our spring operations, as I thought that it would be better to devote a separate chapter exclusively to the account of the details of sledge equipment. But it must not be supposed, because I have omitted to say anything about the sledging during the winter, that it was neglected, and that our time was entirely occupied with our amusements and observatory duties. Such was not the case. The preparations for the spring campaign and the organization of our sledge parties in all its details were very carefully thought over and matured during the long dark hours of the winter. All works on this subject had been diligently read, in order that we might benefit by the experience of our predecessors. Nothing was neglected that could in any way conduce to the success of the enterprise, and everything that could possibly add to the health and comfort of those to be employed on work of such an arduous nature was carefully considered. The sledges, tents, and other equipments necessary for travelling had been constructed under the personal superintendence of Sir Leopold McClintock, who is the highest living authority on Arctic sledge travelling. A few alterations, which we trusted would also be improvements, were suggested by the experience gained during the autumn, and these were all carried out before the return of the sun. The results justi-

SLEDGE UNDER SAIL.

fied our anticipations. Out of the four different kinds of sledges supplied to the expedition those which found most favour with us, and with which the greatest part of the work was done, were the eight-men sledges.* These dragged easier, and were

* The eight-men sledge has six uprights eighteen inches apart. It is eleven feet long, three feet two inches wide, eleven inches high, and weighs 130 lbs. complete. In former expeditions sails were frequently used on the sledges to great advantage, when travelling over smooth ice. But we were seldom so fortunate as to meet with ice which was suitable for sailing, in any of our sledge journeys. May and Egerton got their sledges under sail on an extensive floe

stronger than either the smaller or larger description of sledges. So long as the travelling remains good, that is smooth and level ice with hard snow on its surface, these sledges may be loaded to 240 lbs. for each man to drag, and a good day's work to be accomplished. This weight, of course, would only be dragged on first leaving the ship, or a depôt, and decreases at the rate of about 3 lbs. per man per diem, the amount of provisions consumed by each individual. What are called the "constant" weights, which include the sledge, tent, robes, cooking apparatus, pickaxe, shovel, etc., remain unaltered during the journey. The question of weight is one requiring the closest attention.

Every trifling article, even to a small packet of a *dozen pins* placed in the medicine chest, has to be weighed and recorded in the general equipment. The following table shows the weight of the various articles (being constant weights) required for the equipment of an Arctic sledge for forty-five days:—

in Robeson Channel, when they crossed over to the Greenland side; but as a rule the ice we met with was far too rough to make the use of sails practicable. In rigging a sail on the sledge two tent poles are lashed together as a yard, with a spare pole as a foot yard. The other two tent poles are used as shears, and at their ends a mast-head iron, or shear head, is fitted, consisting of two rings united by a piece of iron about three inches long, from the centre of which there is a hook on each side for the steadying guys, and a small block for the halyards is seized on to the iron between the rings. A spare cross-bar is placed on the top of the lading, over the midship uprights, and lashed down to the bearer. It is fitted with a span seized along its top-side, and the bights, with a thimble in each, project just beyond the cross-bar. The ends of the shears are then stepped into the thimbles attached to this cross-bar, and the sail hoisted. On smooth ice, with the wind aft or on the quarter, a sledge will travel under sail at a good pace. But smooth ice was almost unknown in the region explored by our expedition.

EQUIPMENT OF AN EIGHT-MEN SLEDGE, PROVISIONED FOR AN ABSENCE OF FORTY-FIVE DAYS.

	lb.	oz.
Sledge (complete)	130	0
Tent (complete)	44	0
Tent poles, five in number	25	0
Coverlet	31	8
Extra coverlet (used only in cold weather)	20	0
Lower robe	23	0
Waterproof floor-cloth	15	0
Sail	9	4
Eight sleeping bags	64	0
Eight knapsacks (packed)	96	0
Two pickaxes	14	8
Shovel	6	8
Store bag	25	0
Cooking gear	29	0
Gun and ammunition	25	0
Medical stores	12	0
Instruments	15	0
Constant weights	584	12
Forty-five days' provisions for eight men (including packages)	1080	0
Total	1664	12

which, dragged by seven men, is equivalent to about 238 lbs. per man to drag.

This should never be exceeded, nor should it even be kept up for any length of time.

It will thus be seen that it is impossible for a sledge party to be absent from the ship for more than seven weeks, at the outside, on its own resources. In order, therefore, to enable it to remain away for a longer period, depôts of provisions are established during the autumn on the line of route, and auxiliary sledges are despatched in the spring from which the extended parties may be replenished with provisions after they have been away from the ship some two or three weeks. These auxiliary sledges, on their return, are again completed with provisions and sent out to meet the extended parties on their way back. By these means, a sledging party may remain away for as long as twelve or thirteen weeks.

Depôts can only be laid out when there is a continuous coast line, and under circumstances when a *cache* containing provisions can easily be discovered. When the frozen ocean has to be traversed, depôts cannot be depended upon; for a movement of the ice, or the misfortune of wandering off the outward bound track during thick weather, would deprive the travellers of any chance of finding their supplies. The result in such a case would probably be fatal. The only way of ensuring an extended absence to a party sledging over the pack, is by sending with it an additional sledge. This, of course, entails the necessity of traversing the same road three times over. For the men must never under any circumstances (other than unavoidable necessity, caused by the sickness of some of the crew) be allowed to drag more than the outside weight of 240 lbs. at any one time.

It would, I think, and I am now speaking from experience, be preferable, when such a journey is necessary, to send a sledge away for only six weeks rather than to provision a party for three months, and compel the men to undergo the monotonous and wearisome work of going over the same ground so often; and, I believe, quite as much work would be accomplished.

The tents were all made of the lightest duck,*

---

* The tents were of light, close, unbleached duck. The eight-men tents were nine feet four inches long at the bottom, and eight feet at which was sufficient to protect us from the falling or drifting snow, and the keen cutting wind. The space inside was, of necessity, very limited; the width in which each man had to sleep being only fourteen inches. Whilst his head was touching one side of the tent, his feet were in contact with the other. The slightest movement of the sleeper during the night would disturb his neighbours on either side.

The entrance to the tent had a porch attached to it, which was, of course, always carefully closed, and served to exclude the fine snow-drift that would otherwise have penetrated into the interior. The opposite side of the tent was fitted in a similar manner for the protection of the cook whilst engaged in preparing the meals. The duties of the cook during intensely cold weather entail hardships which it is scarcely possible to overrate. The poor cook is never in his sleeping bag until two or three hours after the rest of the party have been comfortably settled for the night, and he has always to rise in the morning a couple of hours before his comrades are disturbed, and this after a hard and fatiguing day's work. His cooking apparatus consists of a spirit lamp, a stearine lamp, a kettle, and a stew-pan. His fuel is either spirits of wine, or cocoa-nut stearine; and as the allowance of either is strictly limited, he has to be as economical as he possibly can. Should his fuel be consumed before the meal is cooked, he will get no more, and the pemmican will have to be eaten in a semi-frozen state. The odour and smoke emitted by the stearine

the top, seven feet wide and high, and weighed 44 lbs. The tent ropes are six fathoms long of one and a quarter inch, and the tent poles eight feet six inches long.

can only be appreciated by those who have served their apprenticeship as cooks to an Arctic sledge party! Many experiments were tried during the winter to improve our cooking apparatus, but few were attended with success. Mr. White devoted a good deal of thought and time to this important matter. By introducing a cone into the kettle and stew-pan he succeeded in gaining a decided advantage in rapidity of cooking, but then his plan also had its disadvantages, a difficulty of cleaning and an encroachment on valuable space being the chief objections to it. By giving the bottom of the pans and kettles a little more concavity, we gained a slight advantage in point of time, and time in cooking also means an economy of fuel. The tent robes, coverlets, and sleeping bags were all made of duffel. The knapsacks were made of duck, and contained the only spare clothing that each man was allowed to take. The contents consisted of two pairs of blanket wrappers, one pair of wadmill hose, one pair of moccasins, a skull-cap for sleeping in, a woollen cap presented to each person in the expedition by H.I.M. the Empress Eugénie, two pairs of mitts, a flannel shirt, a pair of drawers, a comforter, a pair of snow-spectacles, a towel, and a piece of soap. The latter was rather a superfluous article until the thaw set in.

The store bag contained the pemmican chopper and board, a snow-knife and saw, some spare lashings of hide for the sledge, matches, slow match, twine, and various other small and useful articles.

The scale of provisions to be used whilst sledging was almost identical with that of preceding expeditions, the only difference being that we reduced the allowance of spirits by half and doubled the amount of tea and sugar. The following was the daily ration for each man:—

	lb.	oz.
Pemmican	1	0
Bacon	0	4
Biscuit	0	14
Preserved potatoes	0	2
Chocolate	0	1
Sugar for ditto	0	0·5
Tea for two meals	0	0·5
Sugar for ditto	0	1·5
Salt	0	0·25
Pepper	0	0·05
Onion powder or curry paste	0	0·125
Rum	0	2
Spirits of wine	0	2
Stearine	0	3
Tobacco (weekly)	0	3·5

This we found a very ample allowance, and one that could not, in my opinion, be improved upon. The different articles were excellent of their kind, and of very superior quality.

Since our return to England, fault has been found with our leader because lime-juice was not included in the scale of dietary for the sledges, during April, as a daily ration. Our scale of diet was necessarily based on that of preceding expeditions, and we had no reason to expect that we should suffer from that dread disease, scurvy, any more than did our predecessors. Lime-juice had never before been taken as a daily ration by an extended sledge party, and Sir Leopold McClintock, the highest living authority, has since publicly declared that, in following the precedents established by former experience as regards the lime-juice, Sir George Nares acted exactly as he would have done under the same circumstances. Moreover, the lime-juice was supplied in a form that made it impossible to use during an Arctic March, April, or May, away from the ship. It was in bottles or very large heavy jars, and, of course, the moment such vessels were placed near a fire to thaw their contents, in such a temperature, they would have been cracked to pieces. This is a conclusive answer to those who, without experience, and ignorant of the conditions under which we travelled, have expressed opinions on this subject. After May, when it was possible to use it, lime-juice was always taken by our sledge parties as a daily ration. When we came home, the use was suggested of lime-juice lozenges, and the Medical Director General has proposed that lime-juice should be mixed with pemmican. It is certainly very much to be regretted that some such arrangements were not made and carried out before the expedition left England. It will be seen (if lime-juice would really have prevented the attack of scurvy) how terribly we had to suffer from the consequences of the omission.

Lieutenant Parr and myself each took two bottles of lime-juice, with the intention of using it when the warm weather of June arrived. It was not possible to use it to any advantage, hard frozen in a bottle, during March, April, or May.

Dr. Colan drew up very careful medical instructions for the commanders of sledges, and each received some elementary surgical instruction. The doctor also paid most anxious attention to the contents of the medical chest, the weight of which was not allowed to exceed 12 lbs.*

---

* The medical stores for each sledge were :—2 phials of sal volatile and aromatic spirits of ammonia; 2 phials of laudanum; 2 phials of

The clothing worn by the men engaged in the sledging operations was somewhat different from that in use during the winter. Our under clothing was made of thick flannel. Over this we wore one or two flannel or check shirts, long sleeved woollen waistcoats, thick knitted guernseys, and duffel trousers, the latter reaching about a foot below the knee. All wore broad flannel belts, commonly called cholera belts, round their loins. On our heads we had woollen helmet caps, called by the men "Eugenies," and over this was worn a thick seal-skin cap with ear and neck flaps attached.

Our feet were encased in blanket wrappers, one or two pairs according to the temperature, a pair of thick woollen hose reaching above the knees and worn *over* the trousers, and moccasins. The latter, as supplied to us, only came up round the ankle, so we fitted them with leggings. Those who were provided with chamois leather made their leggings of that material, but the majority cut the sleeves off their check shirts which, when sewn on to the moccasin, answered admirably, their chief use being to keep the snow from penetrating into the trousers. Some of the moccasins were also soled with leather, obtained by

wine of opium; a small tin of Gregory's powders; 12 papers (10 grains each) of Dover's powders; 32 papers (15 grains each) of chalk powders; 30 papers (4 grains each) of sugar of lead; a bottle of turpentine liniment; a phial of carbolic acid; glycerine ointment; white ointment; carbolic plaster; 4 dozen purgative pills; oil silk. Sponge, pins, expanding splints, and carbolized tow, cotton wool, a catheter, a tourniquet, a truss with pad, a lancet, twill, Persian gauze, 2 eye shades, small splint, scissors, flannel ice goggles, tape, mustard, 3 calico bandages, 2 flannel bandages, and lint. These stores were in a wooden case, and a medicine tin for bottles, together weighing 4 lbs.; while their contents weighed 7 lbs. 11 ozs., together, 12 lbs.

cutting off the upper part of the fishermen's boots, a pair of which had been supplied to each person. As a rule these soles were quickly worn out, and the men were soon reduced to the bare moccasin, which, however, lasted wonderfully.

Large gauntlet mitts were made during the winter, of fearnought covered with duck, and worn with a strap round the neck. These were only supplied to the sledgers, and were found very useful. At nighttime they were used on the feet in the sleeping bags, and certainly assisted very materially in keeping them warm. Finally each person was provided with a suit of duck overalls, to act as "snow repellers," which were always worn whilst on the march. As an extra precaution against snow-blindness, the men were ordered to paint some device on the backs of these snow jumpers in order to afford a certain amount of relief to the eyes of their comrades. The designs of these devices or crests were left entirely to the artistic imaginations of the men, and they caused a good deal of merriment. They were certainly more quaint than elegant. Donkeys and Polar bears in various wonderful positions appeared to be in the greatest favour. Each crest was accompanied by a motto, invariably a Latin one. Whether these devices relieved us from severe attacks of snow-blindness or not it would be difficult to decide. They served at any rate to amuse us, and often formed the topic of conversation when other subjects were getting scarce. Snow-spectacles were invariably used by the travellers, and were only taken off after the party had halted for the night and had sought the shelter of their tent. In consequence of the adoption of these snow-goggles when we first set out on our travels, we were comparatively exempt from that painful disease, snow-blindness, from which other expeditions have more or less suffered, and which renders the patient so attacked utterly helpless. We occasionally had a few cases, but with one or two exceptions they were in a very mild form.

Such were the details of the general equipment of the sledging parties that were despatched from the "Alert" in the spring of 1876. Officers and men shared alike in everything; they had the same provisions, their costume was identical, they shared the same couch and tent, and each showed the same zealous desire to perform his duty, and the same eager anxiety to bring to a successful issue the service on which they were employed.

Although the whole of the available force on board the "Alert" was engaged in the sledging operations of the spring, we were only able to despatch *two* extended parties.* The rest of the men and sledges were required to act as auxiliaries to the advanced parties, and were continually employed during the summer until the return of all the travellers brought our sledging operations to a conclusion.

The programme to be carried out, and which was determined upon after very mature and careful deliberation, was for one party, the command of which was given to Aldrich the first lieutenant, to continue the discoveries of the autumn by exploring the coast line to the westward; whilst a larger party, which was entrusted to my conduct, was to push across the

* Our available force was much smaller than that of the expeditions under Sir Horatio Austin (1850-51), and Sir Henry Kellet (1852-54). They enjoyed the great advantage of having a third larger force—ninety instead of sixty men.

rugged polar pack, and endeavour to reach as high a northern latitude as possible. The exploration of the north side of Greenland, to the eastward, and the examination of the fiords in Robeson Channel, were left to the sledge parties from the "Discovery."

The difficulties to be encountered and the serious obstacles to be overcome in the journey due north over the frozen sea were well understood. We had made ourselves acquainted with the nature of the travelling to be anticipated by various short excursions on the ice in the vicinity of the ship, and were, therefore, fully aware of the serious character of the work that was before us. None were so rash as to indulge in any extravagant ideas of successfully reaching a very high position. The parallel of 84°, or perhaps 85° by the more sanguine, was regarded as the highest that could possibly be attained.

It was a well-known fact, before the ship went into winter quarters, that the polar pack, composed of extraordinarily heavy ice, was in motion at that season. This motion, or perhaps a general disruption, would occur, it was calculated, in about July or August, possibly in June. It was, therefore, not only a measure of prudence, but one of absolute necessity, that the party destined to travel over this frozen ocean should be provided with the means of safety to themselves, if a disruption should take place at an earlier period than was anticipated. It was therefore decided that two boats,* capable of convey-

* The sledges for carrying boats have the two end cross-bars fitted with two cleats, one on each side of the boat's keel. These cleats are seven inches long, and are securely lashed to the cross-bars. Two battens of American elm, each two inches wide and half an inch thick, are lashed in a fore and aft direction to the top of the cross-bars three and a half inches apart, that is to say one and three-

ing the whole party from one floe to another, should form part of the equipment of the northern division. This additional weight, of course, seriously augmented the labour of the men.

The only previous attempt to advance over a frozen sea, away from the land, was made by Sir Edward Parry, in his memorable journey towards the North Pole in 1827.*

quarters inch on each side of the central bearer. They are sufficiently long to allow of being secured to all the cross-bars. When the boat is placed on the sledge the keel rests on the cross-bars between the cleats, and is held in an upright position by one long cushion of stout canvas, stuffed with cork cuttings, on each side, and these are kept in their places by lashings.

* As Sir Edward Parry's attempt to reach the Pole was the only extended journey that was ever undertaken due north across the Polar Sea, until the second attempt was made by the northern division of sledges under my command, it will be well to give, in this place, the details of Parry's equipment and the result of his expedition.

Sir Edward Parry sailed from England in the "Hecla," on April 3rd, 1827; when placing her in a safe harbour on the north coast of Spitzbergen, he commenced his memorable attempt to reach the Pole on June 21st. He had two boats, the "Enterprise" and the "Endeavour." Parry himself, with Mr. Beverley, was in the former, James Ross and Edward Bird in the latter. Ten seamen and two marines formed the crew of each boat. The boats were flat-bottomed, with the extreme breadth of seven feet, carried well forward and aft, and twenty feet long, the timbers of tough ash and hickory. On the outside frame a system of planking was adopted with a view to securing elasticity in the frequent concussions with the ice. This consisted of a covering of waterproof canvas coated with tar, then a thin fir plank, then a sheet of felt, and, lastly, a thin oak plank, all secured to the timbers by iron screws. On each side of the keel there was a strong runner shod with metal, like that of a sledge, on which the boats entirely rested when on the ice. A hide span across the fore-part of the runners had two horse-hair drag ropes attached to it. The boats had two thwarts, a locker at each end, a light framework along the sides for containing provisions and spare clothes, a bamboo mast, and tanned duck sail, fourteen paddles, and a steer oar. They started with seventy-one days' provisions. The weight of each boat was 1,539 lbs., and the total weight, with provisions,

For reasons already stated, the northern party was unable to lay out depôts on the ice, nor could our sledges be met by supporting sledges until after their return to the land. It therefore became necessary that they should carry with them sufficient provisions to last for the whole time of anticipated absence. This, with the boats, obliged the two sledge crews composing the division to take with them a *third* sledge, so that under the most favourable conditions of travelling, they would be compelled, after advancing two sledges, to return over the same road and drag on the third. This we fondly hoped on starting we should be able to accomplish; little did we think that the fearfully rugged nature of the road would neces-

3,753 lbs., or 268 lbs. per man; besides four light taboggan sledges weighing 26 lbs. each. The daily allowance for each man was 10 ozs. of biscuit, 9 ozs. of pemmican, 1 oz. of cocoa, and 1 gill of rum. Parry took no lime-juice. They slept in the boat with sails as awnings, and travelled during the night.

They sailed in the boats until June 23rd, when it became necessary to haul them on the ice in 81° 12′ 51″ N. The actual travelling then began over floes of small extent, intersected by hummocks. After a journey of thirty days, Parry reached his most northern point on July 23rd, in latitude, by dead reckoning, 82° 45′ N. No actual observation for latitude was obtained at their extreme northern point. They had travelled ninety-two miles over the ice, and two hundred in the boats before they hauled them on to the floe, but were only one hundred and seventy-two miles from the "Hecla." Such had been the drift of the floes to the southward. The boats returned to the "Hecla" on August 21st, and Parry arrived in England again on October 6th.

This journey was made in the middle of summer after the disruption of the ice. The daily allowance of food for the men was insufficient, and the weight of 26 lbs. for each man was too great. But these were points which could only be learnt by experience, and Sir Edward Parry was the pioneer of Arctic sledge travelling. He attained the highest northern latitude ever before reached by man, and it was forty-eight years and two months before any explorer succeeded in going beyond the parallel which Parry reached in 1827.

sitate the same distance being traversed five or even seven times.

For the same reason that the men were ordered to emblazon arms and crests on the backs of their clothes, we had the boats which were to accompany the sledges painted with gay and brilliant devices. The rose, shamrock, and thistle were painted on the hulls, and the royal arms decorated their sterns. Moss, on this as on other occasions, was the artist; his great difficulty in accomplishing the work being that in spite of the quantity of turpentine with which the paint was mixed, it persisted in freezing in the brush, rendering that article more like a stick than an artist's pencil.

The sledges were, of course, all named by their commanders.

CHAPTER XX.

THE JOURNEY OF EGERTON AND RAWSON.

> "You were used to say,
> Extremity was the trier of spirits,
> That common chances common men could bear,
> That when the sea was calm, all boats alike
> Showed mastership in floating."
>
> SHAKESPEARE.

It was a part of Captain Nares's scheme for the spring campaign that, before the departure of the extended parties, a dog sledge should be despatched to communicate with our consort wintering some fifty miles to the southward of us.

The officers and men of the "Discovery" were, of course, in total ignorance of our position and even of our safety, for no communication had taken place between the two ships since the day of our departure from Discovery Harbour, seven months before. As soon as there was sufficient light to admit of travelling, the important and necessary duty had to be undertaken of conveying information to her respecting our position, so that the anxiety of her people concerning our safety might be relieved, and also that the Captain of the "Discovery" might be made acquainted with our intentions regarding the routes of exploration allotted to our sledge travellers. The parties from the "Discovery" would then adopt other routes, and thus the area of unknown country to be explored would be extended to the utmost limit possible. The work of the expedition, consisting of the journeys of the different parties from the two ships, taking different routes, would thus embrace all that human effort could achieve with the means provided.

The duty of communicating with the "Discovery"

DOGS AND SLEDGE.

was entrusted to Egerton; and Rawson, who was naturally desirous of re-visiting his ship, was allowed to accompany him. Their sledge was dragged by a team of nine dogs, and the party was provisioned and equipped for an absence of ten days. If they failed in accomplishing their object in that time, and their supplies became exhausted, they could replenish their stock from the large depôt that had been established during the previous autumn at a point about midway between the two ships, in Lincoln Bay. Petersen, the Danish interpreter, accompanied the two officers in the capacity of dog driver.

In consequence of the very low temperature experienced during the first week in March, their time of departure had to be deferred. Sunday, the 12th of March, was the day eventually selected for the start of this the first sledging expedition of the season.

The temperature on that morning was low, but rose gradually towards noon, until it seemed inclined to remain stationary at 30° below zero.

There were further indications of a continuance of fine weather, from the day being bright and clear and the barometer steady. Letters to our friends on board the "Discovery" were hastily finished. Immediately divine service had been performed the colours were hoisted, and amidst the cheers of "all hands," who had assembled on the floe to bid the travellers God speed, H.M. sledge "Clements Markham," with its bright standard fluttering out bravely before a light breeze, started with the object of renewing intercourse with our comrades in the "Discovery."

For the next two or three days our thoughts on board were constantly with the absent ones, especially as the temperature, shortly after their departure, had again fallen very low. This, however, caused us little uneasiness, for we knew that everything that lay in our power had been done to protect them from any sudden and extreme cold, and we all had the greatest confidence in the skill, discretion, and sound judgment of our two messmates. Many a silent prayer was offered up in their behalf, that they might accomplish their mission in safety, and return speedily with good news of those who, like ourselves, were wintering in the ice.

On the third day they returned unexpectedly with a sad tale of woe and suffering, and with the poor Dane utterly prostrate and helpless on the sledge. I cannot do better than relate the sad story in Lieutenant Egerton's own words.

We read in his official report, that not five hours after they had left the ship "frost-bites became so numerous, that I thought it advisable to encamp."

This was only the beginning of the story, for they appear to have passed a comparatively comfortable night.

At any rate they were up early the next morning and again under weigh; at about one o'clock, when they halted for lunch, Petersen complained of cramp in his stomach and was given some hot tea. He had no appetite, which perhaps was as well, for we read of the bacon, which is always used for lunch, "We were unable to eat it, being frozen so hard that we could not get our teeth through the lean." They still continued their journey, encountering some very rough travelling, which necessitated severe physical labour on the part of the two officers. "The dogs were of little or no use in getting across these slopes, as it was impossible to get them to go up the cliff, and Petersen being unable to work, Lieutenant Rawson and I had to get the sledge along as best we could." Towards the end of the day we read: "Petersen began to get rather worse, and was shivering all over, his nose being constantly frost-bitten, and at times taking five or ten minutes before the circulation could be thoroughly restored. Lieutenant Rawson had several small frost-bites, and I escaped with only one."

On halting for the night, directly the tent was pitched they sent Petersen inside with strict injunctions to shift his foot gear and get into his sleeping-bag, whilst they busied themselves in preparing supper and attending to the dogs; but when they entered the tent, they found "that he had turned in without shifting his foot gear, was groaning a good deal, and complaining of cramp in the stomach and legs."

Having made him change, they gave him some tea, and then administered a few drops of sal volatile, which appeared to give the poor fellow a little ease.

The next morning the wind was so high and their patient in such a weak state that they did not think it prudent to attempt a start. He had passed a very restless night, and still complained very much of cramp.

Later in the day he appeared to get worse, "shaking and shivering all over and breathing in short gasps. His face, hands, and feet were all frost-bitten, the latter severely, and he had pains in his side as well." After restoring the circulation they rubbed him with warm flannels and placed one of their comforters round his stomach.

In such a wretched state was the poor fellow that they agreed it would endanger his life if they proceeded on their journey; and that when the weather moderated the only course they could pursue was to return with all haste to their ship.

As it was impossible to keep their patient warm in the tent, these two young officers burrowed a hole in a snow-drift, and into this cavity they transported the sick man, themselves, and all their tent robes, closing the aperture by placing over it the tent and sledge.

They deprived themselves of their own clothing for the benefit of the invalid, whose frozen feet they actually placed inside their clothes in direct contact with their bodies, until their own heat was extracted and they were themselves severely frost-bitten in various parts. The poor fellow was now in a very low state; he could retain neither food nor liquid. "About 6 P.M. he was very bad; this time worse than before. There appeared to be no heat in him of any kind whatever, and he had acute pains in the stomach and back. We chafed him on the stomach, hands, face, and feet, and when he got better wrapped him up in everything warm we could lay our hands upon," namely, their own clothing, which they could ill afford to lose; but they entirely forgot their own condition in their endeavours to ameliorate that of their comrade. Lighting their spirit lamp and carefully closing every crevice by which the cold air could enter, they succeeded in raising the temperature of the interior to 7°; but "the atmosphere in the hut became somewhat thick!" This was, however, preferable to the intense cold. Let us follow the story out, and learn how nobly these two officers tended their sick and suffering companion. "We were constantly asking if he was warm in his feet and hands, to which he replied in the affirmative; but before making him comfortable" (fancy being *comfortable* under such circumstances!) "for the night, we examined his feet, and found them both perfectly gelid and hard from the toes to the ankle, his hands nearly as bad. So each taking a foot we set to work to warm them with our hands and flannels, as each hand and flannel got cold *warming them about our persons*, and also lit up the spirit lamp. In about two hours we got his feet to, and put them in warm foot gear, cut his bag down to allow him more room to move in, and then wrapped him up in the spare coverlet. His hands we also brought round and bound them up in flannel wrappers, with mitts over all. Gave him some warm tea and a little rum and water, which he threw up. Shortly after I found him eating snow, which we had strictly forbidden once or twice before. In endeavouring to do this again during the night, he dragged his feet out of the covering; but only a few minutes could have elapsed before this was detected by Lieutenant Rawson, who, upon examining his feet, found them in much the same state as before. We rubbed and chafed them again for over an hour, and when circulation was restored wrapped him up again, and so passed the third night."

The patience and endurance of the two officers are beyond all praise. It is difficult to realize the misery of that night. Wearied with the severe physical exertions of the two previous days, having their own meals to prepare and the dogs to look after, they had to pass a sleepless and anxious night in their endeavours to keep life in the body of their half-frozen comrade.

On the following morning Petersen appeared to be slightly better, so thinking it was preferable to run the risk of taking him back as he was, than to pass such another night as the last, they put him on the sledge, and, having hurriedly eaten their breakfast, they started for the ship with all despatch. They had a rough journey before them of eighteen miles; but they knew it was a case of life and death, and they encouraged the dogs to their utmost speed. The dogs, being homeward bound, were willing enough and needed little persuasion, so that, for a time, they rattled along at a good pace. But actual progress could not have been very rapid, for we read in Egerton's report that the patient's "circulation was so feeble that his face and hands were constantly frost-bitten, entailing frequent stoppages whilst we endeavoured to restore the affected parts." The difficulties of the homeward journey may be gathered from the following extracts: "On arriving at the Black Cape we had to take the patient off the sledge, and while one assisted him round, the other kept the dogs back, for by this time they knew they were homeward bound, and required no small amount of trouble to hold in. After getting the sledge round and restoring Petersen's hands and nose (which were almost as bad again a few minutes after), and securing him on the sledge, we again set off. At the next cape the same difficulties were experienced, in fact rather more, for the sledge took charge down a 'ditch,'* about twenty-five feet deep, turning right over three times in its descent, and out of which we had to drag it, and while clearing harness (which employed us both, one to stand in front of the dogs with the whip, while the other cleared the lines), the dogs made a sudden bolt past Lieutenant Rawson, who was in front with the whip, and dragged me more than a hundred yards before we could stop them. At length, after the usual process with Petersen (that of thawing his hands and nose, which we did every time we cleared harness, or it was actually necessary to stop), we got away, thankful that

---

* By a "ditch" is meant a hollow formed between a high snow-drift and a hummock or any projection. Some of these ditches were very steep and precipitous.

our troubles were over. The dogs got their harness into a dreadful entanglement in their excitement to get home; but we were afraid to clear them lest they should break away from us, or cause us any delay, as we were both naturally anxious to return with the utmost speed to the ship, and so relieve ourselves of the serious responsibility occasioned by the very precarious state in which our patient was lying. Upon arriving alongside at 6.30 P.M., we were very thankful that Petersen was able to answer us when we informed him he was at home."

Poor fellow! it was the last home he ever reached alive, for in two short months his remains were carried from the ship and laid in their last resting-place in this world, on the summit of a low hill overlooking the scene of his last sledge journey! In conclusion, Egerton says, "I regret exceedingly that I have been compelled to return to the ship without having accomplished my journey to H.M.S. 'Discovery;' but I trust that what I have done will meet with your approval, and that the course I adopted may be the means of having lessened the very serious and distressing condition of Petersen." Gallant fellow! of course his doings meet not only with the approval but the admiration of all Englishmen who take pride in the noble and heroic deeds of their countrymen. The work of these two brave young officers on this occasion stands out conspicuously amongst the many deeds of daring and devotion with which the annals of Arctic adventure abound.

It must be remembered that during the time they were away the sun had only just made its reappearance, and was therefore at a very low altitude, so that little benefit could be derived from its rays; and it only afforded sufficient light to enable the travellers to keep on the march for about eight or nine hours a day.* On the 20th of March, five days after the return from their calamitous journey, the same two officers made another and a more successful start. On this occasion they were accompanied by a couple of sailors, and their sledge was dragged by a team of seven dogs. In five days, after a severe and toilsome journey, rendered doubly so by the extreme cold and the heavy nature of the road over which they had to travel, they reached the "Discovery," conveying to her officers and crew the pleasing intelligence of our safety, and receiving in return an account of the happy winter passed by them.

Poor Petersen never recovered from the effects of this journey. He rallied a little after he arrived on board, and was placed under the tender and skilful treatment of Dr. Colan, who for some time held out slight hopes of his recovery; but the injuries he had received were of too serious a nature to admit of much hope, and he gradually sank until he expired peacefully on the 14th of May. Perhaps it was better that it should be so, for the poor fellow would not only have been disfigured by losing portions of his nose and ears, but he would also have been a cripple, for the doctor had been compelled to amputate both his feet in order to stop the mortification from extending. These frost-bites are indeed very dreadful, and must always be quickly taken in hand so as to avoid any serious result.

* In previous expeditions parties have left their ships in March; but the March of 75° N. is very different from the March of 82° N. In the former position the sun has been many days longer above the horizon than in 82° N.

So cold were the frozen limbs of poor Petersen, that his companions said it was like touching cold steel, and produced frost-bite almost as rapidly as if they were really touching a piece of metal!

Although this chapter is rather a mournful one, and has a very melancholy termination, I make no apology for having devoted it entirely to our first sledging expedition of the season, believing that my readers will feel both pride and pleasure in hearing of the noble conduct of my two messmates.

CHAPTER XXI.

THE ROUTINE OF SLEDGE TRAVELLING.

> "We are well persuaded
> We carry not a heart with us from hence
> That grows not in a fair consent with ours;
> Nor leave not one behind, that doth not wish
> Success and conquest to attend on us."
> *Henry V.*

On the morning of Monday, the 3rd of April, an unwonted bustle and excitement on board and around the "Alert" betokened that something unusual was taking place. Men in their travelling costumes might have been observed busily engaged in adding the last finishing touches to the already well-packed sledges. Officers, also in travelling attire, were carefully conveying delicate instruments from the ship to the row of sledges drawn up in "line of battle" on the floe, whilst the white ensign flying from the peak bore witness of some important event.

The day was indeed one of memorable import, for it was the one that we had all, during the long dark winter, looked forward to as that on which our real work was to commence. It was the day on which we were to start forth with the object of achieving all that was possible with the means at our disposal, in the great and glorious work of increasing the stock of geographical knowledge respecting the Polar regions. No wonder, then, that the scene of our winter quarters presented an animated and unwonted appearance on that bright but intensely cold morning.

The sledges, seven in number, on two of which were placed the boats to accompany the northern division, were drawn up in single line, one before the other, according to the seniority of their respective leaders. They were all fully equipped and provisioned, and were "manned" by a force of fifty-three officers and men; a chosen band, eager to emulate the deeds of their predecessors, and willing to risk their lives in bringing to a successful issue the task they had resolved to accomplish.

A strict medical examination had been held a day or two previously, and the rather unnecessary question, "Do you feel yourself fit and able in every way to go sledging?" was put to all. It is needless to record the answer!

On the previous day, being Sunday, Pullen preached a capital sermon, drawing comparisons between the undertaking in which we were about to engage, and the march of the Israelites to the Promised Land. The hymn " for those at sea " was sung and the Holy Communion celebrated, at which latter service there was an exceptionally good attendance, the number of communicants amongst the men having largely increased.

From each sledge flew the bright colours of its commander's standard : a swallow-tailed flag bearing the armorial colours, and emblazoned with the crest of its owner, each charged with the red cross of St. George. In addition, the two boats displayed from their mast-heads Captain Nares's Union Jack and a white ensign. Worked by the fair hands of some loved and cherished one at home, these standards, as they fluttered out bravely before a gentle breeze, kindled our enthusiasm, whilst they materially added to the spirit and gaiety of the scene.

The sledges were arranged in the following order:— "Marco Polo" (with a boat), "Challenger," "Victoria" (with a boat), "Poppie," "Bulldog," "Alexandra," and "Bloodhound;" the latter was only a small sledge party ordered to accompany us for three or four days, then supply us with three days' provisions, and return to the ship to report our progress.

At eleven o'clock, everything being in readiness fo a start, all hands assembled on the floe, and prayers were read by Pullen. The hymn, "God, from whom all blessings flow," was then sung, after which the order was given to "fall in," and, amidst the hearty cheers of those few who were left behind, the sledging parties moved off. The captain and officers accompanied us for a short distance, when, wishing us Godspeed, they turned to go back. This was a signal for three cheers from the travellers, after which they settled down to their work, and the march was steadily commenced.

The first day's march was necessarily a short one. It was to many their introduction to the "drag-ropes," and symptoms of fatigue were soon detected, caused by the energetic exertions of the inexperienced, who, unlike the veterans of the previous autumn, overtaxed their strength in their ardour to perform a good day's work.

The temperature at starting was 33° below zero, and at this it remained steady the whole day, rendering the task of writing up our journals when we halted extremely unpleasant and painful.

The scene of our first encampment was an animated and picturesque one. We had marched about six miles from the ship, and the site selected was at the base of a low brow, forming a connection or isthmus between a long projecting tongue and the mainland. Here we pitched our seven tents, from each of which the smoke from the cooking utensils issued, ascending in spiral columns until lost amidst the clouds. In our rear were the snow-clad hills, whilst in front was the illimitable frozen sea. Men hurried about in the execution of various duties incidental to "pitching for the night," such as the issuing of provisions by the several sledge-captains, the banking up with snow of the exterior of the tents, the re-packing of the sledges, or the careful covering up of the lading so as to ensure its protection from snow-drift; all of which duties must be sedulously carried out before rest and repose can be sought in the sleeping-bags. A pleasing aroma of cooking tea was mixed with the fragrance of stewed pemmican, and made us smack our lips in anticipation of the meal that was preparing.

Not the least hard part of a day's work is that of camping after a toilsome and weary journey, especially when the temperature is low and a cold sleepless night anticipated; but when the weather is warm enough to obtain a good night's rest, the order to halt is always received with very great satisfaction, more especially when a good day's work has been accomplished, with the prospect of fair travelling on the morrow.

As soon as the tents are ready for the reception of the men, they enter one by one, take off their "overalls" for which their duffel coats are substituted, change their foot gear and get into their sleeping-bags. This change of foot gear in the morning and evening is the whole extent of the toilet performed by the sledgers until their return to the ship!

The following morning we were under weigh pretty early, having spent a cold wretched night, only too glad to be up and doing something, the temperature inside our tent, with all the men in their bags, being as low as 15° below zero. The experience gained during the autumn had a very salutary effect on the travellers, the apprehension even of frost-bite being in itself sufficient to banish all idea of sleep.

The operation of dressing and undressing, although it is entirely limited to the clothing of the feet, is without doubt one of the most disagreeable duties connected with sledge travelling. Our hose and blanket-wrappers, although they were invariably kept *inside* our sleeping-bags during the night, were frozen so hard in the morning that they were with the greatest difficulty folded over our feet. Sometimes the wrappers were tied round the knees at night-time to protect them from the cold, for that part of our body seemed more sensitive to the temperature than any other.

Not the least trying part of our toilet was lacing and tying the stiffly frozen strings of our equally hard moccasins with fingers either aching from cold or devoid of all sensation. Not only was this a very painful operation, but it was one that sorely taxed and ruffled the equanimity of our tempers.

The snow over which we travelled was very soft and, unfortunately for us, was also very deep, making the dragging with our heavily laden sledges most laborious, in fact so much so that we were frequently compelled to resort to "double banking;" that is to say, the two crews would be employed in first dragging on one sledge and then return to advance the other. This, of course, made our progress very slow. After the long confinement of the men during the darkness of the winter, they were, in spite of the careful attention that had been paid to daily exercise, hardly in what might be called first-rate condition, so that fatigue for the first few days was felt by the majority, and not wishing to impose too much on their zealous desire to push on, short journeys were in consequence performed.

On the second day out, the temperature fell to 45° below zero, or 77° below freezing point. The cold then was so intense as to deprive us of sleep, the temperature *inside* the tent being as low as − 25°, the whole period of rest being occupied in attempting to keep the blood in circulation. Several frost-bites were sustained, but they were all attended to in time, and resulted in nothing worse than severe and very uncomfortable blisters.

So hard were our tent robes and sleeping-bags frozen that they resembled sheet-iron, and care had to be taken to prevent them from coming into contact with the face, for an abrasion of the skin would undoubtedly follow!

Our curry paste, a small quantity of which we used to mix with our pemmican to make it more palateable, looked, as the cook of the day observed, exactly like a piece of brass, and was equally hard. Cramp in the legs was complained of by many during the first few nights, but gradually wore off, having in all probability been induced by the severe and unaccustomed exercise. Thirst was also a subject of complaint, and this, except at meal times, it was impossible to alleviate; for although each man was supplied with a tin water-bottle covered with duffel, the water could not be prevented from freezing, in spite of the bottles being kept inside the waistbands of the men's trousers. The practice of quenching thirst by putting snow or ice into the mouth is a very dangerous one and was never permitted.

On the fourth day out we parted with our little sledge, the "Bloodhound," which, having fulfilled its mission, returned to the ship, taking back one of our party, who appeared unable to stand the fatigues of sledging, and leaving one of their crew to fill his vacancy. We were thus able to send back intelligence of our progress so far, and to report the health of the men to be satisfactory, and that all were in capital spirits. On the 10th of April the six sledges in company arrived at the depôt of provisions established near Cape Joseph Henry during the autumn, and found it undisturbed. The remainder of that day was employed in bringing the provisions off to the sledges, which were left on the ice, and in distributing them. The next morning was thick and foggy, the atmosphere being rendered doubly obscure by a heavy fall of snow.

> "The cold, uncomfortable daylight dawned,
> And the white tents, topping a low ground fog,
> Show'd like a fleet becalmed."

On this day the supporting sledges "Bulldog" and "Alexandra," having performed the duties allotted to them, bade farewell to their companions and returned to their ship. The two extended parties advanced on their solitary missions; the northern division leaving the land and pushing straight out on the rugged polar pack, whilst the western party continued the exploration of the coast to the westward.

It was a strange farewell that was taken on that cold dull day on the inhospitable ice-floe, amidst bristling hummocks and heaped up snow-drifts, as the several parties pursued their different courses, one returning to their Arctic home, the others to unknown difficulties, but to hoped-for discoveries.

Brief was the parting, but sincere were the wishes for each other's success. Hearty British cheers resounded in that icy wilderness, hitherto undisturbed by the presence of mortal man, as we bade adieu to our fellow-travellers, the echoes from which had scarce died away before their forms vanished from our view in the thick driving snow that shrouded in obscurity the surrounding objects.

It was, however, no time for reflection; for now all our energies, both mental and physical, had to be devoted to the furtherance of the great work with which we were entrusted. The men resolutely seized their drag-ropes, and with light and willing hearts commenced their toilsome advance.

In order to enable my readers to follow us during the time we were engaged in the sledging operations, I will endeavour to explain, as briefly as possible, the ordinary daily routine invariably carried out by those so employed belonging to the "Alert."

The cook for the day is an important personage, and his duties, as I have before related, are of a very onerous and trying description. Each individual composing the sledge crew has to perform this office in turn during twenty-four hours, and it is one that sorely taxes his patience and powers of endurance, especially in very cold weather. He gladly transfers his functions as cook to his successor, happy in the assurance that his "turn" will not come round for another week, unless sickness or any other unforeseen event should prostrate any of his comrades.

The cook's work commences at an early hour, when, after having lighted his lamp and converted sufficient ice or snow into water for the morning meal, he re-enters the tent, and walking unconcernedly on the sleeping forms of his companions, proceeds deliberately to brush from the top and sides of the tent the condensed moisture that has been accumulating during the night, and which falls in minute frozen particles on the coverlet. This operation being concluded, to the no small relief of those over whom he has been walking, the coverlet is removed, well brushed, shaken, folded up, and placed on the sledge. He then busies himself with the important preparations for breakfast. In about two hours from the time that the cook is called, the cocoa is reported ready, when the rest of the party are awakened.

If the weather is very cold, breakfast is discussed in our bags, in which we all sit up; a comical-looking lot in our grey skull-caps and duffel coats! The biscuit bag is then laid in the centre of the tent, spoons are produced, and the pannikins, each containing one pint of warm cocoa, are handed in. The only articles that were not considered as common property amongst us were our spoons. These were slightly larger than an ordinary table-spoon, were made of horn, and supplied to each sledger by a beneficent Government. We generally carried them slung round our necks by laniards, or in our pockets.

The pannikins being emptied they are returned to the cook, who has in the mean time been preparing the pemmican. So hard is this article frozen that the portions for use have to be chipped off with a chopper before they can be put into the stewpan.

While the cook's anxiety is momentarily increased by the fear that his fuel will be consumed before the repast is prepared, and his fingers are alternately burnt and frost-bitten in his endeavours to trim and adjust the lamp, prayers are read to those inside, the foot gear is changed and the sleeping-bags rolled up. By the time this has been done, the pemmican is ready, passed in, and eaten. Orders are then given to strike tent, pack sledge, and prepare to march.

The great secret in packing a sledge properly is to have the weights as nearly as possible in the centre —as far from the extremes as it is possible to get them, so that the sledge may rise easily over obstacles. When all is ready, the drag-ropes are manned, and with a "one, two, three, haul," and a good pull altogether, the sledge is started and the march commenced.

Care should be taken to scrape the pannikins out with a knife, before the refuse inside has time to freeze, otherwise it will be difficult to remove. Water for washing purposes, of any description, whilst sledging is quite out of the question. After marching for about five or six hours, a halt is called for lunch. This meal consists of four ounces of bacon, a little biscuit, and a warm pannikin of tea to each man.

Although the most refreshing and enjoyable of all our meals, luncheon was, when there was much wind, or the weather intensely cold, a very trying one The halt is of necessity long. Frequently an hour or an hour and a half elapses before the tea is reported ready, during which time the men are compelled to keep constantly on the move to avoid frost-bites. When there is much wind the tent is pitched; but this adds little to our comfort, for it is too cold to remain inside for any length of time. If we were not all suffering from the same cause, we should be disposed to laugh at the strange antics of our companions in their efforts to keep their feet from getting frost-bitten. One man is "marking time" at the double; another jumping up and down in a frantic manner; another is sitting down cross-legged like a Turk, or a tailor, and is occupied in belabouring his feet with his mittened hands, in his energetic endeavours to restore circulation; whilst another, unable any longer to endure the cold, commences furiously to kick the sledge, or a hummock, with both feet like one bereft of his senses. Although halted, little rest is enjoyed; anxiously is the kettle watched, and many are the tender inquiries concerning the state of the water inside. "Does it boil?" is a question frequently asked, and unless the cook is blessed with an amiable disposition, the perversity of the kettle is sufficient, at times, to drive him almost distracted. The old saw, "A watched pot never boils," is fully exemplified. At length, to the relief and delight of all, the announcement is made that the tea is ready, when all troubles are forgotten in the pleasure and enjoyment of a warm pannikin of tea. Sometimes little difficulties would arise in consequence of the haste with which it was necessary to prepare and discuss this meal. These, although serious at the time, served afterwards to amuse, and were soon forgotten. On one occasion, the water having been boiled, and the cook having, as he thought, carefully added the tea and sugar, which were as carefully stirred up, the allowance of tea was served out and eagerly drunk by the wearied sledgers, who were only too glad and thankful to receive anything warm. It was not until some time after the allowance had been consumed that the cook discovered he had omitted to put in the *tea*, and had served out simply a decoction of warm water and brown sugar! Sometimes the tea was made from salt-water ice, the cook having inadvertently mixed it before tasting the water! In such a case we had either to drink it, or get none at all!

Our bacon was, as a rule, frozen so hard as to be like a piece of granite, and it was only by thawing it in our warm tea that it became eatable. This had the effect of converting our tea into a sort of soup!

The time of halting for the night varied considerably; but it was generally after ten, eleven, and sometimes twelve hours' steady marching. The first thing to be done is to select a suitable site as level as possible and where the snow is not too deep, for pitching the tent, which should be carefully banked up outside with snow to the height of two or three feet. Every one assists in this work except the cook, who is busily engaged in the necessary preparations for the evening meal. As soon as the tent is ready, the men enter, change their foot gear, and struggle into their half-frozen bags, their toes and feet having previously been examined by the officer for the detection of frost-bites. If a frost-bite is discovered, circulation is immediately restored, and the injured part dressed by the application of a little glycerine ointment and some lint.

As a rule the moccasins, hose, and blanket wrappers are so firmly frozen together that they are with difficulty separated, and are taken off the feet as *one* article of clothing. It is amusing to witness the frantic exertions made by some of the men in their efforts to struggle into their duffel coats. They are frozen so stiff and hard that this operation is always

GETTING READY TO "BAG."

an intensely aggravating one, and even when it is accomplished, the men are utterly helpless until the warmth from their bodies has partially thawed the coats and rendered them supple. They were, with a very great deal of truth, likened to "strait-jackets."

By the time that the whole party are comfortably

settled in their bags, supper, consisting of tea and pemmican, is ready and served; after which pipes are lighted, conversation ensues, and the allowance of grog is served out. This is undoubtedly the most delightful and happiest part of the day's proceedings, and I should deprecate very strongly any attempts to deprive the poor Arctic sledger of his small modicum of rum and water, provided it was always issued at the same time as ours, and *never* during the fatigue and exertions of the day. The quantity is so small that the most fanatical theorist cannot seriously maintain that it can do harm. But experience proves that it tends very materially to cheer and invigorate the men during the short time that they can really call their own in the whole twenty-four hours, and it certainly imparts a glow which induces sleep—a very important effect of its use. Sometimes singing will be the order of the day, or rather evening, or perhaps a book will be read aloud; but whatever amusement is resorted to for the purpose of thoroughly enjoying the half-hour after supper, whether it is singing, reading, or yarning, all are cheerful, contented, and happy.

Home is, of course, a great topic of conversation, and what each man intends doing on his return to England is freely discussed. We know all about each other, and frequently detect ourselves confiding secrets that we should under ordinary circumstances divulge only to our bosom friends. Sometimes a hot argument is maintained between two men belonging to different counties on the relative merits of the pigs of their own counties and their manner of feeding; or perhaps they will get into a discussion on the liberality of large landed proprietors near whom they may be living. For instance, one man who lived in Devonshire was extolling Lord Mount Edgcumbe. "Ah! he was a noble lord! he opened his grounds once a week for the admission of the public." But another man, hailing from Lancashire, answered by saying, "He didn't see that he was any better than any other lord; for," he said, "Lord Derby admitted the public into his park every day, and if it was raining he would send his carriage for you!" This argument, although I fear not strictly correct, was unanswerable, and the west countryman had to give in to the more liberal experiences of his friend.

Before composing ourselves to sleep, the cook, having made the necessary preparations for the morning's meal, passes in our coverlet. This is always the last thing done before closing the door of the tent for the night.

How is it possible to describe what this coverlet is like when handed in? Those who have never been initiated into the mysteries of Arctic sledge life would be unable to realize what it resembles when unpacked from the sledge. It is more like a piece of wood or sheet-iron than an article of woollen material. With the utmost difficulty it is unfolded; but as for spreading, that is quite out of the question: it stands up in the centre like a second tent, and refuses to lie flat, in spite of the beating with which it is assailed. It is only after it has been some time in this position that it gradually thaws, when it becomes a "wet blanket" indeed!

The contents of this chapter may give some idea of the ordinary routine of a sledge traveller's life. The details were invariably carried out by the different sledge parties despatched from the "Alert." In the succeeding chapter we will follow the fortunes of the northern division, and I shall endeavour to depict briefly the difficulties it had to contend with, and the manner in which they were surmounted.

CHAPTER XXII.

THE NORTHERN DIVISION—TRAVELLING IN APRIL.

> "These high wild hills, and rough uneven ways,
> Draw out our miles and make them wearisome;
> And yet your fair discourse hath been as sugar,
> Making the hard way sweet and delectable . . . .
> But I bethink me, what a weary way!"
> *Richard II.*

THE different sledge parties having branched off, as related in the preceding chapter, I must request my readers to follow the fortunes of the northern division, which was under my command.

The serious obstacles that so persistently impeded our progress were immediately encountered. The retreating forms of our comrades, who had assisted us thus far, were scarcely out of sight before we were busily engaged in constructing a road along which to drag our sledges. These roads were rendered necessary in consequence of the rugged nature of the ice over which we had to travel, the floes being of the smallest dimensions as regarded superficial area, and surrounded by broad fringes of squeezed-up hummocks. The hummocks proved most formidable impediments to our advance. No sooner had we congratulated ourselves upon successfully accomplishing a passage through one line of these obstacles, than

T

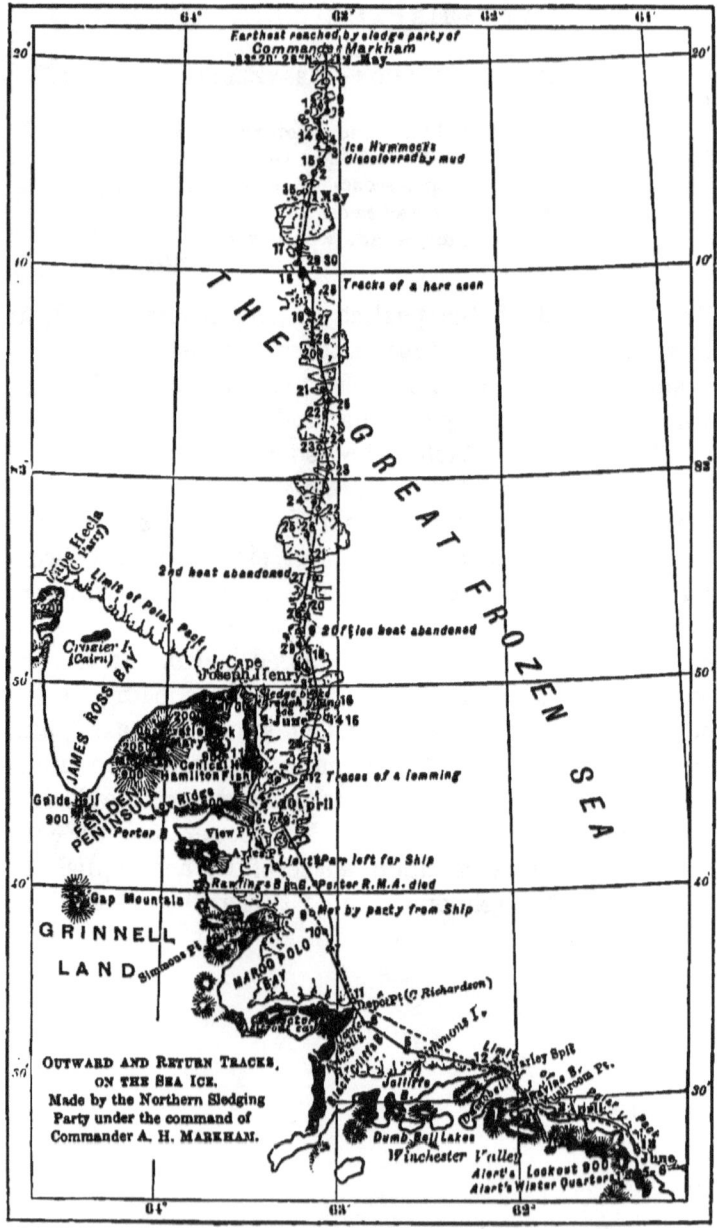

another, and perhaps a more rugged and apparently impassable hedge, appeared in front of us. It seemed as if a terrible conflict had been fought between these ponderous masses of ice, which had so shattered and split them up as to suggest to us the idea that they resembled a tempestuous broken sea suddenly frozen.

To make any advance at all, pickaxes and shovels were in constant requisition, and with these implements we succeeded in hewing and cutting a road for our sledges, by which we were able to make a snail-like progress. The roughness of the road was not our only difficulty. Around and about the hummocks the snow had drifted to such a depth that the men were frequently floundering in it up to their waists, and passages through this had to be cleared with shovels before the sledges could be dragged on. Occasionally the sledges would have to be unpacked and lightened considerably before they could be dragged through this deep soft snow.

We, at first, attempted to console ourselves with the idea that this irregular and broken sea of ice was only caused by our proximity to the land; and that we should, as we advanced in a northerly direction, meet with smooth level floes, on which we should be able to travel along merrily, and so make up for the time expended in struggling through the hummocks.

How delusive proved our hopes and anticipations the sequel will show! The belts of hummocks that separated the floes varied from twenty yards to half a mile in breadth, and were from fifteen to fifty feet in height.

Road-making, as we called it, was a work of daily, I may say of constant, occurrence. We regarded our pickaxes with great affection, and they were consequently treated with the utmost tenderness and care. Any mishap to them would have been indeed a serious misfortune, as we should have nothing to supply their place, and would therefore have been in a predicament in which we could neither advance nor return. The anxiety with which they were watched may therefore be imagined.

Instead of giving simply a brief *résumé* of our sledging life, it will, I think, be more interesting to follow the sledge parties day by day in their arduous march to the northward, and their still more irksome and wearisome return journey. To do this, it will be as well to extract portions from my daily journal, avoiding repetition as much as possible, and commencing on the day after that on which we were left by our supporting sledges to prosecute our undertaking.

April 12*th.* — A most gratifying and unexpected change of weather enabled us to pass a comparatively comfortable night, the temperature inside our tent being as high as $+16°$. Hitherto it has stood at, and generally far below, zero. With the thermometer in the air registering a few degrees below zero, it is just possible to keep ourselves warm enough inside our tents to sleep; but with a temperature ranging from $-35°$ downwards sleep is almost out of the question.

In order to keep the sun as much as possible at our backs during the time we were on the march, we adopted the system of travelling, whilst on our outward journey, between noon and midnight. The cooks were, as a rule, called at about half-past nine in the forenoon, and the sledges were generally on the move about half-past eleven. This time of travelling was selected more with a view to the prevention of snow blindness than anything else.

After breakfast the road-makers, six in number, were advanced for the purpose of constructing a road through an ugly fringe of hummocks on the southern side of which our camp had been pitched; the rest of the party being employed in striking the tents, packing and bringing on the sledges, one by one, as far as the road was practicable. Being a bright sunny day the tent robes and other gear were triced up to the boats' masts and yards to dry. The sun was powerful enough to extract the moisture from the woollen substance, which would freeze, forming a sort of hoar-frost that could with ease be brushed or shaken off.

On these bright clear days, the snow on the surface of the floes over which we were journeying was so highly crystallized that it sparkled and glittered with the most brilliant iridescent colours. The ground upon which we trod appeared to be strewn with bright and lustrous gems, of which the most prominent were diamonds, rubies, emeralds, and sapphires. It was indeed a fairy-like scene; but our duties were too matter of fact to admit of our indulging for any time in romance or sentiment.

A glance at our comrades would quickly recall us to the reality of our situation. Their dirty and rough-clad forms were strangely at variance with the scene of enchantment that might be conjured up. With faces scarified by the combined action of sun and frost, and black with smoke, with the tips of their fingers senseless from repeated frost-bites, with sore shoulders and aching limbs, the wearied sledgers pursued their way, not altogether indifferent to the beauties that surrounded them, but careless of the difficulties and discomforts they encountered.

During the afternoon, being about three miles from the nearest land, we observed, to our surprise, the fresh traces on the snow of a little lemming! It is hard to tell what inducement this little animal could have had for straying so far away from the land, and consequently from its means of obtaining the wherewithal to support life!

We passed through a dense mass of hummocks, emerging, eventually, on a heavy floe of "ancient lineage," whose surface was undulating, and adorned with veritable "ice-mountains" some twenty feet in height. These were generally of a rounded form and of a smooth surface, and appeared to be the result of long and continuous snow-drift. We camped on the northern edge of the floe, the men being employed in cutting a road through the hummocks whilst supper was preparing, in readiness for our start on the morrow.

A journey through, and over, hummocks is the most unsatisfactory kind of travelling that can possibly be imagined. "Standing pulls" must be the order of the day, and the incessant "one, two, three, haul" is constantly heard. The trudging backwards and forwards to drag the different sledges to the front along the same road is decidedly monotonous; but this had no effect on the cheerfulness and general good spirits of the men, who were all actuated by the same zealous desire to do their best. The temperature all day had been delightful, ranging from 8° to 20° below zero.

April 13*th*.—A dull, cloudy day, with the sun shining at intervals, and the temperature as low at one time as $-33°$. We cut a road and dragged the sledges through a fringe of hummocks about two hundred yards in breadth, then crossed a fine large floe that afforded us capital travelling for nearly a mile in a northerly direction, then through another long fringe of large and troublesome hummocks, until we were completely brought to a standstill by a mass of enormous fragments of ice, piled up in an irregular form to the height of from twenty to thirty feet. Through this obstacle we resolved to cut a road: in fact, no other alternative offered. It was a long and tedious job; but with such a hearty good will did the men work that we had the satisfaction of dragging our sledges over a very rough road and encamping for the night with the difficulties in our rear. Parr with pickaxe and shovel was a first-rate "navvy," and worked like a horse.

Our routine was for one or other of us to select the best route through the hummocks. This being done, one, with a gang of road-makers, proceeded to construct the road, whilst the other, with the remainder of the party, dragged the sledges on one by one. Great care had to be taken that our boats, on the exceedingly rough road over which they were dragged, did not sustain any injury. Sometimes it was a very delicate matter, and one that required skilful handling, after the sledges had been hauled up to the top of the hummocks, to lower them down in safety on the opposite side. The ease and facility with which the ice yielded to the dexterous blows of the pickaxes, wielded by strong and determined men, was almost incredible. Apparently impenetrable masses of ice vanished before their efforts, and left a fairly good road by which we advanced.

April 14th.—Last night our sleeping-bags were frozen so hard that it was with great difficulty we succeeded in getting into them. Even when this was accomplished, the warmth we derived from them was inappreciable, and we felt more as if we were confined in a wooden box or coffin than in a woollen bag! My blanket wrappers, although I laid on them all night,

INTERIOR OF TENT.

were so stiff this morning that I had the utmost difficulty in bending them over my feet! Being Good Friday, our prayers in the morning were of longer duration than usual.

Crossed an old floe having a hard incrustation on its surface—not sufficiently strong, however, to bear the weight either of the men or the sledges; consequently at every step we broke through, and would then sink deeply into soft snow. This was not only very laborious but very aggravating work.

On portions of the road, where these patches of level soft snow occurred, the flat-bottomed taboggans, used in the Hudson Bay Company's territory, would be suitable. But the greater part of the road was over heavy broken-up hummocks and hard fragments of ice, lying at all kinds of angles; on the whole we

A PACKED SLEDGE.

found the eight-men high-runner sledge which we used, and which was originally designed by Sir Leopold McClintock, infinitely preferable. Long experience has conclusively proved its excellence. It was the kind of sledge with which the North West Passage was discovered and the Parry Islands explored, and with us it once more did most admirable service in many directions, and over the roughest ground imaginable.

The temperature was too low to allow us to stop for the purpose of obtaining a meridian altitude, which we invariably get at noon. There was an unpleasant nipping breeze from the northward; our faces, more especially our noses, being "touched up" constantly by Jack Frost.

The floes off Cape Joseph Henry, although actually smaller than most of those we have crossed, were far more heavy. In all probability they are reduced in size by great and continual pressure off the cape. The wind freshening, and the weather becoming very thick, we halted an hour earlier than we otherwise would have done.

John Shirley, one of my sledge crew, complained of pains in his ankles and knees. On examination they appeared slightly swollen, and I treated him according to the instructions laid down for the guidance of the sledging officers by our doctor.

Although at the time ignorant of the fact, this was the first appearance of that dreadful disease, scurvy, which shortly afterwards laid its destroying hand upon us, and reduced us to such a helpless and prostrate state. From this day we were deprived of the services of Shirley, who gradually but surely got worse, and was never again able to render the slightest assistance even in the most minute details of our routine.

April 15*th*.—A N.W. gale, with an exceedingly low temperature, and an impervious snow-drift, rendered travelling quite out of the question.

Extreme wretchedness, I might almost say abject misery, was our lot to-day.

We appeared to receive little benefit, in the way of warmth, from our tent robes, and the temperature inside our tent, with our whole party huddled close together, was 22° below zero! Gladly would we have pushed on had it been possible. A hard day's work, even amongst the most impenetrable hummocks, would have been infinitely preferable to our present forced detention and inactivity. Unable to stir outside the tent, on account of the blinding snow-drift that was whirling around, too cold to read or even to sit up in one's bag for the sake of conversation, tent robes and bags frozen hard—a combination of these evils renders the position of those who suffer from them an unenviable one indeed. It is a remarkable fact that we this day experienced a lower temperature during a gale of wind than we did during the whole winter at the "Alert's" winter quarters. This appears to point conclusively to the fact that there can be no large body of water either to the northward or westward of us.

The thermometer invariably rose during the southerly gales experienced in the winter, and this was very naturally attributed to the wind blowing across a large expanse of open water.

April 16th.—Easter Sunday.

The gale, although it had moderated, was still blowing too fiercely to allow us to proceed. We were therefore compelled, sorely against our inclination, to remain encamped. We unanimously came to the conclusion that this was by far the most wretched and miserable Easter Sunday that we had ever spent. Forty-eight hours in a gale of wind, tied up in a bag off the most northern known land, with a temperature 67° below freezing point, is certainly not the most pleasant manner that any one would select for passing an Easter Sunday!

For forty hours I did not have the slightest feeling in my feet, and could not really declare that I was in possession of those useful members—as for sleep, under the circumstances, that was quite out of the question. In spite of the cold and dismal surroundings, we did not neglect last evening the usual Saturday night's toast, on receipt of our small allowance of grog. It most decidedly had the effect of cheering us up considerably, and for the time assisted in making us forget the discomfort of our position. At half-past four in the afternoon, the wind having subsided, it was determined to make a move. We felt that anything was preferable to the tedium and dreariness of our compulsory detention. The tents were accordingly struck, sledges packed, and the march renewed. Shirley, being unable to walk, was placed in his sleeping-bag, rolled up in the tent robes, and tied securely on one of the sledges. This seriously added to the weight to be dragged, whilst it also reduced our motive power; however, we hoped that by thus giving him complete rest, he would the more rapidly recover and resume his place on the drag-ropes.

Alas! how little did we think that the fearful and wasting disease, the premonitory symptoms of which were now exhibited, would insidiously steal its way amongst us, and assailing the party one by one reduce us so disastrously as to bring us to the verge of destruction!

We cut our way through a hedge of hummocks about one-third of a mile in breadth, and then on to a floe apparently of great thickness; but, unfortunately for us, not more than three hundred yards across. Between these stupendous floes we would occasionally meet with some young ice amongst the hummocks which, when it trended in the right direction, would afford us easy travelling; but these leads were never of any extent.

The gale had accumulated the snow in deep drifts, which rendered the task of dragging the sledges harder than ever. Our progress was necessarily slow. We halted and encamped at half-past ten. The men appeared to be more easily fatigued after lying so long idle in their bags than if they had performed a hard day's work. Our camp this evening was pitched almost abreast of Cape Joseph Henry, though some miles off it.

When viewed from seaward, or more correctly speaking, "iceward," this headland presents a bold and rugged appearance, rising nearly perpendicular from base to summit, to a height of about eight hundred feet, whence the land recedes, gradually ascending until it culminates in a peak about three or four hundred feet higher. It appears to be of limestone formation, with regular stratifications dipping to the southward at an angle of 6° to 10° from the horizontal. The Cape itself terminates in a knife-like edge from summit to base, in shape very much resembling the ram-bow of an ironclad. Conical Hill, situated immediately to the southward of Cape Joseph Henry, when observed on the same bearing, presents more the form of a hog's back than a cone, but possesses the same bold, rugged aspect. It is about the same height as the peak surmounting Cape Joseph Henry, and is of the same formation; but, unlike its neighbour, the strata dip to the southward at an angle of about 6° or 10° from the vertical, giving it altogether a rather distorted appearance. There is a great deal of similarity in the surrounding hills, all being more or less coniform, and of an altitude of from one to two thousand feet.

April 17*th*.—Shirley no better this morning, and to add to our troubles, George Porter, one of Parr's sledge crew, was also suffering in the same manner from swollen and puffy knee joints.

Two men *hors de combat* out of our little force diminishes our strength very materially, and as they have both to be carried on the sledges it adds seriously to the weights to be dragged. The morning was bright and sunny, with a temperature as high as 24° below zero, so we congratulated ourselves that it was now really on the turn, and that we should no longer encounter any more extreme cold. The men take kindly to their snow-goggles, and never attempt to take them off whilst on the march—perhaps my expatiating largely on the excruciating agony and acute pain inseparable from snow blindness, is in some way connected with their submissiveness in this respect! Alfred Pearce was, yesterday, rather severely frost-bitten on one of his fingers; but circulation was rapidly restored, and to-day, with the exception of a little soreness, he suffers no ill effects from it. The travelling to-day was nearly a repetition of what we had hitherto been encountering: large masses of ice thickly compacted together, squeezed up into every conceivable, but indescribable, shape and form to a height of about twenty-five feet; but these had to succumb to the strenuous exertions of Parr and his indefatigable road-makers.

Energy and perseverance performed wonders. The men worked uncommonly well—my only fear was that they would overtax their strength. Poor fellows! they get little rest during the day, for even when we halt for lunch, they are compelled to be continually on the move to keep their blood in circulation. To sit or lie down for any length of time would be fatal. No wonder, then, they are fatigued at the end of the day's work.

Some of the floes over which we travelled to-day were of greater thickness than others, and it was no unfrequent occurrence for us to drop a height of six or seven feet from the top of one floe to the surface of another; or, *vice versâ*, to have to haul the sledges up the same height. This was no easy work with our heavily laden sledges and boats. Snow commenced falling at 3 P.M., and continued all night.

April 18th.—The old story last night with our sleeping-bags! So hard were they frozen that it occupied us a considerable time before we could struggle into them. The night, however, was not so cold, and we succeeded in sleeping pretty comfortably. Before starting this morning we lightened our heavy sledge by making a redistribution of the weights on all three sledges. By these means we hoped to be able to get on a little better.

We found the helmet worsted caps that were so kindly given to us by the Empress very warm and comfortable for sleeping in. They are much appreciated by the men, who call them "Eugenies," and they constantly refer with gratitude to her Majesty's kind and thoughtful present.

The travelling to-day was excessively heavy, in consequence of the unevenness of the floes and the deep soft snow with which they were covered. After lunch we arrived at and crossed some "veritable palæocrystic floes"—apparently of gigantic thickness, and studded with numerous rounded snow hillocks;

the height of some of the latter being as much as thirty feet above the surface of the floe. In crossing one of these, the "Victoria" sledge capsized, but was soon righted without damaging either the sledge or the boat, or injuring the invalid who was lashed on top, and who received only a slight shaking. As we proceeded northwards we opened out the land to the westward, and a large bay which has since been called Clements Markham Inlet. A S.E. breeze sprang up in the evening shortly before we halted, which, strange to say, sent the temperature down rapidly to $-33°$, and we had, in consequence, to be cautious about frost-bites.

April 19th.—A fine clear day. Our bags last night were rendered a little more habitable by having been exposed during the day to the heat of the sun, which was sufficiently powerful to extract the greater part of the moisture which had been absorbed by them. Our plan is on fine days to suspend as much as we possibly can from the masts and yards of the boats, and to spread the gear out over the sledges, so that it may dry as we travel along. This answers admirably and enables us to pass more comfortable nights.

After toiling hard for three and a half hours, during which time we had advanced the sledges barely a quarter of a mile, I came to the determination to abandon our largest boat. It was heart-breaking to witness the men slaving in their endeavours to drag on the heavy sledge and boat—to see the continual standing pulls, the incessant "one, two, three, haul," and no result.

I did not arrive at this decision until after very mature deliberation. My conviction was that amongst such ice as that over which we were travelling, should a disruption occur, our boats would be of little service to us, except as a means of ferrying from one floe to another. For this purpose I retain the smaller boat.

Leaving the boat in as conspicuous a position as possible, with her mast stepped and yard triced up, and having obtained a round of angles in order to fix her position, so as to facilitate our finding her on the return journey, the march was resumed, every one well pleased at being rid of the incubus, as the large boat was always regarded. We travelled over deep and uneven snow ridges, and experienced great difficulty in getting from one floe to another, on account of the perpendicular drop. Before halting we got on to some young ice amongst the hummocks, along which we rattled gaily, actually performing a distance of about half a mile in something like two hours! This is good work for us. It must be remembered that we have to advance *three* sledges, and to do this we have to walk over the same road five times!

If our invalids would only show some symptoms of improvement we should have more hope of reaching a higher latitude; but at present they compensate in weight and loss of power for the abandonment of the boat. I regard each man carried as about 200 lbs. extra weight, and the loss of their services on the drag-ropes is about equal to another 200 lbs. weight to be added—therefore the two invalids reckon as much as 800 lbs., exactly equivalent to the weight of the deserted boat! So long as they remain ill, we gain nothing upon the actual weights dragged before their sickness commenced. Instead of their getting better, we have the prospect of an increased sick list, for this evening Alfred Pearce was compelled to fall out from the drag-ropes, suffering from a badly swollen ankle, and exhibiting in fact the same symptoms as the other men.

April 20*th*.—This morning we were unable to make a start in consequence of the thickness of the weather. Snow was falling slightly, but the fog was so dense that it was imposible to see the length of the sledge ahead. As I had brought with me one of Dickens's works, "The Old Curiosity Shop," I read aloud to the men, who were much interested in the story.

By 2 P.M., the weather having cleared slightly, we determined to push on and find our way through the fog and hummocks as best we could. The snow was very deep and the hummocks appeared to be interminable. The task of selecting a road was by no means easy—nothing to be seen but hummocks in every direction. At eight o'clock, the fog lifting a little, we succeeded in extricating ourselves from our difficulties, and crossing a large heavy floe got on to a lead of young ice which gave us good travelling. Although this young ice enabled us to travel quicker, and rendered the work of dragging easier, still I was sorry to see it, as I was rather apprehensive that the pack might break up earlier than we anticipated, and so place us in an exceedingly awkward predicament. We halted and camped at half-past ten, having (considering the lateness of our start) performed a fair day's work.

April 21*st*.—A keen piercing wind from the northward. Travelling much the same. Although the temperature was only 17° below zero, the cold was more intense than we had yet felt it since leaving the ship. The wind seemed to cut us in two, and was the cause of numerous superficial frost-bites. One man, Thomas Simpson, was rather severely frost-bitten in the big toe, which was, however, quickly attended to and brought round.

Our greatest enemies, whilst crossing a floe of any extent, were the numberless cracks and fissures in the ice, radiating in all directions and treacherously concealed by a covering of snow. Into these we frequently fell, and as some of them were of great depth it seemed almost miraculous that we escaped without a fractured limb! These cracks must be produced either by enormous pressure or intense cold.

April 22*nd.*—The wind blew in heavy squalls last night, and continued fresh this morning; but as we all dreaded a longer detention in our tent we resolved to push on at all hazards.

It was painful to witness the efforts of the poor fellows in their endeavours to protect their faces from the cold cutting wind as they plodded along, dragging the heavily laden sledges; but they seemed cheerful enough, and treated the numerous frost-bites that appeared on their cheeks as rather a good joke than anything else. The sun peeped out for a few moments during the afternoon; but a heavy mist hung over the land, entirely obscuring it from our view. The floes over which we travelled to-day were more level than any we had yet crossed, and infinitely larger; but as a set-off against this, we found the snow very deep, which rendered the dragging excessively laborious. Few hummocks adorned the edges of these floes. They appeared to have come into contact with each other in a most amicable manner, and then immediately united before any pressure could be exerted, so as to form the immense hedges of heaped-up masses of ice that have hitherto been our great bugbear. One floe crossed to-day was estimated at about a mile and three-quarters in length, and about six miles in circumference.

April 23rd.—Progressing but slowly. The travelling was very heavy, through deep soft snow, and we were delayed considerably by being obliged to make roads over broad belts of heavy hummocks.

We camped for the night on the verge of a floe, with enormous hummocks squeezed up together immediately in front. The prospect of advancing was not cheering! A S.E. breeze, springing up in the afternoon, sent the temperature down suddenly to $-24°$. Our invalids did not appear to be improving, and we were rather puzzled at some of their symptoms.

April 24th.—The greater part of the day was employed in cutting a road through a perfect sea of hummocks. They appeared to be interminable. From the highest we could see nothing like a floe, nothing but an uneven range of massive and shapeless blocks of ice. The road-making was very hard and *very* cold work, and the men had to be relieved pretty often with the tools.

Skill is of more avail at this sort of work than brute force. A skilled workman will soon demolish a large hummock, on which a strong but inexperienced man is wasting all his energy and strength in fruitless blows.

We had the satisfaction to-day of crossing the eighty-third parallel of latitude,* and of knowing

---

* By the Act of Parliament (58 Geo. III. cap. xx.) passed in 1818, a reward of £1000 was assigned to any one who should cross the latitude of 83° N. But in 1828 this Act for the encouragement of Polar discovery was repealed by 9 Geo. IV. cap. lxvi.

that we were the first party of men that had ever reached such a high position. The wind to-day, although decidedly unpleasant, was of some service, for being from the southward we were able to make sail on our sledges and thus utilize the otherwise unwelcome breeze.

April 25th.—A beautiful day, but with a low temperature. A slight breeze from the eastward reminded us that we possessed noses. These latter appendages have been voted decided nuisances, and could easily be dispensed with whilst sledging! The travelling to-day was a slight improvement on our preceding day's work. Indeed at one time we were able to advance our two light sledges "single banked," that is with their own individual crews, instead of employing both crews to drag on one sledge at a time; but this was only for a very short distance. The snow was very deep and of a tenacious consistency, clinging to the sledge runners and thereby seriously impeding our progress. So powerful were the rays of the sun this afternoon that my thermometer, when exposed to them, rose rapidly from $-17°$ to $-8°$. At 6 P.M. I observed faint parhelia showing prismatic colours. We were delayed towards the end of the day by a broad belt of hummocks, through which a road had to be cut. The large hummocks passed to-day, although smooth and rounded on the top and on one side, were precipitous on the other and were fully thirty feet high. Some of them appeared like isolated fragments in the centre of a floe, and resembled the large grounded floe-bergs in the vicinity of the "Alert's" winter quarters. They were undoubtedly portions of the floe which had been broken off and squeezed up under irresistible pressure.

April 26*th*.—Temperature to-day as high as $-2°$. For the first time, since we have been away, were we able thoroughly to enjoy our lunch. On account of the increased warmth, our bacon was more palateable, and we could throw our wearied forms on the soft snow and discuss our pint of tea without running the risk of having our toes frost-bitten. The sensation of possessing feet was a novel and delightful one. Several of the men have of late been attacked by violent bleedings of the nose; but this, in all probability, is due to the rise of temperature. No improvement in our travelling—still the same old story—hummocks and snow-drifts, snow-drifts and hummocks. So dense were the latter that, when we halted for the night, it really seemed as if we had arrived at "the end of all things;" for in front of us was an apparently impassable sea of hummocks extending north, east, and west as far as the range of vision. A dismal prospect, indeed! But we did not despair, and still hoped we might cut our way through these obstacles, and emerge upon floes along which we should have little difficulty in advancing.

April 27*th*.—A hard day's work! Road-makers incessantly employed, and the sledges "double banked" the whole day, progress being necessarily slow. Our invalids showed no signs of amendment, indeed two others exhibited symptoms of the same disease; for such it appears to be.

Another great misfortune that happened was that both our shovels came to grief—the handles breaking off at the junction between the wood and iron. We, however, succeeded in "fishing" and thus rendering them serviceable. We should be in a sorry plight if any accident happened to our pickaxes as well as to our shovels. As an instance of the amount of walking we had to perform, I may mention that to-day I had, of necessity, to cross the same floe, on which the snow was knee-deep, no less than thirteen times, "and didn't I hate that blackguard floe!"

April 28*th*.—The temperature actually rose as high as $+ 2°$! This is the first day that we have registered the thermometer above zero! It is a decided improvement.

Last night, inside my tent, the temperature was as high as 33°, and, in spite of a hard day's work, we were all busily employed, after supper was over, in some way or another. A couple were splicing lanyards in their drag-belts; one was tailoring; another repairing his moccasins; one was darning his mitts, and another patching up his stockings with an old blanket wrapper; whilst I was both reading aloud and dressing and bandaging my patients' legs. All were smoking except myself. The effect in a small confined tent may be imagined!

Two of the men, who are not tobacco smokers, smoked what they called "herb" tobacco, which diffused a rather pleasing aroma, and served to deaden the unpleasantness of the tobacco smoke. It is composed of various dried aromatic herbs, and is, I believe, recommended by the faculty for many disorders.

The travelling was as bad as ever—through heavy hummocks and deep snow-drifts. We had the misfortune to capsize the sledge, on which was one of the invalids; but a slight delay was the only inconvenience caused. The weather in the afternoon became very thick, making it extremely difficult to select a route. Everything was of one uniform colour:

above, below, behind, and before; all was alike, and it was quite impossible to tell whether we were going up or down hill until a fall would inform us of the fact. To our great surprise, this evening, we came across the traces of a hare in the soft snow. They were apparently recent, and travelling in a southerly direction. The little creature was evidently very tired, as the footsteps appeared to be close together. Poor Pussy! it must have wandered out on the floe and lost itself, for we were quite seventeen miles from the nearest land. I have no doubt, if we had followed up the track, that we should have found the poor little animal lying dead or exhausted under some hummock, famished for want of food.

April 29*th*.—Small floes surrounded with high hummocks and covered with deep snow, were still encountered, with occasionally a short lead on some young ice that we sometimes met twining round the larger floes. It was difficult to account for the presence of so much young ice, and I can only suggest that, after the disruption in the summer, the pack remained some length of time in a quiescent state, and so allowed the young ice to form between the floes; for if once in motion, no ice of a single season's formation could withstand the tremendous pressure that would be exerted by these stupendous floes, but must inevitably be pulverized and broken up into small fragments. Our wretched cook last night made our tea and cooked our pemmican with the water obtained from salt-water ice. We all in consequence suffered from intense thirst, without being able to obtain anything to alleviate it.

April 30*th*.—After halting last night the wind freshened into a gale, the clouds thickened, and snow began to fall heavily, and this continued all day without intermission, so much so that we were unable to make a start. It was impossible to see the length of the sledge ahead, and, surrounded as we were by hummocks, it would have been folly to have attempted a move. We consoled ourselves by saying that the rest would do us good, and that the invalids more especially would benefit by it.

CHAPTER XXIII.

THE MOST NORTHERN POINT EVER REACHED BY MAN.

> "And here on snows, where never human foot
> Of common mortal trod, we nightly tread
> And leave no traces, o'er the savage sea,
> The glassy ocean of the mountain ice;
> We skim its rugged breakers, which put on
> The aspect of a tumbling tempest's foam
> Frozen in a moment."
>
> BYRON.

MAY 1st.—A fine sunny morning ushered in the month of May, all the more appreciated in consequence of the enforced idleness of the preceding day. The bright sun had a wonderful effect upon us all. It seemed to cheer and invigorate our spirits, whilst it stimulated us to renewed exertions in our endeavours to reach as high a northern latitude as possible. Our invalids, however, were very faint and weak. They exhibited no favourable symptoms of improvement, and were a great clog and drawback to our progress. With our diminished crews we found it hard work to drag the sledges over the rough hummocky road, and through the deep soft snow-drifts that were constantly met. Road-making became a necessary part of the daily routine. Floes of any extent were rarely seen, and we had to thread our way through a perfect labyrinth of piled-up masses of ice, with little or no prospect of its improving. It was a dreary and wild-looking scene: no living thing in sight but our own little party, no colour or object to relieve the eye; nothing but a chaotic and illimitable sea of ice. Sometimes a fog was observed gradually rolling itself towards us, like a large mantle, until we were completely enveloped in its dense folds; when, continuing its onward course, it would roll as rapidly away, leaving a bright luminous band stretching across the horizon in the direction whence it had come.

May 2nd.—Although we had been told that there was not the slightest chance of our being attacked with scurvy, still, from the utter prostration of our invalids, combined with other symptoms, we were almost inclined to believe that we were really afflicted with this dire and wasting disease. It was a terrible idea that forced itself upon us, and one that we were loath to indulge in; but we feared that the symptoms pointed unmistakeably to the fact that this fearful disease, so dreaded by the mariners of old, was gradually but surely laying its hand upon us, completely prostrating those it attacked and rendering them helpless from pain and exhaustion. Parr and myself spoke of it only when we were by ourselves, as we considered it of the utmost importance that the men should remain in ignorance as long as possible, and not even suspect the nature of the disease which had crippled so many of their number. Swollen joints and discolouration of the skin, attended with faintness and great weakness, were the principal symptoms. Great as were the natural difficulties which surrounded us, still, should our surmise be correct, we could not but regard this as the most formidable of all obstacles to our advance that could possibly be imagined. Our only hope was that the five men now afflicted might, through their habits or disposition, have been more prone to the attacks of this insidious disease, than the remainder of our party, who, we hoped, might escape scathless. We camped this evening amidst a pile of hummocks, after one of the hardest day's work we have yet performed. So rough was the road and so deep was the snow that the sledges could only be advanced by "standing pulls." This was disheartening, for we had all been cherishing the hope that as we advanced northwards we should find larger and more level floes and less snow; the reverse, however, was the case. Several times did one or other of us disappear through deep rents in the floe, but we always succeeded in scrambling up again unhurt.

May 3rd.—A dull, dark, foggy day rendered it extremely difficult to select our road, and we were occasionally compelled to unload the sledges before they could be dragged through the deep soft snow-drifts which were continually met across our route, making the work all the more hard and distressing. The fog persistently hung over us all day; but was not sufficiently dense to retard our progress altogether, though it materially increased our labours and augmented our difficulties.

May 4th.—Everything appeared to combine against us: weather, snow ice, and sickness! In spite of these evils our tents were struck and a start made; but after advancing for half a mile, which took us exactly three and a half hours to accomplish, we arrived at such a confused heap of hummocks that, with the dense fog prevailing and the falling snow, it was impossible to make any headway. To persevere would have been imprudent. The tents were accordingly pitched, and we consoled ourselves by saying that the rest would be productive of much good to our sick companions, for even those that had to be carried on the sledges could get no rest whilst being dragged and jolted and sometimes capsized over the roughest road imaginable. After lunch, the weather clearing a little, we employed ourselves in cutting a road through an amorphous conglomeration of ice for quite three-quarters of a mile. The pack over which we were travelling appeared to consist of numerous small floes, the largest being barely one hundred yards across at its widest diameter, but the majority much smaller, and each of these floes was surrounded by a mass of hummocks piled up and lying one on top of the other to the height of twenty and thirty feet: the belts of hummocks being from thirty to forty yards in breadth.

Observing one large hummock to be very much discoloured, we found, on approach, that this discolouration was caused by the adhesion of mud or clay, a line of which extended for some distance along the edge of the floe, and gave one the idea that it had rubbed against, or in some manner had come into contact with, the shore. Mud it undoubtedly was, and we bottled a quantity of it for the purpose of subjecting it to microscopic investigation when we should return on board. This was conclusive evidence that a periodical, if not an annual, disruption of the pack occurs, and that these floes, although now at such a distance from the land, had at some time or another been in very close proximity. Moreover, this must have occurred at a recent date, otherwise the summer thaws and the autumn snow would have obliterated all such traces as those we had discovered.

May 5th.—The weather was still as thick as pea-soup! However, we were able to avail ourselves of the road that we had constructed yesterday, and moved our camp so far. To do this, although the road was fairly good and the distance only three-quarters of a mile, the time occupied was four and a half hours! The scene that surrounded our encampment was a dreary one indeed—a desolate, cold, and inhospitable scene: everything of the same uniform colour; no object to relieve the eye; no signs of life; nothing to break the stillness and solitude of this waste of snow and ice. Surely Shelley must have contemplated such a scene when he wrote the following lines:

> "Those wastes of frozen billows that were hurled
> By everlasting snow-storms round the Poles,
> Where matters dared not vegetate nor live,
> But ceaseless frost round the vast solitude
> Bound the broad zone of stillness."

It was a relief, indeed, to turn from such a scene, and rest the eye upon our little encampment, while listening to the cheerful voices of our men, as, oblivious to hardship and suffering, they sat "yarning," in their tents, and relating to each other their adventures in other parts of the globe. To our great satisfaction and comfort the temperature was at, or about, zero all day, and for the first time, since leaving the ship, we were able to eat our bacon without in the first place thawing it in our tea!

May 6th.—A fine, bright day; but the rest of yesterday had produced no beneficial results. Our invalids were gradually getting worse; even those who were apparently in good health complained of aching limbs, and exhibited some of the first symptoms of those who were already ailing. Four of the men had also been suffering for the last few days from snow blindness, though not in a severe form. A sugar of lead lotion afforded them great relief, and acted as a cure. We had been so far extremely fortunate in our comparative exemption from this painful and irritating affliction. We must attribute our immunity from it to the constant use of our snow-goggles, which were never taken off until the time of "bagging!"

In getting under weigh in the morning, and also when we are encamping, the sick men cause us no little delay; for they are perfectly helpless, and require assistance in every little detail connected with their dressing and undressing, being totally incapacitated from doing anything themselves.

The travelling was very heavy. We appeared to have arrived at a perfect barrier of hummocks, with portions of large floes intermixed, all broken and squeezed up together and covered with deep snow. As far as reaching a high latitude was concerned, we might as well have turned back at once, for our advance must needs be slow; but it was not impossible that this sea of hummocks, with which we were contending, might be the limit of our rough road, and that if we could succeed in struggling through them for a few miles, we might emerge upon large and level floes on which we should be able to travel with greater ease and celerity. Possibly the rugged nature of the ice might be due to the junction of two tides, which, from the commotion produced, would create the obstacles that were impeding our progress. After halting for the night, a party of men were employed road-making whilst the tents were being pitched and supper preparing. All were very glad to get into their bags and rest after the fatigues of the day. A slight air from the S.E. sent the temperature down rapidly to 11° below zero. The minus quantities still prevailed.

May 7th.—We started this morning carrying three of our invalids; but before we had gone many yards it became painfully evident that the two others were quite unable to walk, although the gallant fellows struggled along manfully.

Our only resource was to advance the sledges and then return with them empty to bring on the other disabled sufferers. We had now a third of our little band *hors de combat*, our strength was diminishing daily, and our weights on the sledges in consequence were increasing. The travelling appeared to be getting, if possible, worse; the hummocks were higher and the snow-drifts deeper. One of the former, on being measured by means of a lead line, was found to be, from the top of the floe to its summit, forty-three feet three inches.

We halted earlier than usual, and, having constructed a pedestal for the magnetic instrument out of solid snow, obtained a series of observations for the inclination of the needle and for the total magnetic force.

May 8th.—We at length forced ourselves to believe that the disease from which our men were suffering was really scurvy. We issued to those who were afflicted daily allowances of lime-juice from the small stock that we brought away with us.

But it was with the utmost difficulty that a small allowance for each could be thawed. The lime-juice was in two bottles. On putting one near the cooking apparatus to thaw, the bottle cracked and fell to pieces. At last I adopted the plan of placing the other bottle between my legs when in the sleeping-bag, and, after a long time, I succeeded in thawing a small quantity. But it is now known that this was of no use; for the state of the lime-juice used by Dr. Coppinger at Polaris Bay showed that the whole volume must be thawed and remixed before it can be used with any advantage. This can only be done in the warmer weather of June or July.

The loss of appetite, depression of spirits, with other symptoms were, we thought, decidedly scorbutic, and we feared, without fresh meat and vegetables, that there was little chance of seeing the sick men on the drag-ropes again during the journey. Being a fine, bright day, the invalids were made to come out and bask in the sun, whilst the rest of the party, with pickaxes and shovels, were engaged in cutting a road through the hummocks. A double series of magnetic observations were obtained, together with sights for latitude, longitude, and variation of the compass. The hummocks amongst which our tents were pitched were of various heights and bulk, from small fragments of ice to huge piles over forty feet high. Some of them consisted of a number of small hummocks squeezed up into one large mass, whilst others were apparently the regular floe-bergs, and, although perhaps of greater bulk, were not quite so high.

Between these hummocks, and consequently along the only road where we could drag our sledges, the snow had accumulated in drifts to a great depth, and this, formed into ridges by the wind, rendered the travelling all the more difficult. Occasionally the tops of these ridges were frozen hard, and it was of no uncommon occurrence to step from deep snow, through which we were floundering up to our waists, on to a hard, frozen piece, or *vice versâ*.

Sometimes these ridges were only partially frozen, or covered with a slight crust, just hard enough *not* to bear our weights, and this made it exceedingly disagreeable and laborious to travel over.

May 9*th*.—Another beautifully warm day, with the temperature only a degree or two below zero! It was impossible to remain idle on such a day, so we resolved to push on.

Lightening two of the sledges of about half their loads, two of the sick men were placed on them, and these were dragged to the limit of the road made yesterday. Here the tent was pitched, the two invalids placed inside, the sledge unpacked and dragged back. In this manner we succeeded in advancing during the day a distance of about three-quarters of a mile; but so tortuous was our road, and so often had it to be traversed, that to accomplish this short distance we had to walk about seven miles, and this through very deep snow. Rawlings, Simpson, and Ferbrache were complaining of aching limbs, and their legs exhibited slight discolouration.

May 10*th*.—We advanced the sledges in the same manner as yesterday, accomplishing about the same distance; but so distressing was it to see the exertions of the men in their endeavours to perform a good day's work, and so painful was it to witness the sufferings of the sick, that I very reluctantly came to the conclusion that our camp this evening must be our most northern one. With five of my little force disabled, and as many more showing decided scorbutic symptoms, it would have been imprudent to persevere farther, however much inclination might prompt such a proceeding. Besides, our provisions must be taken into consideration, and we had only thirty days left to take us back a distance that occupied us forty days to advance, so that our turning back became an imperative necessity. We might, I think, console ourselves with the knowledge that the motto engraved on my flagstaff, and which had been presented to me by my friend and former Captain, now Commodore A. H. Hoskins, had been fully carried out. It was happily chosen, and although the lines are expressed in the first personal pronoun they had reference to the whole party:

> "I dare do all that may become a man:
> Who dares do more is none."

We felt that the absence of any greater success could not be attributed either to a lack of energy or of perseverance. It was, however, a bitter ending to all our aspirations, for which even the knowledge of being homeward bound failed to compensate. In justice to my brave companions I must say that no men could have done more under the same circumstances.

May 11*th*.—Having arrived at the determination of dragging the sledges no farther in a northerly direction, I deemed it desirable to try what good two days' perfect rest would do for our invalids; and, as there were many useful observations to be taken in this high latitude, I determined to devote the two following days to obtaining them. As soon as breakfast was discussed, a snow pedestal was erected for the instrument for determining the magnetic force and inclination of the needle, a double series of observations being obtained. Sights were taken in order to fix our position both by latitude and longitude, and also for the variation of the compass.*

Some of the men were employed in cutting a hole through young ice that existed between the hummocks in order that we might obtain deep sea temperatures with a Casella's thermometer, which we had brought with us for the purpose.

In three hours this work was accomplished, the ice being only sixty-four inches in thickness. On attempting to get soundings, to our great surprise we succeeded in finding bottom in seventy-one fathoms (four hundred and twenty-six feet).

At this depth we managed to obtain, by various contrivances that were lowered down, a specimen of the bottom, which was carefully bottled, in order to be carried to the ship, there to undergo microscopic examination.

Wishing to possess any specimens of animal life that might exist in this high latitude, a bread bag, filled with the scrapings of our pannikins and a little pemmican, was lowered to the bottom, and, having been kept there some hours, was hauled up, and to our great joy found to be almost alive with numerous

---

* The original from which the annexed illustration is a copy, was painted by Admiral R. B. Beechey, and exhibited in the Royal Academy in 1877. It is now in the possession of Mr. Clements Markham.

HIGHEST NORTHERN CAMP.

small crustaceans * and foraminifera ; specimens of which were, of course, collected and preserved, being the most northern animal life yet discovered. With our thermometer a series of temperatures was taken at every ten fathoms, whilst the specific gravity of the surface water was also obtained.

Tidal action was apparent; but, with the means at our disposal, we were unable to observe the rise and fall of the tide, or to make any accurate measurement regarding it. Altogether the day was not unprofitably spent.

May 12*th.*—This 12th of May must always be regarded as an eventful day in the lives of our little party, for it was that on which we had the honour, and no small gratification, of planting the Union Jack on the most northern limit of the globe ever attained by civilized man, or, in fact, so far as our knowledge goes, by mortal man! In order to insure being within four hundred miles of the North Pole, we started immediately after breakfast to the northward, carrying with us the sextant, artificial horizon, and all our colours and banners. We were a party of ten,† two men being left behind to attend to the wants of the five who were sick, and who were left comfortably settled inside the tents.

* *Anonyx nugax*, a fine adult male example, and several smaller ones. The length of the largest specimen is 1½ inch. This species is one of the commonest and most abundantly distributed of the northern *Amphipoda*. It was discovered by Captain Phipps in 1773, and is found along the shores of Arctic America, in the White Sea, on the coasts of Greenland, Iceland, Spitzbergen, Norway, and in the Sea of Okhotsk

† The names of these men are—Commander A. H. Markham, Lieutenant A. A. C. Parr, Thos. Rawlings, Ed. Lawrence, John Radmore, Thos. Jolliffe, Daniel Harley, Wm. Ferbrache, Wm. Maskell, and John Pearson.

The walking was undoubtedly severe, at one moment struggling through deep snow-drifts, in which we floundered up to our waists, and at another tumbling about amongst the hummocks.

Some idea may be formed of the difficulties of the road, when, after more than two hours' hard walking, with little or nothing to carry, we had barely accomplished one mile!

Shortly before noon a halt was called, the artificial horizon set up, and the flags and sledge standards displayed. Fortunately the sun was favourable to us, and we were able to obtain a good altitude as it passed the meridian, although almost immediately afterwards dark clouds rolled up, snow began to fall, and the sun was lost in obscurity.

We found the latitude to be 83° 20′ 26″ N., or three hundred and ninety-nine miles and a half from the North Pole. The announcement of our position was received with three cheers, with one more for Captain Nares; then all sang the "Union Jack of Old England," our "Grand Palæocrystic Sledging Chorus," winding up, like loyal subjects, with " God save the Queen."

No words of mine could describe the scene that surrounded us better than those of Coleridge in his "Ancient Mariner":

> "The ice was here, the ice was there,
> The ice was all around."

For nought else but snow and ice could be seen in any direction.

In spite, however, of these dreary surroundings, suggesting everything that was desolate and miserable, mirth, happiness, and joy seemed to reign paramount amongst our little party. Perhaps there was something in the idea of having been farther north than any other man had hitherto penetrated, that promoted such feelings! Whatever produced them, they were shared in by all. Even the sick, on our return to camp, prostrate and suffering as they were, participated in the general hilarity and rejoicing. They knew their toilsome journey had terminated, and that each day would bring them nearer to their ship and to those supplies that were necessary to save their lives.

On returning to the tents, a magnum of whiskey, kindly sent by the "Dean of Dundee," for the express purpose of being drunk at our highest northern position, was broached, and for supper we had divided amongst the two sledge crews a hare that had been shot by Dr. Moss on the third day after leaving the ship. Could men in our position want more? Never were the bones of a hare picked so clean! No dog would have benefited much from the scraps remaining from our repast!

Absent friends were duly toasted, and the evening was brought to a close with songs, in which even the invalids joined. All appeared happy, cheerful, and contented.

CHAPTER XXIV.

RETURN OF THE NORTHERN DIVISION.

> "Is not short payne well borne, that brings long ease,
> And layes the soule to sleepe in quiet grace?
> Sleepe after toyle, port after stormie seas,
> Ease after warre, death after life, does greatly please."
> *Faërie Queene.*

AT three o'clock on the afternoon of the 13th of May the homeward march was commenced, our main object, of course, being to get back to the ship as speedily as possible.

Before starting, a couple of records, inclosed in two tin cases, were deposited on the floe. One was placed as near the centre of the floe as possible, the other was secured on the top of a hummock.

On the records was stated the latitude and longitude of the position, together with a few words regarding the condition of the party. If these are ever picked up it will be very interesting and important, as throwing light on the drift or tide in these high latitudes.

It is unnecessary to describe the incidents that occurred on each successive day during the return journey. Day by day did our strength diminish. Gradually, but surely, the men, one after the other, began to feel the cruel grasp of the disease, as they struggled manfully on, dragging their poor, helpless companions, in spite of racking pains and aching limbs. Although themselves attacked by the dreadful malady, the men who were still able to work suppressed their own sufferings in their endeavours to ameliorate those of their more helpless and ailing comrades. Unmindful of their own miserable plight, they devoted themselves to the tender and soothing functions of nurses with a thoughtful and careful tenderness that would have done credit even to those of the weaker sex.

Often had the same road to be traversed, as the sledges were advanced one at a time, and most fortunate was it that we were able to adhere to the road constructed during our outward journey. To do so, however, during the thick weather which constantly prevailed, was a task of great difficulty and very trying to the eyes; but we knew that if by ill-luck we should wander away and lose it, our chances of ever seeing the ship again would be poor indeed! The hours selected for travelling were between 6 P.M. and 6 A.M. By choosing this part of the day, or rather night, for working, we kept the sun as much as possible at our backs, and slept during the warmth of the day. Towards the end of May, although the temperature of the outside air was below the freezing point, the sun was so powerful that it would raise the temperature inside our tent, whilst we were sleeping, to as much as 70° or 80°, which would be quite unbearable! Frost-bites had become a thing of the past, and were no longer dreaded. The temperature did not rise above the freezing point until the month of June.

Snow fell heavily during the greater part of the return journey, and fogs were very prevalent. Gales of wind had to be endured, for to halt was out of the question—rest there was none—onward was the order of the day.

As the disease gradually assumed the mastery over the party, so did the appetites decrease, and in a very alarming manner, until it was with the greatest difficulty that anybody could be induced to eat at all. Instead of each man disposing of one pound of pemmican a day, the same quantity sufficed for the entire party in one tent; and even this, occasionally, was not consumed. Nor was the subject of eating and drinking so often discussed. During the outward journey, beefsteaks and onions, mutton chops and new potatoes, and Bass's beer formed the chief topics of conversation. On the return journey they were scarcely alluded to. Hunger was never felt; but we were all assailed by an intolerable thirst, which could only be appeased at meal times, or after the temperature was sufficiently high to admit of quenching our thirst by putting icicles into our mouths.

Aching bones and sleepless nights were the chief causes of our sufferings.

With all these hardships it was a great comfort to be able to put on dry foot gear. If it was fine when we encamped, our blanket wrappers and hose were spread out on the tent in the sun, so that when we got up they were not only dry, but *not frozen*, and were, therefore, limp and supple!

On the 17th of May we again, strange to say, crossed the track of a hare, being at the time about twenty-five miles from the nearest land. Like the track before seen, the footsteps were close together, indicating that the poor little creature was in a very exhausted state. Although the traces were very indistinct, they appeared to be going in a northerly direction.

Though our travelling was slow, we could see a perceptible decrease in the distance between ourselves and the land, whenever the weather was fine enough for us to observe it. "Old Joe," as the men irreverently termed Cape Joseph Henry, loomed nearer and darker, and we all regarded it with anxious, longing eyes.

On the 18th of May the first icicles were observed hanging from the edges of a few hummocks—a sure sign of the returning power of the sun.

Ominous symptoms of a disruption of the pack were seen on the same day, and again on the following one. A crack in some ice had opened considerably since we last passed over it, whilst small hummocks had been formed by the pressure of two floes, one against the other. These little indications made matters assume a still more serious aspect. They may have been due to tidal action, but they were undoubtedly warnings to get off the pack as speedily as possible.

On the 20th the snow crystals that fell actually melted on coming into contact with our clothes or any dark substance. These crystals were all of a beautiful stellar shape. A hummock passed, although composed, apparently, of one piece of ice, was of two different colours, a deep blue and a pale yellow. Portions of each were broken off for the purpose of testing their respective specific gravities, and also to carry back to the ship for analysis. In all probability the discolouration was caused by the presence of diatomaceæ. The hummocks, at about this date, began to assume a different appearance, the mild weather depriving them of their snowy covering, and causing them to lose much of their former resemblance to gigantic wedding cakes!

The men began to have an inkling of the nature of the disease from which they were suffering, although we studiously avoided all mention of it. It went with them by the name of the "Joseph Henry mange!" Their spirits were wonderful, and they joked each other as they hobbled along. Their lameness they called the "Marco Polo limp," and declared on their return to England they would introduce it as the fashionable gait!

Nothing appeared to subdue their courage or their zeal. Orders were always executed with the utmost willingness and good humour, and with as much alacrity as they were capable of evincing.

The men having heard that tea-leaves had been recommended as a good *vegetable*, the contents of the tea-kettle, after lunch and supper, were carefully collected, and devoured with avidity; but there is little faith, I fear, to be placed in their efficacy for warding off or subduing our terrible complaint.

Instead of our sledge loads appearing to diminish in weight as the provisions were consumed, they seemed to drag heavier, and we were at a loss whether to attribute this to the depth and softness of the snow over which we travelled, or to the increasing weakness of our party! It was hard work, and as much as we could do to make any progress at all. The men experienced great difficulty in moving their legs, the slightest exertion caused intense pain, and it was a piteous sight to witness them struggling bravely on, without uttering a murmur or complaint. They all knew that their only hope of safety was to get back to the ship as speedily as possible.

The 24th of May being the Queen's birthday, all the flags and banners were displayed during the short time we halted for lunch, and her Majesty's health was drunk by her most northern and not least loyal subjects. On that day, amongst the entire party, we could only muster four and a half good and sound pairs of legs! Still even those with "game legs" stuck to the drag-ropes nobly, and if they were unable to render much assistance, still the drag-ropes acted as a support, and therefore enabled them to keep up.

On the 25th the eighty-third parallel of latitude was recrossed.

The comparatively high temperative caused the snow over which we journeyed to assume a "sludgy" consistency, which clung tenaciously to our legs and to the sledge runners, rendering the work of dragging and walking all the more laborious.

On the 27th the condition of the party was so critical that it became only too painfully evident that, to insure their reaching the land alive, the sledges must be considerably lightened in order to admit of a more rapid advance. The state of the party was on that day as follows: five men were in a very precarious condition, utterly unable to move, and consequently had to be carried on the sledges; five others nearly as bad, but who nobly persisted in hobbling after the sledges, which they could just manage to accomplish, for, as the sledges had to be advanced one by one, it gave them plenty of time to perform the distance; whilst three others exhibited all the premonitory scorbutic symptoms. Thus only the two officers and two men* could be considered as effective! This was, it must be acknowledged, a very deplorable state of affairs.

I therefore decided to abandon the remaining boat, which would materially lessen the load to be dragged. This decision was only arrived at after long and anxious consideration. I had to decide which was the lesser of two evils.

For I well knew that should a disruption of the pack occur, and we had already observed ominous signs of such an event, without a boat the party would indeed be placed in a hopeless position; but again I knew that in retaining the boat, the weights to be dragged by our weakened crew would be so excessive as to preclude the possibility of reaching the shore before all the provisions would be expended, and starvation would be the result. Again it was of the utmost importance that haste should be made in order to reach the ship, and place the sick under proper medical treatment. The disease was extending so rapidly as to produce a marked change for the worse every day. The boat, therefore, and all superfluous weights were abandoned, and the march was again wearily resumed.

Many a silent prayer was offered up to God to protect and watch over us, for we felt, indeed, that we were in dire distress, and that without His aid and assistance we must perish; and we prayed for strength to enable us to drag our poor helpless and

---

* John Radmore, chief carpenter's mate, and William Maskell, able seaman.

suffering companions to a place of safety. A record was left in the deserted boat, containing a brief account of our state and condition, with the latitude and longitude where it was abandoned.

On the following day great excitement was caused by the appearance of a snow bunting, which was seen fluttering about amongst the hummocks, uttering its sweet and pleasant chirp, which to us was the most

SNOW BUNTING.

pleasing music we had heard for many a long day. No wonder the sudden appearance amongst us of this little warbler was so interesting, for it was the first bird we had seen for nine long months. Even the invalids, as they lay on the sledges, requested that they might have their faces uncovered, so as both to see and hear the little friend that had flown off to us, as if it were a messenger to welcome our party back to life and friends. Long and anxiously was it watched as it winged its course towards the land, whither we also were slowly wending our way.

On the 29th the colours were again displayed at lunch time, in commemoration of the first anniversary of our sailing from England, and allusions were made to that ever-memorable day, comparisons being drawn between our condition then and now! On that evening our tents were pitched close to the boat that we had abandoned on our outward journey, and which we found exactly in the same state as when we left it, with its mast stepped and yard hoisted, standing out like a grim sentinel guarding those icy wastes.

On the 31st, whilst crossing some young ice between two heavy floes, one of the sledges broke through, and we had no little trouble in saving it from complete immersion, and the invalid who was on it from being drowned! These warnings were unmistakeable, and pointed to the necessity of reaching the land as quickly as possible. The falling snow and drift thawed upon our clothes, making us wet and extremely wretched and uncomfortable.

On the 1st of June the temperature was some two or three degrees above freezing point. This had the effect of thawing the surface snow and converting it into a thick sludge. Our foot gear in consequence was in a soaking wet state. Our working force on this day was reduced to six, and all suffering more or less.

On the 2nd the thick weather, which had so persistently clung to us, proved triumphant and robbed us of our road. Up to this date we had been able to avail ourselves of the road constructed with so much trouble and labour on our outward journey. On this day we wandered off it, and in spite of our efforts were unable to pick up the trail again. The severe and monotonous labour of road-making had again to be resorted to. On the 5th, to our very great joy, we succeeded once more in pitching our camp on *terra firma*, after an absence from it of two months. On first landing our hopes were excited on observing the recent traces of a sledge and human footprints, and we congratulated ourselves upon soon obtaining that relief we all so much required; but we were doomed to disappointment, for on reaching the depôt of provisions established near Cape Joseph Henry for our use, and which was found intact, we learnt that a sledge party with Captain Nares had left for the ship only two days previously! This was a bitter blow, for we knew that something more than provisions was needed for the safety of the party.

We learnt also that scurvy had made its appearance on board the "Alert," and that poor Petersen died from the effects of his last sledge journey, on the 14th of May.

Three hares had been kindly and thoughtfully left for us in a crevice amongst the hummocks by Captain Nares, and this furnished us with meals for a couple of days; it is needless to add, they were done ample justice to, not only for the sake of their goodness and the change they afforded, but also because we thought the fresh meat would act as a specific against the scurvy.

The tracks of a wolf were observed near the depôt, and the animal was frequently heard howling in a mournful manner, but we never saw it.

Obtaining a few supplies from the depôt, our march was again resumed; but so rapid had been the encroachments of the disease, that it was only too palpable that immediate succour was absolutely necessary for our salvation. At the rate of progress we were making, it would take us fully three weeks to reach the ship, although only forty miles distant; and who would there be left in three weeks' time? The few who were still strong enough to drag the sledges would barely last as many days! Assistance had, therefore, to be obtained. To procure it, one amongst us was ready and willing to set out on this lonely and solitary mission, with the firm reliance of being able to accomplish what he had undertaken, and with the knowledge that he possessed the full confidence of those for whose relief he was about to start on a long and hazardous walk. On the 7th of June Lieut. Parr started on his arduous march to the ship. Deep and heartfelt were the God-speeds uttered as he took his departure, and anxiously was his retreating form watched until it was gradually lost to sight amidst the interminable hummocks.

> "All waste! no sign of life
> But the track of the wolf and the bear!
> No sound but the wild, wild wind,
> And the snow crunching under his feet."

Although the loss of one strong man, like Parr, from the party was seriously felt, still the knowledge that active steps had been taken to procure aid was sufficient to compensate for this reduction in our strength, and the men gallantly persevered at the drag-ropes, buoyed up by renewed hopes.

On the day previous to that on which Parr left, an Eskimo dog, to our great surprise, was seen threading its way to us through the hummocks. It was soon recognized to be one of our dogs, named Flo; but she was so timid that at first nothing would induce her to approach. After a little time, however, we coaxed her to us, and on having some pemmican thrown to her she ate it ravenously. Poor thing! she was wretchedly thin and emaciated; she, we concluded, had been cast adrift, or made her escape from the last dog-sledge that visited this neighbourhood. She joined our tail of cripples, hobbling, like them, after us and carefully walking in the track of our sledges.

On the 8th of June sadness and despondency prevailed amongst our little band. One of our number had received that summons to which all must at some time attend, and had been called to his long account.

> "His soul to Him who gave it rose.
> God led it to its long repose—
> Its glorious rest."

This was a terrible and unexpected blow to many who regarded themselves as being in a still more critical and precarious condition than was poor Porter. His end was calm and peaceful, and he retained his senses to within five minutes of the time of dissolution.

Sad and mournful, indeed, was the small procession that wended its way slowly to the new-made grave, dug out of a frozen soil, carrying the lifeless remains of their comrade, covered with the Union Jack, on the same sledge on which he had been dragged, whilst alive, for many weeks; and there, with the tears trickling down their weather-beaten and smoke-begrimed faces, with their hearts so full as to choke all utterance, they laid their late fellow-sufferer in his last resting-place.

A rude cross, improvised out of the rough materials that our own equipment supplied, with a brief inscription, marks the lone and dreary spot in that far-off icy desert where rests our comrade in his long sleep that knows no waking, and where probably human foot will never again tread.

> "O World! so few the years we live,
> Would that the life that thou dost give
> Were life indeed!
> Alas! thy sorrows fall so fast,
> Our happiest hour is when at last
> The soul is freed."

Gladly, after the ceremony was concluded, was the order to renew the march received, every one being desirous of quitting a place so fraught with sad and melancholy associations; the day, as if in unison with the state of our own thoughts and feelings, was dull and gloomy.

The late mournful event produced a despondency in our little band to which we had hitherto been strangers.

One and all felt and knew that assistance, to be of any avail, must arrive speedily, and many a wistful glance was directed towards the south, in the faint hope of seeing that succour without which they would surely perish. They felt more their own weakness and helplessness, and dreaded a recurrence of what had recently taken place. The journey was silently and wearily resumed.

As many of the men were unable to eat their pemmican, on account of the soreness of their gums, and from a certain dislike that they had lately taken to it, a new "dish" was tried, consisting of preserved potatoes mixed with bacon fat, and although in flavour, if any was perceptible, it rather resembled what starch might be like, it was decidedly acceptable as a change, and each person consumed about two-thirds of a pannikin.

On the morning of the 9th a rainbow was seen, which, being an unusual sight, afforded much interest. On the same day, shortly after the march had been commenced, a moving object was suddenly seen amidst the hummocks to the southward. At first it was regarded as an optical illusion, for we could scarcely realize the fact that it could be anybody from the "Alert!" With what intense anxiety this object was regarded is beyond description.

Gradually emerging from the hummocks, a hearty cheer put an end to the suspense that was almost agonizing, as a dog-sledge with three men was seen to be approaching. A cheer in return was attempted, but so full were our hearts that it resembled more a wail than a cheer.

It is impossible to describe our feelings as May and Moss came up, and we received from them a warm and hearty welcome. We felt that we were saved, and a feeling of thankfulness and gratitude was uppermost in our minds, as we shook the hands of those who had hurried out to our relief the moment that Parr had conveyed to them intelligence of our distress. Those who a few short moments before were in the lowest depths of despondency, appeared now in the most exuberant spirits. Pain was disregarded and hardships were forgotten as numerous and varied questions were asked and answered.

We heard with delight that they were only the vanguard of a larger party, headed by Captain Nares himself, that was coming out to our relief, and which we should probably meet on the following day. A halt was immediately ordered, cooking utensils lighted up, ice made into water, and we were soon all enjoying a good pannikin full of lime-juice, with the prospect of mutton for supper!

After halting for the night Moss made a thorough medical inspection of the whole party. His report was by no means cheering : all were more or less affected, and some were in a very precarious condition. The presence, however, of a medical officer amongst us restored confidence, and acted as a powerful antiscorbutic!

On the following day we met the larger party coming out to our assistance, and with their help arrived alongside the "Alert" on the 14th of June, seventy-two days after our departure from the ship.

What a contrast did that departure afford to our return!

Then, on that bright but cold April morning, all were in the highest spirits, cheerful and enthusiastic, looking forward with confidence to a comparatively successful issue to their undertaking—a fine, strong, and resolute band.

Alas! how different was the return! Out of that party of fifteen men, one had gone to his long home, eleven others were carried alongside the ship on sledges dragged by a party despatched to their relief, and only the remaining three were capable of walking.* Even they were scarcely able to move one leg before the other, and were, on their return, placed with the others under the doctor's hands. It was, indeed, a sad and terrible calamity with which we had been afflicted, totally unexpected and unparalleled in the

* Radmore, Jolliffe, and Maskell.

annals of Arctic sledging experiences. On our arrival alongside the ship, we were, of course, most warmly welcomed by every soul on board; before entering Captain Nares called for three cheers for our party, and then offered up thanks to Almighty God for having preserved us through many dangers and privations, and for guiding us back to our ship without further loss of life.

CHAPTER XXV.

RETURN OF ALL THE SLEDGE TRAVELLERS.

"Now that the winter's gone, the earth hath lost
Her snow-white robes, and now no more the frost
Candies the grass, or calls an icy cream
Upon the silver lake or crystal stream,
But the warm sun thaws the benumbed earth."

CAREW.

THE hearty welcome we received from one and all on board the "Alert," together with the indescribable pleasure of a warm bath, followed by a champagne supper for those whom the doctor reported well enough to indulge in such a luxury, made us all supremely happy; the feeling being increased by the knowledge that our suffering companions were under the tender care of kind and skilful hands, and that all responsibility connected with their treatment had, so far as we were concerned, ceased. Our late hardships and the anxiety we had felt regarding the safe return of the party were almost forgotten, and were it not for the number of cots hanging up outside the wardroom, and the row of beds along the lower deck, each occupied by a sick man, we should almost have felt inclined to regard our late sledging expedition as a dream from which we had suddenly been awakened.

A more thorough break-up of a healthy and strong body of men it would be difficult to conceive. Not only had the men engaged in the extended party under my command been attacked with scurvy, but also those who had been absent from the ship only for short periods, and some, who may be said never to have left the ship at all, or if they did, only for two or three days! The disease then could not be attributed to any special circumstance connected with sledge travelling.

The seeds must have been sown during the time, nearly five months, that the sun was absent, and we were in darkness. Fresh animal and vegetable food is undoubtedly necessary for the preservation of health, and its absence is the originating cause of scurvy. To this originating cause all Arctic Expeditions have been equally exposed. The predisposing causes of scurvy, which actually lead to an outbreak when the originating cause exists, are the long absence of the sun, entailing darkness, damp, intense cold, and bad ventilation. To these predisposing causes our expedition was exposed for a very much longer period than any other which sent out extended travelling parties. For this reason other expeditions were exempt from scurvy while we were attacked. In short, the different result was caused by the difference in latitude. As our winter arrangements, and our scale of diet, both on board and while travelling, were identical with those of former expeditions, the cause of the outbreak could not have had anything to do either with diet or winter routine. Lime-juice, though most useful in warding off for a time and delaying an attack of scurvy, and as a cure, will not, with other circumstances unfavourable, prevent an outbreak.

This is the opinion of all the best medical authorities; and our experience proved it to be an undoubted fact. Some of our men had scurvy who never left the ship and never ceased to take their daily rations of lime-juice, and others were attacked who went away travelling at a time when daily rations of lime-juice formed a part of the sledge dietary.*

In future, when an expedition winters in so high a latitude as 82° N., the prevention of an outbreak of scurvy must be secured by improved measures for mitigating the predisposing causes.

Owing to the condition of the crew of the "Alert," Captain Nares publicly announced, on the 16th of June, that on the return of the sledge parties, he would endeavour to rejoin the "Discovery," and would then send that vessel to England with all the invalids, and those unfit to remain out a second winter. The "Alert" would pass her second winter at Port Foulke, whence, in the ensuing spring, parties would be despatched for the purpose of exploring Hayes Sound, and the adjacent land. This work completed, that vessel also would return to England. The reason that Port Foulke was selected as our future winter quarters was the amount of animal life, principally reindeer, reported to abound in that neighbourhood, and we also anticipated little or no difficulty in breaking out in the following summer.

This resolution was undoubtedly a wise one, for it was certain that in the then state of the ship's company of the "Alert," many lives would be sacrificed if all the men were required to spend another winter

---

* As soon as it was possible to use the lime-juice in the form in which it was supplied to the expedition (that is, in jars or bottles) all sledge parties were invariably supplied with it as a daily ration.

in the Arctic Regions. The idea of soon reaching England acted as a cure upon those who were in the worst stage of scurvy, and conduced more to their recovery than all the medicines and careful nursing that they received from our painstaking and attentive doctor.

In the mean time great anxiety began to be felt regarding the safety of the western sledge party under Aldrich. From the wholesale manner in which the northern division had been afflicted, it was feared that they also would not pass scathless.

Still we hoped they would not suffer to the same extent. Their route was along the coast line, and it was expected that they would have been able to supply themselves occasionally with fresh provisions, such as hares, geese, and perhaps musk-oxen.

On the 18th of June, four days after the return of my party, May, with three men and the dog-sledge, dragged by our remaining six dogs, left the ship in order to obtain intelligence of Aldrich's party, and if necessary to take him relief and assistance. The succeeding days were anxious ones to all on board, and many were the trips taken to the summit of Look-out-hill, in the hope of seeing the returning sledgers. We could not disguise from ourselves the fact that unless they returned quickly they would be placed in a very critical position. In a few days they must be without provisions. This we knew. The temperature, too, had reached freezing point, and frequently stood two or three degrees above it, causing the surface snow to thaw, and therefore making the task of dragging a sledge one of severe and unpleasant toil.

On the 21st the sun reached its highest northern

declination, and every day would bring us nearer to another winter; therefore we knew that to effect our deliverance from the ice this year, it was necessary to get our sledging parties on board as soon as possible, in order to prepare the ship for sea, and to commence the operations requisite for cutting her out of winter quarters.

The snow on the hills to the northward of us was rapidly disappearing; but this might only be due to their southern aspect, for in our immediate vicinity the snow appeared as deep as ever. Towards the latter end of May the hills around the ship were perfectly bare; but the heavy fall of snow, experienced by us during our return journey, had again covered them as they were during the winter.

Water began to form in little pools on the floes near the ship, and every sign betokened the approaching disruption of the pack. On the 23rd, a few king ducks, some Arctic terns, and skuas were seen hovering about the land, and one or two specimens of the latter were shot—their skins swelling our natural history collection, their bodies being reserved for the sick.

On Sunday, June 25th, immediately after Divine Service, on ascending Look-out-hill, to our very great delight we observed the wanderers struggling through the hummocks some six or seven miles off. Hurrying down to communicate the good news, a relief party was speedily formed, and by midnight we had the very great satisfaction of receiving them all on board. It was the old story repeated. All were suffering from scurvy, and only Aldrich and two men were able to walk alongside the ship, one of the latter being so bad that he was under medical treatment for many weeks after his return on board.

Their absence from the ship extended over a period of eighty-four days, during which they did very good service, having explored no less than two hundred and twenty miles of new coast line. May found them near Cape Joseph Henry, not far from the spot where he had before brought succour to my party. They were then struggling bravely on, but were in a very crippled condition. It is most fortunate he succeeded in reaching them when he did. His cheery spirit and strong help did much to assist them, and enabled Aldrich to bring his little party alongside their Arctic home in undiminished numbers. It was a great relief to all on board to know that every one had returned, that no stragglers were absent. So great was the anxiety felt until all the sledging parties had arrived, that the lot of those on board was hardly more enviable than that of the travellers!

Our good ship was now converted into a regular hospital, and might almost be said to be in charge of the medical officers; for those who were not actually under treatment had to be placed at the disposal of the doctor, so as to act as nurses, cooks, or attendants of some kind. Perfect rest and careful nursing were the most essential requisites for a complete restoration to health. Spenser must have had the recovery of similar wayworn and stricken travellers in his mind when he wrote—

> "Now when their wearie limbes with kindly reste
> And bodies were refresht with dew repast."

The medical staff were unremitting in their ceaseless attention to their patients, and it was to their untiring watchfulness that we owed the complete recovery of our sick.

Much had to be done to get the ship ready for sea; but, for some time, only a few officers and *three* men could be employed in any work connected with these preparations, the remainder being engaged entirely with their duties to the sick. The principal work that had to be done, before the ice broke up round the ship, was to get on board and stow away all our powder, besides the provisions and stores that had been landed before the winter. The housing had long been taken down, and the upper deck had been partially cleared of snow, so that daylight was once more admitted through the skylights and illuminators. It is a curious fact connected with those who were for a long period absent from their ship, that the hair on their faces became perfectly bleached, until in fact it was nearly white. The loss of colour was gradual, and, although noticed, was never alluded to, each one imagining that his companion's hair was turning grey from the effects of hardship and anxiety! It was only after our return to the ship that those possessing beards and moustaches discovered the change that had occurred. The colour returned in the same gradual manner that it had disappeared. We all suffered a loss of hair from the head; but this may easily be attributed to our sealskin caps, and other head-dresses, which were constantly worn.

After the long use of moccasins, it took us some time to get accustomed to leather boots, which we were obliged to wear on account of the sludgy state of the surface of the floes and the land. With a temperature some degrees below freezing point, nothing is more comfortable or better suited for travelling over the pack than a good pair of moccasins.

The return of the sledge travellers was celebrated, on the 29th of June, by the best dinner we could afford to put on the table. As our printing-press had long been dismantled, a written *menu* was given to myself and Aldrich as the leaders of the two extended sledge parties. A beautiful sketch of the highest position reached was drawn by Moss, the following being as near as possible a fac-simile:—

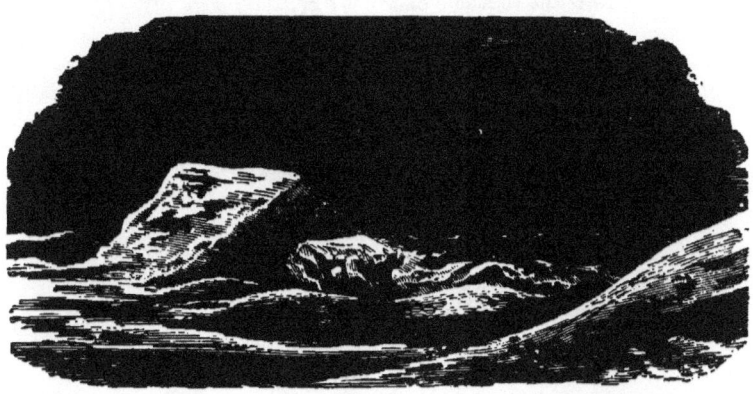

"Marco Polo."   Lat. 83° 20′ 26″ N.

MENU.

Potage olla Podrida.

Petits Pâtes d'Homards.   Fricassée de Pégouse et Sardines.

Rognons aux Champignons saucés dans Attrapez-en-haut.

Rissoles à la Tomato.

Mâchoire de Bœuf.   Jambon au Champagne.

Petits Pois.   Carottes.   Ognons.   Pommes de Terre.

Tourte de Pêches.

Compote de Blancmange et Rhubarbe Fou.   Pouding en Marmelade.

Pains rôtis aux Anchois.

Fromage.   Liqueurs.   Dessert.

Café noir.

H.M.S. "Alert."   *29th June*, 1876.

On the reverse side of the bill of fare were the following verses composed by Pullen for the occasion. It is needless to add that they were not only appreciated, but that they found a response in every breast :—

> Welcome home to the wished-for rest,
> Travellers to north and travellers to west!
> Welcome back from bristling floe,
> Frowning cliff and quaking snow!
> Nobly, bravely the work was done;
> Inch by inch was the hard fight won.
> Now the toilsome march is o'er,
> Welcome home to our tranquil shore.
>
> Rough and rude is the feast we bring;
> Rougher and ruder the verse we sing.
> Not rough, not rude are the thoughts that rise
> To choke our voices and dim our eyes,
> As we call to mind that joyous sight
> On an April morning cold and bright,
> When a chosen band stepped boldly forth
> To the unknown west and the unknown north;
> And we from our haven could only pray—
> "God send them strength for each weary day!"
>
> He heard our prayer; He made them strong;
> He bore their stalwart limbs along;
> Planted their sturdy footsteps sure;
> Gave them courage to endure.
> Taught them, too, for His dear sake,
> Many a sacrifice to make:
> By many a tender woman's deed
> To aid a brother in his need.
>
> And safe for ever shall He keep
> In His gentle hand the two who sleep.
> His love shall quench the tears that flow
> For the buried dear ones under the snow.
> And we who live and are strong to do,
> His love shall keep us safely too:
> Shall tend our sick, and soothe their pain,
> And bring them back to health again.
> And the breath of His wind shall set us free,
> Through the opening ice to the soft green sea.

DECISION TO RETURN TO ENGLAND.

Captain Nares had hinted that, in the present condition of the men, and supposing also that those of the "Discovery" were in the same state, he would not be justified in allowing even one ship to remain another year exposed to the rigours of an Arctic winter and to the same causes that had led to the recent outbreak of scurvy. We were prepared for this announcement; for we well knew that to remain out a second winter, although there were many of us ready and eager to do so, would simply be to sacrifice many valuable lives for no object; for we could not possibly expect to reach a higher northern latitude, or even to extend our explorations much farther to the westward, although the whole force of the expedition should be confined to the one direction. In deciding to return to England, Captain Nares showed great moral courage, and exercised a sound and wise judgment, in the opinion of all his officers.

On the Sunday following the return of Aldrich's party, a special thanksgiving was offered up to Almighty God for our safe return, and prayers were also said for the speedy recovery of our sick comrades.

On the 1st of July, on the usual monthly medical examination being held, only ten men out of our fine ship's company were reported in a fit state for work, and some of these were convalescents! The invalids, however, thanks to the doctor's assiduous care, were improving slowly but surely.

The thaw had by this time commenced. The snow was soft and wet in the valleys, small rivulets were already meandering through the ravines and gorges, whilst the summits of the mountains were covered with brown patches that the wind and thaw combined had left bare. Little tufts of the beautiful purple saxifrage dotted the sides of the hills over which we walked, bringing forcibly to our minds the wild flowers of our own dear country, and creating a longing desire to behold them once more. Footprints of animals, notably musk-oxen, were occasionally observed; but although these traces appeared fresh, they were evidently those of the preceding autumn, which, having been covered with snow and frozen hard during the winter, had thus been perfectly preserved.

On the 5th of July, however, we were so fortunate as to shoot three musk-oxen within three or four miles of the ship, and on the following morning another fell a victim to the prowess of our sportsmen. This was indeed a God-send, for without fresh meat the recovery of our sick would be long and tedious. The actual amount of food obtained from these animals was at the average rate of 120 lbs. from each. The dexterity with which the beasts were operated upon after death would have done credit to the most accomplished butchers. Our first dish of liver and bacon at breakfast was, it is needless to say, done full justice to—the only fault being an insufficiency in amount.

Fresh provisions were indispensable for the restoration of the invalids to health. Shooting parties were, therefore, organized amongst the officers, and the whole country for a radius of many miles was well scoured in search of game. These shooting parties were very enjoyable, especially to those who, like myself, had been engaged on one of the prolonged sledging expeditions—the contrast being very great. No anxiety, little or no responsibility, careless of time, and oblivious of everything save our own pleasure and convenience. Sleeping when we felt tired, and having our meals when we felt hungry, the night the same as the day, the sun at midnight being as bright as at noon, free from all cares, intent only on sport, the time passed in a serene and delightful manner, and we were truly sorry when the time came to relinquish our gipsying life for a more civilized one on board.

On one of these shooting tours I was away from the ship, accompanied by a few choice spirits, for fourteen days. During that time we succeeded in obtaining a couple of musk-oxen, and several brent geese, which were a welcome addition to the fresh meat already obtained for the sick on board the ship. What delightful little meals we used to cook for ourselves, each one taking his turn, and vying with the others in his endeavours to make his dishes excel those of his predecessor!

On one occasion we had for breakfast the livers and gizzards of thirteen geese served up with a little bacon, these being the perquisites of the sportsmen. In the enjoyment of such luxuries it is not surprising that a return to the ship, and our everlasting Australian and New Zealand beef and mutton, was not hailed with delight.

All this time the thaw had been rapidly progressing, the tops of the hills were bare, and the ravines were rendered almost impassable from the mountain torrents that dashed down towards the sea, gaining strength and volume as they neared their outlets. These had to be crossed by the shooting parties, the water reaching up to our waists, and flowing with such force as nearly to carry us off our legs. As for change of clothing, we had none; but on reaching our tents we would get into our sleeping-bags and leave our wet clothes outside to dry; the temperature at this time being about 40°. A warm supper, with a pannikin of hot tea, followed by a glass of grog, soon made us forget the discomforts of the past in the enjoyment of the present.

Some of the scenery, about five or ten miles in the interior, was extremely picturesque. The spot that we selected for our camp was on the borders of a lake that formed one of a chain extending to the south

BRENT GOOSE AND EIDER DUCKS.

westward. Some of the hills surrounding these lakes were beautifully carpeted with the pretty little purple saxifrage, a *draba*, a *potentilla*, and other wild flowers, while the valleys were covered with patches of luxuriant vegetation, consisting of grasses and delightfully soft moss. Altogether the aspect of the surrounding country afforded a striking contrast to what it was but a few short weeks back, when still wrapped in its wintry garb.

On our return to the ship on the 24th of July, we

were glad to hear that our invalids were progressing favourably, and the convalescents regaining strength. It was also a source of great gratification to us to find a broad stream of water forming outside our protecting floe-bergs, and extending from Point Sheridan to as far south as we could see. This was a very agreeable and unexpected surprise. Active preparations were at once made to release the ship from her icy prison. All stores and provisions were re-embarked, instruments were brought on board and carefully packed up and put away, boats were hoisted up, the screw lowered, and the engines reported in good working order. Strict orders were issued that no one was to be absent from the ship, on any pretence, for a longer period than four hours without express permission. Any day might see our release! Anxious eyes were constantly directed towards the pack, which was now acted upon both by wind and tide, drifting north and south as it felt their influences.

A large cairn, fully ten feet high, was erected on the summit of "Cairn Hill," in which was deposited a record stating briefly what had been accomplished by the expedition, and giving a list of the officers and men of both ships. To this document each of the former attached his signature. Will this ever be disturbed by our fellow-men?

Strenuous exertions were made by means of powder to blow up the ice between the ship and the channel of water that almost tantalized us by its existence, and so clear a passage by which we could effect our escape. Countless torpedoes, containing from 1 to 50 lbs. of powder, were used to accomplish this object, and many hours of hard labour were expended in the same endeavour. At length, on the morning of the

31st of July, our exertions were crowned with success, and great was the excitement on board when hurried orders were issued to raise steam with all despatch and to prepare for sea! A fresh south-westerly wind had blown the pack off the shore, leaving a clear channel of water extending as far as could be seen to the southward.

By 7 A.M. the ship was free and afloat, and at eight o'clock the colours were hoisted, and we succeeded, without much difficulty, in steaming clear of the prison that had for eleven long months so securely held us in its icy fetters.

Who can describe the feelings experienced by all on board the "Alert" on again hearing the long-silent throbbing of the engines, and knowing that the ship was once more in motion?

Yet a slight pang of regret was felt at leaving the barren, sterile coast, off which we had passed so many happy days, and we could not but feel grateful to the kind floe-bergs which had, during that time, protected us so well from "ye merciless yce."

CHAPTER XXVI.

THE RETURN VOYAGE IN THE ICE.

"Let our trusty band
Haste to Fatherland,
Let our vessel brave
Plough the angry wave."
THORHALL'S *Saga*.

CAPE JOSEPH HENRY was lost to sight as the "Alert" rounded Cape Rawson; but very heavy ice off Cape Union for a time completely obstructed our progress.

Excessive caution was necessary in handling the ship amongst these ponderous floes. Patience combined with perseverance are essential virtues inseparable to successful ice navigation, and they were constantly called into requisition in order to ensure a safe deliverance from the dangers which surrounded us.

A vigilant look-out had to be kept on the pack, and the ship was moved from time to time in order to avoid a "nip." Frequently we would observe a heavy floe coming into contact with the large grounded masses of ice that lined the coast, forcing them over, or crumbling them into shapeless fragments, thus clearly illustrating our own fate should we be so unfortunate as to be caught between the two.

The orders "up" and "down screw and rudder"

were given and executed several times during each day. As on our outward journey, preparations were now made for abandoning the ship at a moment's notice. Tents, clothing, cooking utensils, and all necessaries for a life on shore were spread out on the upper deck in readiness to be thrown on the ice in the event of such a catastrophe.

The cool way in which we all spoke of the probable loss of our home, and the prospect of being cast adrift at a moment's notice, was very remarkable. Perhaps the knowledge that our consort, the "Discovery," was within some forty miles of us, and therefore within easy travelling distance, might account for the light manner in which such a calamity was regarded; but it was impossible to disguise the fact that the loss of our good ship would be a very serious, not to say uncomfortable, event.

Steam had to be kept ready at a few minutes' notice, so as to take advantage of every little opening that might occur in the ice, even though we should only succeed in advancing a few hundred yards. On one occasion the ship was purposely forced into the pack, with which it drifted to the southward; but on the turn of the tide, when the ice began to drift in the opposite direction, it was no easy matter to free ourselves from the bondage to which we had voluntarily subjected ourselves. If it can be avoided, it is best not to allow a ship to get beset, even when the drift of the pack is favourable.

As we proceeded south, although our progress was slow, the change in the appearance and massiveness of the ice was very palpable. Occasionally we would meet small specimens of our palæocrystic friends, over which we had travelled during the preceding spring, but, as a rule, the ice was of a much lighter description. Still the floes were far heavier than those met with in Baffin Bay, and by no means to be despised.

During the time the ship was detained, waiting for the ice to open to allow her to proceed, our sportsmen were not idle, landing at all hours of the day and night in order to procure fresh food for the sick. So successful were they in their forays that the sick were supplied with a fresh meat meal daily,—geese, ducks, and hares forming the principal part of their "bags." The slaughter amongst the former was tremendous— entire flocks numbering from fifty to seventy birds falling victims to the prowess of not more than two guns, and within the short space perhaps of half an hour! The unfortunate birds being in the act of moulting were, of course, unable to escape the unerring aim of our marksmen.

In addition to crops of mustard and cress that we succeeded in raising on board, we were able to obtain small quantities of sorrel, which the convalescents were sent on shore to gather from the valleys and sides of the hills, often returning with sufficient to enable a limited allowance to be served out periodically. Sometimes the sick men were sent on shore themselves to *browse* on this excellent antiscorbutic.

On the morning of the 5th of August, being within twenty miles of the "Discovery," Egerton, accompanied by one of the men, was sent to give them information of our position. Our own ship was then, and had been for the past forty-eight hours, effectually jammed by the ice and unable to move. In the mean time we on board the "Alert" were endeavouring to get our vessel clean, and into something like order and ship-shape. On the following morning we sustained a slight "nip," caused by the ice setting rapidly in towards us. Our rudder head was badly wrenched before the rudder could be unshipped, and the iron tiller was bent and crippled. We only succeeded in easing the pressure by exploding some charges under the ice. In the forenoon Rawson, with two of the men belonging to the "Discovery," walked on board. We were, of course, delighted to see them and to hear news of our consort.

From them we learnt that poor Egerton had lost his way, and did not arrive on board their ship until after he had been wandering about for eighteen hours! The news from the "Discovery" was what we feared. Notwithstanding the large amount of musk-ox flesh procured by them during the autumn and following summer, scurvy had attacked her crew in almost the same virulent manner as it had ours. The return journeys of some of their sledge parties were simply a repetition of our own. Beaumont's division—the one exploring the north-western coast of Greenland—had suffered very severely, and we heard with extreme regret that two of his small party had succumbed to this terrible disease.

The rest of his men, with himself and Dr. Coppinger, had not yet returned to the "Discovery," having remained in Polaris Bay to recruit their healths. This was, indeed, a bitter ending to our spring campaign, on which we had all set out so full of enthusiasm and hope. It had the effect, however, of confirming Captain Nares in his resolution to proceed to England. With such broken-down crews it would have been folly indeed to have risked the rigours of a second Arctic winter; and there was really nothing left for us to do, Beaumont having done his work so well that it would have been impossible for us to have extended any exploration in that quarter. The "Discovery" had been afloat for some time, and was in perfect readiness to proceed to sea on the arrival of Beaumont and his party. Their absence caused us great anxiety, as the pack, being in motion between ourselves and Polaris Bay, and consequently where they would have to cross, made us fully alive to the risks and dangers they would encounter whilst crossing it. Still we hoped to hear of their safe arrival as soon as we should drop anchor alongside our consort in Discovery Bay.

The most important news was that a large seam of lignite of the Miocene period had been discovered within about three miles of their winter quarters. They had not been able to utilize this coal, but several large specimens had been carried to the ship—the result of experiments made being that it was reported, for steaming purposes, equal to the best Welsh coal.

Whilst imprisoned by the ice and waiting to escape, our naturalist made an interesting discovery within two hundred yards of the ship. On the beach, about twenty feet above high-water mark, he observed some wood which, on examination, proved to be portions of sledge runners and cross-pieces; also a snow scraper, made from the tusk of a narwhal or walrus, and a large lamp, apparently a piece of schistose rock hollowed out.* These relics are the most northern traces of Eskimos yet found. Their position would lead one to suppose that the wanderers had arrived so far north along the shores on the western side of the

---

* I have already referred to this discovery in my remarks on the migrations of the Eskimos, at p. 69.

channel, and from thence crossed over to the opposite Greenland coast; the cliffs to the northward being very steep, and although not actually impassable, great difficulty would be experienced in travelling along their base. This, and the absence of animal life, would readily account for their desire to leave such an inhospitable and sterile land.

On the 7th and 8th of August the ship was subjected to some very severe squeezes. On the latter day a large floe-berg pressed violently against the vessel and forced her on shore, lifting the stern bodily out of the water to a height of about five feet. The noise of the cracking of the beams and the groaning of the timbers was a sound that once heard will never be forgotten. To those below, the crumbling of the pitch in the deck seams sounded like a shower of hail on the upper deck. Fortunately for us the floe-berg was heavy and of deep flotation, and therefore grounded before it had time to cause the destruction of the ship. It was a grand sight to witness some of the neighbouring floe-bergs—great masses of ice from sixty to seventy feet in thickness—turned completely over and swept away by the pack in its irresistible career.

We had no time, however, to indulge ourselves in watching spectacles of such magnificence. Our position was by no means pleasant: any pressure upon the ship, caused by spring tides or otherwise, must inevitably crush her; and the prospect of another winter in the ice began to dawn upon us. There was apparently no escape, as, from our experience of the preceding year, we had cause to believe that, when once the floe-bergs grounded along the coast, they remained immoveable during the whole winter, and

REDUCING A FLOE-BERG.

here were we forced on shore by a floe-berg which had grounded immediately outside us. Our only chance was to reduce the huge mass of ice by which we were imprisoned, so as to lighten it sufficiently to float and drift away at high water. It was a bold idea; but it was no sooner resolved on than every available working man in the ship, irrespective of rank or station, was busily employed with axe, pick, or chisel in demolishing the obstruction. On the third day, so energetically was the work carried out, that the judicious explosion of a heavy charge of powder immediately under the berg had the effect of floating it away at high water, and the ship was released.

The pack being loose, we succeeded in making good progress, and on the following evening had the very great satisfaction of anchoring alongside the "Discovery," after having been separated from her for nearly twelve months. An interchange of visitors immediately took place. Local news, for want of more important intelligence, was fully and freely discussed, and the routine of the winter and the doings of the sledge parties formed topics of interesting conversation. The prolonged absence of Beaumont and his party acted as a damper upon our spirits, for we could not hide from ourselves the fact that their journey across the strait must be a hazardous one. So uneasy did Captain Nares feel regarding their safety that he determined upon going in search of them, even over to Polaris Bay. Accordingly, on Sunday morning, the 13th of August, having transferred all our sick and helpless hands to the "Discovery," and having our own ship's company supplemented by six men from our consort, we again made a start, but were stopped by heavy ice at the entrance of the harbour, through which it was quite impossible to penetrate. On the following day, to our great delight, we observed a tent pitched on the ice about three miles to the southward of the ship. A relief party was quickly formed, and in a few hours we had the extreme pleasure and satisfaction of welcoming Beaumont and his party on board, none the worse for what they had recently gone through, and almost indignant at all offers of assistance that were made to them. On account of the drifting of the pack over which they had been travelling, their work, during the last three or four days, had been excessively severe. On occasions they were compelled to continue the march for thirty-two and twenty-two consecutive hours without resting.

As the ice still remained packed and impenetrable, we were unable to advance, although more than one unsuccessful attempt was made to push on. On several occasions the dredge was hauled and with good and interesting results. The coal seam was also visited by different parties of officers. It exists in a visible seam on the northern side of a ravine, and is about three hundred yards long and twenty-five high. We were unable to ascertain its depth below the surface of the ground, or its thickness.

We were also very fortunate in finding a large number of vegetable fossils in the surrounding limestone, some of the leaf impressions being very clear and perfect. At the head of the ravine is a magnificent cave, formed by the two sides of the gorge and covered with a roof of frozen snow. This roof is apparently permanent, as when we visited the cave it was precisely in the same condition as when it was first discovered twelve months before! The

H.M.S. "ALERT" FORCED ON SHORE.

cave is very large, capable of accommodating easily sixty or seventy men.

During these excursions several butterflies were caught and brought on board as specimens, as also some flies, gnats, and other *diptera*. Many hares were also shot, to the great delight of our doctor, who had been working like a horse in order to bring his patients round.

The scenery in the channel between Bellot Island and the mainland, through which we passed in one of our vain attempts to get south, was very striking: bold cliffs, and hills rising to a height of two thousand feet on either side, intersected by deep ravines and gorges having almost precipitous sides and terminating in bays and little harbours.

On Sunday the 20th, by dint of boring and charging, at the expense, however, of our rudder head, we succeeded in forcing a passage through the ice in Lady Franklin Bay, and into a broad stream of water extending along the coast to the southward, which we fondly hoped would eventually lead us into open water.* But navigation in ice-bound seas is indeed uncertain. For on the following day we were compelled to seek refuge inside a land-locked and apparently well-protected and secure harbour. How deceitful was its appearance! Hardly an hour had elapsed after entering this sheltered retreat, before the "Alert" was severely nipped by a heavy floe and forced on shore.

For many hours the ship remained in a very critical position, as the tide receding left her completely high and dry, and listed over at an angle of 25°.

* At this time the "Pandora" was cruising in the entrance of Smith Sound, with an impenetrable barrier of ice blocking her way to the northward.

So steep was the bank on which we had been forced, that at low water we were able to walk, "dry shod," from the stem to the main chains, whilst aft the water was over our mizzen chains, and within a short distance of the taff-rail. A good sensational photograph and some sketches were made of the ship in this unpleasant position. Strenuous efforts were, of course, at once made to lighten and float the vessel. The fore part was entirely cleared, and the chain cables brought aft. A bower anchor was laid out astern in order to haul the ship off to.

The manner in which this latter work was performed was both novel and ingenious. A small but heavy piece of ice was secured and brought alongside the ship. On this was placed the anchor, as on a raft. It was then towed by boats to the position decided upon, when the raft was destroyed by exploding a charge of gunpowder immediately underneath it, the anchor, of course, sinking to the bottom.

With such good will did all work, that we had the joy and satisfaction of seeing our good ship afloat, and ready to proceed, in about fifteen hours from the time of the accident taking place. The bay, which was the scene of our mishap, was called Rawlings Bay, after one of our men, who was my sledge captain in all my expeditions. A musk-ox skull and the horn of a reindeer were picked up by Feilden close to where the ship was aground, proving that the neighbourhood is occasionally visited by these animals.

From this time, until the 9th of September, we were engaged in a never-ceasing struggle with the ice, frequently detained for many hours, and rarely advancing more than a few hundred yards during the day. The fast-forming ice reminded us unpleasantly of the near approach of winter, whilst the land had again assumed its wintry covering of snow. On the 22nd of August candles had to be used below at midnight for reading or writing. The young ice was found very tenacious, glueing and cementing the broken fragments of floes together. This caused such an impediment to our advance, although the pack was what is termed loose, that we were on several occasions compelled to relinquish all attempts at penetrating farther, and to secure the ships until a more favourable opportunity should occur. Our stock of coal, too, was getting alarmingly small, and had to be very carefully economized. Without the means of steaming, our chance of escape would, indeed, have been small.

On the 24th we rounded Cape Fraser;* on the 27th,† so slow was our progress, that we only just succeeded in getting into Dobbin Bay, where we were detained until the 3rd of September. The temperature had fallen to 19°. Last year we were frozen up on the 3rd of September, and here were we on the same date with as low a temperature and many miles to accomplish before we could actually be clear of the ice!

Snow also began to fall heavily, and everything appeared gloomy and inhospitable. As there was now a prospect of our being forcibly detained for another winter in the ice, and as some of our provisions were getting low, on passing the large depôt established in Dobbin Bay on our way up the

* On this day the "Pandora" succeeded in landing a party on Cape Isabella for the second time, searching for a record.

† On the 27th the "Pandora" was driven out of Smith Sound by a gale.

2 A

previous year, we landed and brought off all the tea, sugar, and chocolate, and such other articles as we were likely to require.

Whilst this work was in progress, a large ground seal (*Phoca barbata*) was shot by Hans, of the "Discovery," on which was found a partially healed wound; on further examination, an iron-pointed harpoon with an ivory socket, evidently of Eskimo construction, was discovered imbedded in its blubber. It would have been very interesting if we could have traced, by the manufacture of the instrument, the tribe to which it had belonged and the locality where the wound was inflicted.

One morning, when some little distance from the land, a small fox, of a mottled colour, wandered off to the ship, being attracted towards us either by hunger or curiosity. The officer of the watch, always on the *alert*, soon spied the little animal cruising about amongst the hummocks and shot it. The skin was preserved with the collection of natural history specimens, whilst the body was eaten by us at dinner and found to be delicious. Passing Cape Hawks, and Allman Bay, an inlet which was named after the distinguished President of the Linnæan Society, we continued to push the ships in the direction of open water to the south, which we at length reached.

It was with no small amount of thankfulness that on the 9th of September we emerged from the cold, grim clutches that seemed only too ready to detain us for another winter in the realms of the Ice King, and that we felt our ship rise and fall once more on the bosom of an undoubted ocean swell. It was, indeed, a joyous sensation to look around and see nothing but blue water, and, with the exception of a few straggling bergs, not a single speck of ice in sight. This broad sheet of water had for some time been known to us, having been observed from the summits of various hills that we had ascended, and all our energies of late had been concentrated into

ALLMAN BAY.

reaching it. We had a hard fight, but perseverance and patience ultimately proved triumphant.

On first reaching it, we found it to be coated with a thin layer of young ice, which offered a great deal of hindrance, although it had not the effect of checking us altogether. Our course through this young ice could be distinctly traced for a long distance astern, by a broad lane of water resembling the Suez Canal. At 6 p.m. we passed Cape Sabine, and distinguished our cairn on the top of Brevoort Island apparently untouched. Ahead was Cape Isabella, towards which we steered.

CHAPTER XXVII.

HOMEWARD BOUND.

> " Still in the yawning trough the vessel reels,
> Ingulfed beneath two fluctuating hills;
> On either side they rise, tremendous scene,
> A long dark melancholy vale between.
> The balanced ship, now forward, now behind,
> Still felt the impression of the waves and wind,
> And to the right and left by turns inclined."
>
> FALCONER.

> "*Montano.*—What from the cape can you discern at sea?
> *1st Gent.*—Nothing at all: it is a high-wrought flood;
>   I cannot, 'twixt the heaven and the main,
>   Descry a sail.
> *Montano.*—Let's to the seaside, ho!
> *3rd Gent.*—Come, let's do so;
>   For every moment is expectancy
>   Of more arrivance. (*Within.*) A sail! A sail!
> *4th Gent.*—The town is empty; on the brow of the sea
>   Stand ranks of people, and they cry—a sail!"
>
> *Othello.*

SHORTLY before midnight, on the 9th of September, Cape Isabella was reached and the ships were clear of Smith Sound. As, on our outward journey, to me had been allotted the duty of erecting a cairn on that prominent headland, and establishing a post office, so, on our return journey, was I assigned the duty of visiting the place in order to ascertain if letters had been deposited there during the period of our absence by any enterprising friend. On reaching the lower cairn, to my great surprise—for we hardly expected that any one would have visited the place since our departure the previous year—I found an additional cask had been placed alongside the one that I had established there. This was quickly opened, and found to contain a small mail for each ship.

Hurriedly leaving a record notifying our visit, we eagerly seized our treasures and made the best of our way to the boat. Great was the excitement when the news spread that a mail from England was actually on board, and we were soon deep in the enjoyment of perusing late letters from home, a pleasure to which we had so long been strangers.

Many were the heart-felt expressions of gratitude that rose to the lips of those lucky recipients of home news towards that gallant officer and friend who had so perseveringly and so generously, in spite of many dangers and difficulties, succeeded in depositing their letters so far north. The bulk of our mail we imagined had been left either at Disco or Upernivik. Had we examined the cairn on the summit of Cape Isabella, we should there have learnt that the same kind and disinterested friend had taken them to Littleton Island, and there safely deposited them. Being ignorant of this fact, and the weather being against our proceeding thither, a course was shaped to the southward; those who were under the impression that our English letters were really on that island being consoled by the fact that we were steering homewards, and that in a short time letters would be no longer necessary or of any value.

Wars, and rumours of wars, were prevalent, for our latest news came from England at the time when all Europe was disturbed and unsettled by the complexion of affairs in the East.

This made us all the more anxious to get home quickly; but alas! everything was against us. Tempestuous weather, with the wind *always* contrary, was our introduction to our own element, and, as our coal was running very short, we were obliged to put the ships under canvas and thrash them at it. Icebergs were innumerable, and, as the nights were increasing in length and the darkness in density, they were anything but pleasant neighbours.

On the 12th of September it was blowing so hard and the weather was so thick, that it was determined to seek an anchorage under the lee of the land in Whale Sound, and there wait until the weather moderated. With this object the ships were worked up under fore and aft sails and steam, eventually anchoring in a small bay (Bardin Bay) in close proximity to the Tyndall Glacier. As we came in we observed an Eskimo settlement on the eastern side of the bay, and several natives were seen running along the land towards us; but as the glacier intervened they were unable to communicate, and the weather was too bad to allow us to send a boat to them. This was much to be deplored, as, irrespective of the fact that these people were the first human beings that we had seen for many a long month, it was desirable that we should propitiate them in favour of white men, and for this purpose we had many little articles of infinite value to them, such as knives, needles, thread, scissors, etc., besides provisions, ready for their acceptance.

These natives were of the same tribe as those who were so kind to Kane and Hayes, and also to the "Polaris," so it would have been a good action, independently of all other reasons, could we have befriended them.

We had not been at anchor, however, more than five hours before a change of wind, accompanied by heavy squalls which came over the hills fast and furious, obliged us to get under weigh, and again put to sea, although the weather was as thick and the wind as strong as ever—added to which hail and snow showers were frequent: altogether a very unpleasant and miserable night was spent, for it was nearly midnight when we were forced to fly from our harbour.

On the 16th we were beating about off the entrance to Lancaster Sound, near Cape Byam Martin. This was all familiar ground to me, and brought back to my recollection scenes on board the old whaler, "Arctic," that had occurred in the same locality three years before. We made many tacks in our endeavours to weather Cape Walter Bathurst, but, for a long time, without success, for the wind invariably headed us on each tack.

On the 20th several eider-ducks, some turnstones, rotges, and snow-buntings were seen, but all going in a southerly direction, apparently anxious to seek warmer climes before the winter should have claimed both the sea and land. How we envied these birds their means of locomotion! for foul and strong winds causing slow progress, were beginning to be very irksome. Our old friends the "mollies" (fulmar petrels), that we had not seen for so long, again joined us, and might be seen continually darting down and picking up in their voracious maws all scraps that had been thrown overboard.

The persistent manner in which the bad weather clung to us was quite marvellous. Hardly a fine day

FULMAR PETRELS ("MOLLIES").

had been enjoyed since we emerged from the ice. The words of Falconer would have been applicable to us, and might have been repeated with truth every morning:

> "A lowering squall obscures the southern sky,
> Before whose sweeping breath the waters fly.
> *   *   *   *   *
> It comes resistless! and with foaming sweep,
> Upturns the whitening surface of the deep."

At length, after being buffeted about for many days, the high land of Disco was sighted on the 25th of September; and on the same day we came to an anchor in the little harbour of Godhavn, and congratulated ourselves once more upon our return to civilization.

The day, as if to make up for our previous bad weather, was a bright sunny one, and perfectly still and calm. This was all the more appreciated after the turbulent seas which had lately almost driven us distracted. The scenery coming in was very beautiful. On one side were the high cliffs of Disco, intersected here and there with deep fiords and bays, whilst on the other lay the perfectly quiescent sea, studded with icebergs of all shapes and sizes. Occasionally the surface of the water would be ruffled and disturbed by the appearance of a seal's head, as the inquisitive little animal would pop it up to gaze curiously at us as we steamed slowly by; or else a whale, as he swam lazily along, would give a flick with his huge tail, or spout a jet of water in the air, which might be taken either as a welcome back to more genial climes, or an angry remonstrance that a monster larger than himself should dare to live in his own particular domain. Birds flew around and alighted near us. One, a ger-falcon, was so bold as to venture to perch upon our fore-royal truck; but, I am ashamed to relate, was fired at for its misplaced confidence. It escaped, however, unhurt. Everything was bright and joyous, and all were happy and elated. Our joy was slightly marred on arrival to find that our mails had really been taken on and left at Littleton Island; but a mail, with letters of a later date than those brought out by the "Pandora," which had been got together and made up for us at

Copenhagen by my cousin, had just arrived in the Danish brig "Tjalfe."

Of course it could not be expected that, during the period of our absence from England, no sad changes should have taken place, and the sorrowful faces of more than one among us testified to the fact that some dear and loved ones would be seen no more in this world.

From Mr. Krarup Smith, the Inspector, we learnt that the "Pandora" had only taken her departure for England four days previously, having been unsuccessful in her endeavours to reach Cape Sabine. The attempt had only been relinquished by her commander when the lateness of the season compelled him to beat a retreat. A supply of beer, sent from England by my cousin, was found awaiting our arrival, and was most acceptable. A cask of beer had also been kindly left for our use by Allen Young, so that we were enabled to supply "all hands" with a glass of beer twice a week during the passage to England. Through the kindness of the Danish authorities, we were able to obtain thirty tons of coal, with a promise of thirty more if we chose to go to Egedesminde, another settlement about sixty miles to the southward. This was an offer too valuable to be disregarded, and was accepted by Captain Nares.

Having shifted our rudder, which, to use an American phrase, was "pretty considerably chawed up," from its treatment by the ice, and made good a few other defects, we took our departure from Godhavn on the morning of the 28th, Mr. Krarup Smith, the Inspector, coming on board to accompany us round to Egedesminde. As we steamed out of harbour the little three-gun battery fired a farewell salute, the ensigns on shore, and on board, were dipped, and the ladies (two in number), from their verandahs, waved with their pocket handkerchiefs a last adieu. It was a fine clear morning as we left; but a thick fog soon overtook us, in which we remained enveloped for the remainder of the day, and it was not until the following morning that we reached our destination.

Our way took us through a perfect labyrinth of small islands, some of the narrow channels through which we had to pass being almost blocked by large grounded masses of ice, remnants of icebergs. The "Alert" and "Discovery" being the first steamers that had ever visited Egedesminde, the natives turned out in force to witness our arrival. Several kayaks came skimming rapidly along the smooth and unruffled surface of the water as we approached, their occupants gazing with evident astonishment at the large "umiaks," whose motive power was to them invisible and incomprehensible. The Danish flag was run up on three separate flag-staves on shore, and a salute of seven guns was fired to welcome our arrival.

There is much similarity about the various Danish settlements in Greenland. The houses are of the same size and colour, and generally of about the same number, whilst all possess their little church, their storehouse, and their cooperage. The settlement is very prettily situated on the northern side of the largest of a group of many islands of all sizes. These are of the same metamorphic formation, and possess a more luxuriant vegetation than we had hitherto seen. The island is covered with numerous small lakes and ponds, and is extremely marshy and swampy. The difficulty of walking, without sinking up to the ankles in a bog, is very great.

The population of Egedesminde, which is the most southern settlement in the Inspectorate of North Greenland, is about one hundred and thirty souls, including the Danes, who with the Governor and his family number about twelve. The entire population of North Greenland is about four thousand three hundred.

The boggy substance, like peat, is dug up and stacked during the summer, and when dried is very generally used as fuel. The chief employment of the inhabitants is, as at the other settlements, that of collecting skins and blubber. Reindeer are obtained on the mainland, but they are not plentiful.

The Governor, Mr. Boldroe, was good enough to present us with a fine large haunch of venison; but, curious to relate, when served up, it had an unmistakeable taste and odour of musk! Our scorbutic patients, who were at this time nearly all convalescent, benefited largely from the quantities of fresh fish, principally cod, obtainable at this place.

On the morning of the 2nd of October, having received on board the amount of coal promised, we bade our kind friends farewell, and steamed away amidst the usual firing of guns and dipping of colours. The stoppages at these two civilized places were very pleasant breaks to us, after our long absence from society of any description, except our own, and were not regretted by any one. Indeed, the kindness and true hospitality extended to us by our Danish friends in the different settlements in Northern Greenland will long be remembered with feelings of gratitude and pleasure.

From the date of leaving this our last port until our arrival at Valentia, we experienced very tempestuous weather. Strong head winds were in constant attendance, and the ship's general state was being " battened down and under close-reefed topsails." Under these circumstances our daily rate of progress was remarkably slow, and on some days we found that we had actually increased our distance from home instead of having lessened it. Few on board had before experienced a longer continuance of really stormy weather. From the severe buffeting we received, our rudder, already crippled, was reduced to such a state as to be absolutely useless, the rudder-head being almost wrenched off, and we were obliged to steer the ship during the remainder of the voyage by means of the rudder pendants.

On the 16th of October, to the intense surprise of everybody, a vessel was sighted ahead, which proved to be the "Pandora." How very small is this world we live in! Here were we in the middle of the broad Atlantic, fifteen hundred miles from England, and out of the course of all ships, and yet actually meeting a vessel that had purposely come out to seek us.

The weather was too bad to allow us to communicate, but an interchange of news was effected by signal. The three ships remained in company for a couple of days, when they lost sight of each other in thick and blowy weather, we having previously ordered the "Discovery" to rendezvous at Queenstown in case of parting company.

Our rudder being in such a dilapidated state, Captain Nares determined upon putting in to Valentia for the purpose of shifting it, the spare one having in the mean time been temporarily repaired. With this object we anchored in the snug little harbour of Valentia, on the 27th of October, and here Captain Nares and several of the officers left for the purpose of proceeding at once to London to report our arrival.

> "Now, strike your sayles, yee jolly mariners,
> For we be come unto a quiet rode,
> Where we must land some of our passengers
> And light this wearie vessel of her lode.
> Here she awhile may make her safe abode."

It is in vain to attempt to describe the pleasure we all felt at beholding trees and green fields once more, with the cattle browsing in them. It is difficult at once to throw off old habits, and there were many on board who expressed their anxiety to land at once with their guns for the purpose of shooting "that herd of musk-oxen." Had we given way to our inclinations, I fear our reception would not have been so warm or so hospitable as it was.

The people of Valentia were the first to bid us welcome. Their kindness and hospitality will never be effaced from our memory. The rudder having been shifted, and sundry repairs executed, we took our departure on the following morning at daylight, being guided out of the place by a most eccentric and original old pilot. On the 29th we reached Queenstown, where we found the "Discovery" had arrived only a couple of hours before. Here again we received a warm welcome and enjoyed that hearty hospitality for which the Irish people are so justly celebrated. That evening we were the guests of the Port Admiral, he and Mrs. Hillyar hearing of no refusal, although we had to sit down to dinner in—well, clothes very dirty and very much the worse for wear. The next day, having taken in a supply of coals, we started for Portsmouth, the two ships remaining in company and arriving in that harbour together on the 2nd of November.

Our reception there and afterwards is a matter of history. Suffice it to say that our exertions received the approbation of our country and of our brother officers, and that the Lords of the Admiralty were pleased to express their satisfaction at the manner in which the expedition had been conducted by our leader, as well as at the way in which the work had been carried out by his subordinates.

My story has now come to an end. My aim has been to describe our daily life during a very eventful service.

I have quoted largely from my journal, and in some instances I have thought it best to copy from it *verbatim*.

Nothing is further from my thoughts than to claim for this narrative any literary merit whatever. I simply wish it to be regarded as a plain but accurate statement of facts—an unpretending account of the cruise of one of the ships of the late expedition—by one of its members.

In launching my little book upon the ocean of literature, I venture to quote the words of brave old

Master Beste, who, being engaged in compiling a record of another Arctic expedition, humbly apologizes, as I do, for submitting his work to the public:—"And herein I humbly pray pardon, for my rude order of writing, which proceedeth from the barren brayne of a souldier and one professing armes, who desireth rather to be wel thought of with your honour for his well meaning than for anye hys cunning writing at all."

FAREWELL!

INDEX.

Admiralty, Lords of, visit to the Polar ships, 9; satisfaction at the results of the expedition, 368.
Admiralty Inlet, remains of Eskimos on shores of, 68.
Albert Head, 65.
Aldebaran, erratic conduct of, 200.
Aldrich, Lieut. Pelham, R.N., skill in managing a kayak, 30; starts on a reconnoitring expedition in the autumn, 128; second autumn journey with dog-sledge, 133; starts on a third autumn journey, 136, 137; ascends a hill near Cape Joseph Henry, 147; glees by, 169, 216; his lecture on meteorology, 169; orchestra for the Royal Arctic Theatre, 171, 175, 214; plays the harmonium at church, 187; one of his dogs lost, 190; plays at Christmas, 194, 195; commands the extended party to the west, 241; anxiety for his safety, 331; return, 332.
Ale, prepared specially for the expedition, 17. (*See* Beer.)
"Alert," H.M.S., 1, 2; special fittings, 3; departure from Portsmouth, 9; leaves Berehaven, 12; commencement of the voyage,15; a lively ship, 17; arrival at Godhavn, 26; departure from Godhavn, 34; on shore, 43; proceeds to Cary Islands, 48; Port Foulke, 51, 56; perilous position of, 65, 91; at Hannah Island, 100; in Discovery Harbour, 104, 108, 393; on shore near Cape Beechey,

112; in the palæocrystic ice, 117, 118; crosses the threshold of the unknown region, 119; danger at Floe-berg Beach, 125, 134; precarious winter quarters, 125, 135, 136; housed in, 154; internal winter arrangements, 156; printing establishment, 165; departure of sledges from, 257; scurvy breaks out on board, 321; succour from, reaches N. division, 325; freed from winter quarters, 342; forced on shore, 351; afloat again, 347; at Valentia, 367. (*See* Winter Quarters.)
"Alexandra," H.M. sledge, 217, 259, 263.
Alexandra Bay, 61, 63.
Amusements in winter quarters, 167; importance of, 163. (*See* Theatricals.)
Anonyx nugax: crustacea brought up at the extreme northern point, 309 (*n.*).
Arctic Circle crossed by the expedition, 26.
Arctic Highlanders, 48. (*See* Eskimo.)
Arctic school, 166, 167. 213.
Arctic theatre. (*See* Theatricals.)
"Arctic," whaler, reminiscences of, 360.
Astronomical observatory, 153, 180.
Astronomy, lecture on, by Captain Nares, 169; by Commander Markham, 169.
Atanekerdluk, fossil plants at, 36.
Atlantic, gales of w'nd in, 17, 18.

Auks, Little. (*See* Rotges.)
Autumn depôt. (*See* Depôts.)
Autumn travelling, 128, 129, 133, 137 to 150; discomfort, 141; severe work, 147, 148; return from, 148, 149; results, 149.
Auxiliary sledges, 234.
Ayles, Adam, song by, 216.

Bache Island, of Hayes, not an island, 64.
Baffin, William, gave name to Woman Isles, 41.
Bag (sleeping), 139, 233, 235, 240, 279, 283, 287.
Baird Inlet, 57.
Baird, Cape, stopped by ice off, 103.
Banks Island, heavy pack on west coast, 200.
Bantry Bay. (*See* Berehaven.)
Bardin Bay, 359.
Barrow, Cape John, 93.
Bears, hunt in Melville Bay, 46; recent tracks, 86.
Beaumont, Lieutenant, H.M.S. "Discovery," his journey along the north coast of Greenland, 346; return of, 350.
Beechey, Cape, Eskimo remains at, 69; lane of water in direction of, 102, 112, 113; rounded, 114.
Beer at Godhavn, 363.
Bellot, Cape, 103, 112; Island, 112, 351.
Berehaven, expedition at, 12.
Bessels Bay, entrance passed, 100; description of, 101.
Bessels, Dr., observation as to meetings of tides at Cape Fraser, 92; coast-line correctly delineated by, 99.
Beverley, crimson cliffs of, 48.
Bide-a-wee Harbour, 58. (*See* Payer Harbour.)
Bills of fare, 185, 186, 196, 335. (*See* Play-bills.)
Birds of the Arctic regions, 24, 35, 50; Brent geese, 345; dovekies, 50, 101; eider duck, 101, 131, 360; falcon, 362; fulmar petrel, 361; glaucous gulls, 50; ivory gulls, 50, 101, kittiwakes, 50; king ducks, 50, 332; knots, 110; looms, 40, 50; ptarmigan, 225; rotges, 46, 50, 360; skuas, 332; terns, 110, 332; turnstones, 360.
Birthdays, celebration of, 184, 185.
Black, Cape, 253.
Blasting the ice, 87, 89, 90, 341, 349.
"Bloodhound," H.M. sledge, 259, 263.
Boats for the expedition, 4; search for, left by Hayes, 53, 55; on a sledge, 58; jolly-boat of "Valorous" landed in Dobbin Bay, 84; turned in on their davits owing to height of ice, 90; advanced to northward of ship, 133; hauled up during winter quarters, 157; on sledges, 242 (*n.*); in Parry's expedition, details of, 243 (*n.*); painted, 245; care of, on sledge, 279; abandonment of, by Commander Markham, 288, 289, 318.
Boldroe, Mr., governor of Egedesminde, 365.
Botanical collections, 31.
Botany. (*See* Vegetation.)
Bottle-nose whales, 20.
Brent geese, 345.
Brevoort Island, 57; cairn on, 356.
Brevoort Cape in sight, 103.
"Bruin," largest dog on board, 210.
Bryant, Geo., H.M.S. "Discovery," serving in the "Alert," 169.
Buchanan Strait, Eskimo remains at, 69.
"Bulldog," H.M. sledge, 217, 259, 263.
Burroughs, Geo., ship's steward, H.M.S. "Alert," acts in *Chops of the Channel*, 173.
Butterflies, 351.
Byam Martin Cape, 360.

Cairns at the Cary Islands, 49; at Life-boat Cove, 53; at Cape Isabella, 56; on Brevoort Island, 356; ancient cairns on Washington Irving Island, 85; on Hannah Island, 101; at Lincoln Bay, 117; at the "Alert's" winter quarters, 384.

Cairn Hill, 219, 220, 221, 225; cairn built, 341.
Cane, Fredcrick, armourer, H.M.S. "Alert," songs by, 169, 215.
Carl Ritter Bay, 99.
Cary Islands, 48; depôt on, 49, 84.
Castletown. (*See* Berehaven.)
Cave in the snow, 350.
Cetaceans, various kinds, 20, 21.
"Challenger," H.M. sledge, 217, 259.
Chlorine observations, 180.
Chops of the Channel, play acted by the men, 173.
Chorus, grand palæocrystic, 216.
Christmas in the Arctic regions, 192 to 197; bill of fare, 196; poem on, 196.
Clavering, Captain, Eskimo seen by, on east coast of Greenland, 69.
"Clements Markham," H.M. sledge, 217; starts for "Discovery," 248.
Clements Markham Inlet, 288.
Clothing during winter, 159, 160; sledging, 239. (*See* Foot-gear.)
Coal, discovery of, 350; offer of, at Egedesminde, 363.
Cod-fish, 21, 25, 365.
Colan, Dr., H.M.S. "Alert," his lecture on food in the Arctic regions, 169; medical instructions to officers of sledges, 238; skilful treatment of Petersen, 255; attention to scurvy patients, 333, 338, 345.
Cold, extreme, 208, 222, 224. (*See* Temperature.)
Collinson, Cape, 94.
Cook, while sledging, 235, 265.
Cooking apparatus, weight, 233; description, 235.
Copenhagen, letters sent out from, 363.
Coppinger, Dr., H.M.S. "Discovery," state of lime-juice found by, in Polaris Bay, 305; journey with Lieut. Beaumont, 346.
Cress. (*See* Mustard and Cress.)
Crimson cliffs of Beverley, 48.
Crinoids dredged up, 73.
Crow's-nest, description, 3; Captain Nares constantly in, 66; a cold berth, 98.
Crozier Island passed, 98.
Crustaceans dredged up at the extreme northern point, 309.
Cryolite mine in Greenland, 20.
Crystal Palace Glacier, 50.

Dancing at Christmas, 197; old year, 204.
Darkness, approach of, 127; in sledge travelling, 141; in winter, 178, 182; monotony of, 207.
Davis, John, musicians in the expedition of, 8; gave name to Cape Desolation, 22, 23.
Davis Strait, 18, 19, 20.
Daylight. (*See* Light.)
Deaths. (*See* Petersen, Porter, "Discovery.")
Depôts on Cary Isles, 49; Cape Isabella, 56; Dobbin Bay, 85, 353; Cape Collinson, 95; Cape Morton, 102; Lincoln Bay, 117, 248; Floe-berg Beach, 122, 124; near Cape Joseph Henry, 147, 149, 263, 321; to southward of Floe Berg Beach for "Discovery" sledges, 255; for sledge parties, 234.
"Deptford," snow storehouse so called, 154.
Desolation, Cape, 22.
Diptera, 351.
Disco, 6, 18, 34, 358, 362; tradition of, 33, 34; view from hills of, 31. (*See* Godhavn.)
Disco Bay, 31.
"Discovery," H.M.S., 95; departure from Portsmouth, 9; commencement of voyage, 15; sighted off Greenland coast, 25; towed by the "Alert," 41; following, 45; sent to communicate with natives at Cape York, 48; at Port Foulke, 56; perilous position, 65; grounds off Cape Louis Napoleon, 90; in great danger, 91; blown from her anchors, 95; lands a depôt at Cape Morton, 100; in harbour, 104; winter quarters of, 107; sledge crew from, joins the

374   INDEX.

"Alert," 108; theatre on board, 174; a health to, 217; depôts laid out for sledges of, 227; work of sledge parties, 242; arrangement for opening communication with, from "Alert," 246, 255; to return to England, 330; joined by "Alert," 344, 345; scurvy among crew of, 346; two deaths, 346; rendezvous at Queenstown, 367.
Discovery Harbour, 104, 106, 112; "Alert" arrives at, 347.
Distant, Cape, walk to, 110; "Alert" passes, 112.
Divine service, 187; on Christmas day, 195; before sledges start, 258, 259.
Dobbin Bay, 83, 86; depôt at, 84, 353.
Dock cut in the ice at Dobbin Bay, 86.
Dockyard. (See Portsmouth.)
Dog-driver. (See Petersen.)
Dogs, Eskimo, 29, 38, 78, 79; disease, 79; wailing, 88; habits, 130; sledging, 80, 81, 128; dog "Sallie" lost and found, 190, 191; alarm of during winter, 199; nearly steal musk-ox beef, 207; alarm caused by, 210; regularly fed, 210; team sent with sledge to "Discovery," 247, 255; trouble with, 253. (See Bruin, Sallie, Flo, Nellie.)
Dovekies, 50, 101, 115.
Draba, 57, 340.
Dredging, 25, 73, 102.
Driftwood, 112.
Drip. (See Snow.)
Drip, inconvenience of, in winter, 182.
Ducks. (See Birds.)
Dumb-bell Bay, 131.
Dundas Harbour, remains of Eskimos at, 68.
D'Urville, Cape, passed, 83.

Edinburgh, H.R.H. the Duke of, visit to Arctic ships, 8.
Egedesminde, offer of coals at, 363; expedition at, 364, 365.

Egerton, Lieut. George Le Clerc, R.N., officer of the watch when the ship touched the first ice, 22; starts on autumn travelling, 133; stage manager of the Royal Arctic Theatre, 171; parts taken by, 174, 214; sails his sledge, 231 (n.); sent to open communication with "Discovery," 247; his efforts to save Petersen, 249 to 254; second start for the "Discovery," 255; sent to the "Discovery," 345.
Eider ducks, 131, 360.
Electricity, observations on, 180.
Ellesmere Land, 50.
Eskimo, Frederic, 29, 128; Hans Hendrick, 39, 48, 354; pilot, 42. (See Dogs.)
Eskimos, 33; at Proven, 38; Cape York, 48; Etah, 52; traces of, in Payer Harbour, 58; in Twin-glacier Bay, 61, 62; wanderings, 67, 69; Admiral Sherard Osborn and Mr. Clements Markham on wanderings of, 68, 69; remains on Capes Sabine, Hilgard, Louis Napoleon, Hayes, Fraser, shores of Buchanan Strait, Radmore Harbour, and Bellot Isle, 69; at Admiralty Inlet and Dundas Harbour, 68; at Cape Beechey, 69, 347; in Whale Sound, 359.
Etah, native village, 52, 69.
Eugénie, H.I.H. the Empress, present of woollen caps from, 7, 236, 239, 287; visits the Arctic ships, 8.
Exercise during winter, 181, 187; for sledging crews, 227, 228.

Falcon, 362.
Farewell banquets, 8; to the expedition at Portsmouth, 9, 10, 11; to the "Valorous," 35.
Farewell Cape, 19, 23, 69.
Feilden, Captain, naturalist, H.M.S. "Alert," ascends hill above Bessels Bay, 101; visits Distant Cape, 110; his lecture on geology, 169; picks up skulls in Rawlings Bay, 352. (See Naturalist.)

INDEX. 375

Ferbrache, Wm., sledge crew, N. division, symptoms of scurvy, 306.
Figure-heads of the Arctic ships, 4.
Finner whale, 20.
Fire, precautions against, fire-hole, 160, 161; alarm of, 226.
Fishing on the Torske bank, 25
Fiskernaes, expedition off, 24.
Fitting out the expedition, 1 to 8.
"Flo," Eskimo dog, met with adrift, near Cape Joseph Henry, 323.
Floes. (See Ice.)
Floe-bergs, description of, 114; "Alert" secured inside a fringe of, 122, 125; split by intense cold, 211.
Floe-berg Beach, depôt at, 122, 124; desolate scene at, 126; view from, 127; winter quarters at, 132.
Flowers. (See Vegetation.)
Foot-ball on the ice, 77.
Foot-gear, while sledging, 260, 261, 268, 280.
Foraminifera brought up at the extreme north point, 309.
Fossils, collections in Bessels Bay, 102; in the coal, 350.
Fossil plants, at Atanekerdluk, 37; in the coal near Discovery Harbour, 350.
Foulke Port, 51, 56, 69, 330.
Foxes, traces of, 60, 107; fox shot, 354.
Fox trap, 68.
Francombe, Reuben, H.M.S. "Alert," parts and songs by, 173.
Franklin Pierce Bay, 72.
Fraser, Cape, 55, 72; Eskimo remains on, 68; passed by the ships, 92; meeting of the tides, 93; rounded, going south, 353.
Frederick VII., Cape, ship in danger off, 114.
Frederic, 29, 128. (See Eskimo.)
Freezing, experiments in, 223.
Fresh meat, 186. (See musk-ox, hares, Brent geese.)
Frost-bites, danger of, 81; Petersen frost-bitten in the autumn, 129; danger of, in autumn travelling, 142; many frost-bites in return autumn journey, 147; Lieut. May's severe frost-bite, 148; other frost-bites and amputations, 148; sufferers during the winter, 198; precautions against, 199, 208; on the dog sledge, in journey to "Discovery," 249.
"Frost-bite Range," 148.
Frozen ocean, 200, 215; depôts cannot be laid out on, 234, 244; difficulty of travelling over, 242; movements of, 242. (See Palæocrystic Sea. Sledgings.)
Fulmar petrels, 361.

Gales of wind in the Atlantic, 17, 18; in Smith Sound, 59; in Robeson Channel, 119; at Floe Berg Beach, 124; furious gale during autumn travelling, 133 134; in winter quarters, 205 206; while sledging, 282, 283, 285, 296, 297; on the voyage home, 366, 367.
Geese. (See Brent.)
Geology, lecture on, by Captain Feilden, 169.
Geological collections, 31, 102, 116, 350. (See Fossils.)
Geological formation, 64, 67, 68; physical aspect of the coast lines, 99.
Ger-falcon, 362.
Giffard, Lieut. R.N., H.M.S. "Alert," magnetic observer, 154; in charge of the printing, 164 (n.), 169, 175, 215, 216; lecture on magnetism by, 169; parts taken by, in theatricals, 214.
Gilbert, Sir Humphrey, musicians on board ship of, 7.
Glaciers: of Jacobshavn, 32; of the Waigat, 36; of Omenak fiord, 38; near Cape York, Petowik, 48; Crystal Palace, 50; my brother John's (of Kane), 52; twin glaciers, 60, 61; of Grinnell Land, 64, 73, 83; in Bessels Bay, 99; Tyndall, 359.
Glaucous gulls, 50.
Godhavn, arrival at, 26; lovely

376 INDEX.

weather at, 33; hospitality of the people, 33, 363, 364.
Godthaab, expedition off, 24.
Good, Joseph, petty officer, H.M.S. "Alert," song by, 168.
Gore, Wm., stoker, H.M.S. "Alert," song oy, 216.
Grampus, 21.
Grand palæocrystic chorus, 216.
Greenland, streams of ice, sweep down east coast of, 23; coast of, 25; natives on east coast, 69; insularity of, argument from tides, 92; distant view from Floeberg Beach, 128; exploration of northern coast, 242, 346.
"Greenwich," observatory at winter quarters so called, 152.
Grinnell Land, description of, 67, 72; coast line, 94.
Gulls, 50, 101, 332, 360.
Guy Fawkes' day celebrated, 179.

Hair frozen into solid masses, 209; effect of sledge travelling on colour of, 334.
Hakluyt Island, 50.
Hall Basin, 100, 101.
Haloes, 200.
Hannah Island, ships anchored inside, 100; visit to, 101.
Hans Egede, 24.
Hans Hendrik, Eskimo engaged at Proven, 39; endeavour to engage his brother-in-law, 48; seal shot by, 354.
Hares, traces of, 60, 107; at "Alert's" winter quarters, 211; traces of, on the Polar Sea, 296, 314; left by Captain Nares for N. division, 321; shot, going south, 345, 351.
Harmonium, obtained from the "Valorous," at church, 187.
Hartstene Bay, arrival at, 51.
Hawks, Cape, 83.
Hayes, Dr., 51, 52, 53, 72, 73, 85, 99, 360.
Hayes, Cape, Eskimo remains on, 69; ascent of, 90.
Hayes Sound, 60; tides in, 62; intended exploration, 330.

Henry Island of Hayes, not an island, 64.
"Hercules," H.M. sledge, Lieut. W. H. May, R.N., 137, 217.
Hilgard, Cape, Eskimo remains on, 69.
Hoskins, Commodore A. H., sledging flag-staff presented by, 307.
Housing for winter quarters, 154, 155, 156.
Hudson's Bay Company's Toboggans, suitable in soft snow, 281.
Hummocks, difficulty of marching over, on the Polar Sea, 278, 279, 281, 284, 301; discoloured by mud, 301; great barrier of, 303; great size, 304, 305; different colours of, 316.
Hunt,Wm., ward-room cook, H.M.S. "Alert," songs by, 214.
Hydrostatics, lecture on, by Lieut. May, 169.

Ice, first seen, 22; stream of, near Cape Farewell, 23; the middle pack, 44, 45; dangers, 65, 66; occupations when detained by, 66; ships stopped by, 57, 65, 73, 82, 90, 95, 103, 110, 113, 121, 344; amusements on the, 77; dock cut in the, 86; great height of, 89; increasing thickness, 96; extending across Hall Basin, 100; pressure on Cape Frederick VII., 114; of the Polar Ocean, 127, 147, 200; the dangerous state of the, in autumn travelling, 141; movement of, during winter, 184; character of, in travelling over the Polar Ocean, 284, 291, 300; symptoms of disruption, 315, 320; state of, on the voyage southward, 344. (See Palæocrystic, Blasting, Floe-bergs, Hummocks.)
Ice navigation, most important maxim in, 45; uncertainty of, 57, 64; qualities required for, 82.
Icebergs first sighted, 22; constantly seen, 23; in Disco Bay, 32, 34; danger from, in the

INDEX. 377

Waigat, 38; indicate shoal water, 60; danger from, off Albert Head, 65; ships endangered by, 91; number decreasing, 96; innumerable, 359.
Independence, Cape, of Kane, 98.
Insects collected, 351.
Isabella, Cape, 356, 357; Captain Markham lands at, 56, 57, 95; letters at, 358.
Itivdliarsuk glacier, 36.
Ivory gull, 46, 50, 101.

Jacobshavn, glacier of, 32.
John Barrow, Cape, 93.
Jolliffe, Thos., petty officer, H.M.S. "Alert," in N. division sledge party, holds out to the end, 326 (*n*).
Joseph Henry, Cape, 127; Aldrich starts for, in the autumn, 136; depôt near, 147; dog "Sallie" lost at, 190; arrival of sledges at, 263; floes off, 282; encamped abreast of, 285; description of, 285; northern division of sledges reaches, 321; last seen, 343.

Kane, Dr., his open polar sea, 72, 98, 360.
Kardluk Point, in the Waigat, 36.
Kayak, difficulty of using, 30; adventure of Mr. Wootton, 30; Eskimo pilot in, 43.
Kennedy Channel crossed, 103; musk-oxen on east side of, 103.
"Kew," magnetic observatory at winter quarters so called, 154.
Kew Observatory, thermometer tested at, 223.
King ducks, 50, 332.
Knapsacks, sledging, contents, 235, 236.
Knots, seen and secured at Distant Cape, 110.

Lady Franklin Inlet, 103, 111.
Lafayette Bay (of Kane), 98, 99.
Lancaster Sound, geology, 67; remains of Eskimo on shores of, 68; "Alert" off mouth of, 360.
Lemmings, traces of, 107; description, 115, 116; eaten by "Nellie," 212; traces away from the land, 278.
Letters at Cape Isabella, 358; at Godhavn, 363; at Littleton Island, 358, 362.
Lieber, Cape, 102.
Lievely, 26. (*See* Godhavn.)
Life-boat Cove, visit to, 53.
Light, lecture on, by Lieut. Parr R.N., 169; return of, 207, 225.
Lime-juice, regular daily issue of, 16; impossibility of using, while in a frozen state, away sledging, 238; taken on the sledges by Commander Markham and Lieut. Parr, 238; served out to sledge crew by Commander Markham, 305; useless unless the whole volume is thawed, 305; its use in the treatment of scurvy, 329; used on all sledge journeys when its use was possible, 330.
Lincoln Bay, 115; coast between, and Cape Union, 121; depôt, 117, 248.
Little Vulgar Boy, play acted by the officers, 214.
Littleton Island, visit of Captain Nares and Commander Markham to, 53, 55; not visited, going south, 358; mail at, 358, 362.
Looms (*see* Birds), 40, 41.
Loom soup, 40.
Louis Napoleon, Cape, Eskimo remains at, 69; passed by the ships, 90.
Lyngenmarkfjeld, in Disco, ascent of, 31.

M'Clintock, Admiral Sir Leopold, sledge of, the best, 281; superintends outfit of expedition, 2; his detention in the Melville Bay pack, 44; sledge equipments superintended by, 231; on the absurdity of taking frozen limejuice on sledges, 238; tea-leaves recommended by, 316.
Magnetic observations, 31; while sledging, 73, 180, 305; snow observatory for, 152, 153, 209.

INDEX.

Magnetism, lecture on, by Lieutenant Giffard, R.N., 169.
"Marco Polo," H.M. sledge, 137, 217, 259.
Marine shells found above sea-level, 116.
Markham, Commander Albert H., R.N., visit to Littleton Island, 53; to Cape Isabella, 56; to Hannah Island, 101; to Distant Cape, 110; starts on an autumn reconnaissance, 128; starts on second autumn sledge journey, 133; on main autumn sledge journey, 137, 144; in charge of magnetic observations, 154; lecture on astronomy, 169; parts taken by, 174, 214; followed by a wolf, 228; takes lime-juice on his sledge, 238; in command of the northern division of sledges, 242, 311; attains the most northern point ever reached by man, 309, 311; resolves to abandon large boat, 288, 289; serves out lime-juice, 305.
Markham, Clements, on Eskimo wanderings, 68. (*See* Clements Markham.)
"Markham Hall," store-house at winter quarters, 152; demolition of, 210.
Maskell, William, H.M.S. "Alert," songs by, 169, 216; parts taken by, 174; sledge crew, N. division, holds out to the end, 317, 318 (*n.*).
May, Lieutenant W.H., R.N., starts on autumn travelling, 137; severely frost-bitten, 147; suffers amputation, 148; astronomical observer, 152; his lecture on hydrostatics, 169; manager of the theatre, 214; glee sung by, 216; sails his sledge, 231 (*n.*); comes to the rescue of the northern division, 325; goes to succour Aldrich's party, 331, 332.
Medical staff, their tests of the physical capacity of the officers and men, 15; unremitting care of the sick, 333.

Medical inspections, 187, 204, 258, 326, 337.
Medical stores for sledges, 238 (*n.*); weight, 233.
Medical instructions to commanders of sledges, 238.
Melville Bay, 18, 44; passage through, 44; bear hunt in, 46.
Melville Island, remains of Eskimo at, 69; musk-oxen at, 106.
Men of the expedition, selection of, 4; tests of physical capacity, 15; regular daily issue of lime-juice to, 16; always reliable in an emergency, 125; sufferings and excellent conduct in autumn travelling, 134, 145; their good humour and wit, 146; frost-bites and amputations, 148; clothing during winter, 159, 160; school for, in winter, 166, 167, 213; theatricals, 171, 173; Christmas cheer, 195; fondness for dancing, 195, 197, 204; excellent health, 204; paleness on return of sun, 211; heroic conduct while sledging, 277, 286, 287, 291, 302, 310, 311, 313, 316, 352.
Meteor, brilliant, seen at winter quarters, 201.
Meteorites at Ovifak, 31.
Meteorological observations, 162, 180, 183, 223.
Middle pack, Captain Nares's resolve to take the, 44.
Miocene Period, coal of, discovered, 347.
Mollies, 361.
Moon, 181. (*See* Paraselenæ.)
Moravian missionaries, 24.
Morton, Cape, 100, 102; depôt of, 100.
Morton, Mr., his "open polar sea," 93; description of Cape Constitution, accurate, 98; unable to ascend cliff, 98.
Mosquitoes, plague in Greenland, 32.
Moss, Dr., surgeon, H.M.S. "Alert," reading by, 168; lecture on mock moons under the microscope, 169; makes a balloon on Guy Fawkes'

day, 180; paints scenery for theatre, 171; succours the northern division, 326; sketch for bill of fare by, 335; paints the boats, 245.
Murchison Sound, 50.
Musical instruments, 7. (*See* Harmonium, Piano.)
Musicians in the ships of Sir H. Gilbert and John Davis, 7, 8.
Musk-oxen, traces of, 60, 61; hunting, 104; range of, 106; traces in Discovery Harbour, 107; beef presented by "Alert" to "Discovery," 108; hunt in Shift-Rudder Bay, 113; quantity of meat from, 186, 204; meat nearly stolen by dogs, 207; in the summer, 338.
Mustard and cress grown in the "Alert," 205, 211, 345.

Nares, Captain George S., R.N., resolves to take the middle pack, 44; visits Life-boat Cove and Littleton Island, 53; constant vigilance, 66; visits Hannah Isle, 101; ascends hill above Cape Morton, 102; selects winter quarters for "Discovery," 107; observes opening in the pack, 114; catches a lemming, 115; desirous of finding a more sheltered spot for winter quarters, 128, 135; his account of sledge travelling, 140; lecture on astronomy, 169; gives name to the Palæocrystic Sea, 200; excellent health and spirits of those under his command at the commencement of the New Year, 204; lecture on sledging experiences, 215; arrangement for opening communication with "Discovery," 246; unjust attack upon, regarding lime-juice, 237; absurdity of the charge against him, 238; his Union Jack taken with northern division, 258; at Cape Joseph Henry Depôt, 321; leaves hares for northern division, 321; comes to the relief of the northern division, 325, 327; decision to return home, 337, 346;
anxiety for safety of Beaumont, 349; accepts offer of coal at Egedesminde, 363; lands at Valentia, 367; satisfaction of the Admiralty with his conduct of the Expedition, 368.
Narwhal hunting, 59.
Naturalist, zeal in a gale of wind, 19; visit to Ovifak, 31; finds Eskimo remains at Cape Beechey, 69; ascends hill in Bessels Bay, 101; at distant Cape, 110. (*See* Feilden, Captain.)
"Nellie," Commander Markham's black retriever, coveted by Eskimos at Proven, 39; dislike of Eskimo dogs, 78; surprise at the tabogganing, 188; stood the cold well, 188, 189; adventure with, in the unifilar house, 209, 210; eats the lemmings, 212; followed by a wolf, 228.
Nelson, Lord, an old Arctic officer, 179.
New Year's day, 202, 203, 204.
Nip, preparations for, 65, 71, 83; off Cape M'Clintock, 94; south of Cape Beechey, 348. (*See* Ice.)
Norman-Lockyer Island, Eskimo remains on, 69, 74; visited, 73.
North extreme, camp, 307, 308; farthest point ever reached, 309, 311.
"North Water," of Baffin Bay, 47; of Smith Sound, 72, 97.
Northumberland Island, 50.
Norton Shaw Cape, passed by the ships, 94.

Observations, scientific, in winter quarters, 180; difficulties, 180; while sledging, 305; at farthest northern point, 307, 310. (*See* Magnetic, Meteorological, Astronomical.)
Observatories, wooden, for transit instrument, 152; magnetic, 154, dismantling of, 227.
Officers, selection, 4; tests of physical capacity, 15; amusements, 167; lectures by, 169; theatricals, 169, 173; scientific observations, 180; birthdays celebrated, 184;

Christmas, bill of fare for, 196; approval of decision of Captain Nares to return, 337. (*See* under names.)
Omenak fiord, discharging glaciers in, 38.
Orchestra, Royal Arctic Theatre, 171.
Osborn, Rear-Admiral Sherard, C.B., dedication to, v.; on Eskimo wanderings, 68.
Ovifak, visit of naturalist to, 31.

Pack. (*See* Ice.)
Palæocrystic Sea, name given, 200, 234. (*See* Frozen Ocean.)
Palæocrystic floes in Robeson Channel, 92, 114, 118.
Palæocrystic grand chorus, 216; sung at the most northern position ever reached by man, 310.
"Pandora" brings letters to Cape Isabella, 358; at Godhavn, 363; sighted in the Atlantic, 366.
Paraselenæ, 181, 200.
Parr, Lieut. A. C. C., R.N., ascends the hill above Bessels Bay, 101; starts on autumn travelling, 133, 137, 144; sledge goes through the ice, 144; in charge of astronomical observatory, 152; lecture on light by, 169; takes limejuice on his sledge, 238; an indefatigable road-maker, 286; sent to the ship for help, 322, 325.
Parry, Sir Edward, his farthest northern point passed, 150; his sense of the importance of exercising and improving the minds of the men in winter quarters, 163, 166; attempt to reach the pole, 243 (*n.*).
Parry Islands, Eskimo remains on shores of, 68.
Payer Harbour, 58.
Pearce, Alfred, H.M.S. "Alert," songs by, 216; severely frost-bitten, 286; attacked by scurvy, 289.
Pemmican, 237, 270.
Pendulum Islands, Eskimos met with near, 69.
Petermann fiord, 100; fine view of, 103.

Petersen, Danish dog-driver, autumn travelling, 128, 129; starts for "Discovery," 248; frost-bitten, 248; efforts to save his life, 248 to 254; brought back to the ship, 254; death of, 255, 321.
Petowick glacier, 48.
Photographing at Godhavn, 31.
Pinkey and Collins' patent topsails, 3.
Plants, 31, 57, 60, 74, 107. (*See* Vegetation.)
Plays. (*See* Theatricals.)
Play-bills, 173, 175, 176, 214.
Plymouth, visit from Commander-in-Chief, 11.
Polar Ocean, 122, 128, 215, 234, 242; Parry's attempt to sledge over, 243 (*n.*); march of the northern division over, 276, 311 (*see* Hummocks), 285, 301; young ice, 296.
Polaris Bay, 100; state of limejuice found in, 305; sledge-crew recruiting at, 346, 349.
"Polaris," visit to her second winter quarters, 53, 54; her cruise, 72; Dr. Bessels of, 92, 99; land seen from, 101; musk-ox shot by crew of, 106; Eskimo kind to crew of, 360.
Polarization of light, observations, 180.
"Poppie," H.M. sledge, Lieut. Giffard, 217, 259.
Poppies, 57, 74.
Popular entertainments in winter quarters, 168, 169; programmes, 175, 176.
Portsmouth Dockyard, ships fitting out at, 1; harbour, departure of expedition from, 9, 10; return to, 368.
Potentillas, 340.
Prayers, 187. (*See* Divine service.)
Presents to the expedition, 6, 7, 193, 194.
President Land has no existence, 101.
Prince Patrick Island, heavy pack on west coast of, 200.

INDEX. 381

Prince Regent Inlet, formation of cliffs, 64, 67.
Printing office in winter quarters, 164, 165; prospectus, 164; bills of fare, 185.
Prologue, Royal Arctic Theatre, 172, 173.
Protococcus nivalis, 48.
Proven, arrival at, 38; survey of, 39.
Provisions for sledging, weight, 233; scale, 237.
Ptarmigan, 225.
Pullen, Rev. W. H., chaplain, H.M.S. "Alert," glees by, 216; lecture on Arctic plants, 169; author of the prologue, 171, 172, 176; leads the choir, 187; Christmas bill of fare by, 196; lines on the New Year by, 202; a burlesque operetta written by, 214; grand chorus composed by, 216; service on departure of sledges, 258, 259; lines welcoming return of sledges by, 336.

Queenstown, rendezvous at, 367.

Radmore, John, chief carpenter's mate, H.M.S. "Alert," sledge crew in northern division, holds out against scurvy, 318; to the last, 326 (n.).
Radmore Harbour, Eskimo's remains at, 69.
Rainbow, 325.
Rawlings, Thos., petty officer, H.M.S. "Alert," captain of sledge, northern division, attacked by scurvy, 306.
Rawlings Bay, 352.
Rawson, Lieutenant Wyatt, R.N., joins the "Alert" from the "Discovery," 108; visits Distant Cape, 110; glees by, 169; parts taken in theatricals by, 174, 214; skill in tabogganing, 187; visit to snow hut built by, 212; accompanies Egerton on journey to "Discovery," 247; his efforts to save Petersen, 249 to 254; arrives from "Discovery," 346.

Rawson Cape, 219, 343.
Records left at Cape Isabella, 57; in cairn on Hannah Island, 101; at extreme northern point, 312; at Cairn Point (winter quarters), 341.
Reindeer, Port Foulke, 52; traces, 60; scarce near Egedesminde, 365.
Retrospect on New Year's day, 197.
Reward for crossing 83rd parallel, 292 (n.).
Richardson Bay, 99.
Right whales, 21.
Rink, Dr., on the Eskimo, 33.
Ritenbenk, expedition at, 34.
Road-making on the ice, 273, 275, 277, 279, 286, 292, 294.
Robeson Channel, 69; view of, 110; position on American chart not to be recognized, 115; palæocrystic floes of, 118; examination of fiords, 242.
Rorqual whale, 21.
Ross, Sir John, Arctic highlanders of, 48; red snow, 48.
Rotges, or little auks, 46, 50, 360.
Royal Arctic Theatre, 169, 170; prologue, 172; plays, 173, 214.
Rudder, arrangement for unshipping, 3; head damaged, 67; unshipped for a nip, 83; seriously injured, 113; shifted, 113; frequent necessity for unshipping, 344; head badly wrenched, 344, 351.

Sabine, Cape, 55, 57, 59; Eskimo remains on, 69; passed, going south, 356.
Sails for sledges, 231 (n.).
"Sallie" suspected of robbing Rawson's depôt, 213. (*See* Dogs.)
Salt beef, character of, 154.
"Sanderson, his hope," shooting looms at, 40.
Sanitary condition of the men in winter quarters, 187.
Saxifrage, 57, 74, 340.
Scenery of Greenland, 24; from Disco, 31; in Disco Bay, 35; in the Waigat, 36; near Cape York,

48, 50; of the glaciers, 60; off Cape Hawks, 83; at winter quarters, 126; at the extreme northern point, 310, 311.
School in winter quarters, 165, 166; last assemblage of, 213.
Scientific observations in winter quarters, 180.
Scoresby on the size of the rorqual, 21.
Scoresby Bay, 94.
Scurvy, 237; premonitory symptoms, 284, 285; dread of, 299; increasing symptoms, 303, 304, 305, 313; decrease of appetite, 314; extreme weakness, 317; outbreak on board the "Alert," 321; true causes of the outbreak, 329, 330; cure of patients, 333, 339, 345; patients convalescent, 365; outbreak in sledge crews of "Discovery," 346.
Seals basking on the ice, 24, 45; shot by Hans, 354.
Selection of officers and men for Arctic service, 4.
Self, James, A.B., H.M.S. "Alert," songs by, 216.
Shells, marine, found above sea-level, 116.
Shift-Rudder Bay, 114.
Shirley, John, stoker, H.M.S. "Alert," songs by, 168; attacked by scurvy, 282; on the sledge, 284.
Shooting parties in summer, 338 to 340.
Sick. (*See* Scurvy.)
Simpson, Thos., H.M.S. "Alert," in sledge crew, northern division, attacked by scurvy, 306.
Skating, 77, 110.
Sky, beauty of, 83. (*See* Meteor, Sun.)
Sledges, description of, 231 (*n*.); sails for, 231 (*n*.); weight, 233; boats on, 242 (*n*.); required for northern division, 244; dog sledge sent to "Discovery," 247; departure of sledges in the spring, 257, 258; sledge standards, 258; art of packing, 277; high-runner sledges the best, 281;

(*See* Dogs, Marco Polo, Hercules, Victoria, Bloodhound, Bulldog, Alexandra, Challenger, Poppie, Clements Markham.)
Sledge crews, exercise of, 227.
Sledging, first lessons in 58; with dogs, 79, 80, 81, 128; first experiences, 129; severe work, 133; details of, 137; shore-going notions of, 138; realities, 139; lecture on, by Captain Nares, 215; grand palæocrystic chorus, 216; preparations for, during the winter, 230; equipments superintended by Sir Leopold M'Clintock, 231; weights, 233; auxiliaries and depôts, 234; tents, 235; cooking apparatus, 235; contents of knapsack and storebag, 237; scale of provisions, 237; medical stores, 238 (*n*.); clothing, 239, 240; programme of sledging operations, 241; the first encampment, 260; intense cold, 259, 262; arrival at autumn depôt, 263; daily routine, 264 to 270; roadmaking, 273, 275, 276; increasing difficulties, 304; method of advancing, 295, 304, 306, 313; most northern encampment, 307; extreme northern point, 309 to 311; return journey of northern division begun, 312; northern division reaches land, 321; return of northern division, 327; western division, 331, 332; eastern division, 350. (*See* Autumn, Hummocks, Temperature, Foot-gear, Cook.)
Sleeping-bags, 139, 235, 240; weight of, 233; frozen hard, 280, 283, 287.
Smith, Mr. Krarup, Inspector of North Greenland, his hospitality, 26, 29, 363.
Smith Sound, 47, 49, 69.
Snow, crimson, 48; heavy falls in Smith Sound, 71, 73, 95; in Robeson Channel, 111, 119, 121; heavy falls during autumn travelling, 147; buildings with, 152, 153, 154; temperature at different depths, 162; heavy drifts during

winter, 205; drifts while sledge travelling, 261, 287, 306.
Snow blindness, precautions against, 240; use of goggles, 286, 303.
Snow bunting seen by sledge crews, 319.
Snow hut built by Rawson, 212.
Sorrel, 345.
Soundings at extreme northern point, 308, 309.
Southsea Common, farewell to the expedition from, 9, 10.
Specific gravity observations, 180.
Spectrum analysis observations, 180.
Standards for sledges, 258.
Stanton, Cape, in sight, 103.
Steam, lecture on by Mr. Wootton, 169.
Stone, Geo., of the "Discovery," serving on board the "Alert," songs by, 174.
Store-bag, sledging contents, 237.
Stoves, 158.
Stuckberry, Thos., petty officer, H.M.S. "Alert," parts and songs by, 173, 216.
Summer, 337, 339.
Sumner, Cape, in sight, 103.
Sun, sets at midnight, 127; final disappearance, 141; last view of, 148, 150; date of final departure, 151, 178; longing for the return of, 207; return of, 219, 220, 221, 222; effect of, on the ice, 207, 313.
Sylvester heating apparatus not supplied, 158.
Symons, Robert, A.B., H.M.S. "Alert," printer, 164 (n.), 169, 175, 216; songs by, 214.

Tobogganing, 187.
Toboggans, Hudson's Bay Company's sledges, suitable for soft snow, 281.
Temperature, observations for, 162; variations during winter, 183; extreme cold, 223, 224; while sledging, 259, 262, 278, 283, 286, 290, 294, 295, 302, 313, 314, 320.
Tents, 139; weight, 233; description of, 235, 260.

Terns, 110, 332.
Tests of physical capacity, 15.
Theatricals, dresses, 171; orchestra, 171; prologue, 172; play-bills, 173, 175, 176, 214; plays, 173, 214.
Thermometers tested, 224.
Thermometrical observations, 162, 223. (*See* Temperature.)
"Thursday pops," 168, 169, 175, 176, 215.
Tidal observations at Twin Glacier Bay, 62; in winter quarters, 161, 180.
Tides, meeting of, at Cape Fraser, 92; in Polar Sea, 304, 309.
"Tigress," at Life-boat Cove, 53.
Torske bank, fishing on, 25.
Trafalgar day celebrated, 179.
Turnstones, 360.
Twin Glacier Bay, 61.
Tyndall Glacier, 359.

"Unies." (*See* Narwhals.)
Unifilar House, 209.
Union, Cape, 101, 103, 118; rounded, 121, 122; pressure on, 125, 343.
Union Jack of Captain Nares, taken with the northern division, 258; planted at the most northern point, 309.
Upernivik, 41, 42, 43, 358.

Valentia, "Alert" at, 367.
"Valorous," H.M.S., to take out stores to Disco, 6; joins the Arctic ships, 11; to make the best of her way to Disco, 14; at Disco, 28; kindness of captain and officers, 33; farewell to, 35; lost sight of, 37; jolly-boat landed at Dobbin Bay, 84; harmonium obtained from, 187.
Vegetation at Godhavn, 31; at Cape Isabella, 57; at Twin Glacier Bay, 60; at Norman Lockyer Island, 74; in Discovery Harbour, 107; lecture on Arctic plants by Mr. Pullen, 169; of the Arctic summer, 340.
Ventilation during winter, 158; drip, 182.
"Victoria," H.M. sledge, Lieut.

Parr, R.N., 137, 217, 259; goes through the ice, 144.
Victoria Head, 67.
Von Buch, Cape, 93.

Waigat, scenery of, 36; danger from fogs and icebergs, 37; steam out of, 38.
Wales, H.R.H. the Prince of, visit to Arctic ships, 8.
Wales, Prince of, Mountains, 50.
Walrus seen on the ice, 45, 74; hunts, 74, 75, 76.
Walter Bathurst Cape, 360.
Warming apparatus not supplied, 157.
Warming arrangements during winter, 157, 158.
Washington Irving Island, ancient cairns on, 85.
Weights for sledging, 232; to be dragged by each man, 233; in Parry's expedition, 243 (*n*.).
Welcome of sledge travellers to ship, 335, 336; of the expedition, on return to England, 368.
Whales, 20, 21. (*See* Cetaceans.)
Whale Sound, 49, 359.
White, Mr., engineer, H.M.S. "Alert," lecture on history by, 169; part taken by, at the theatricals, 174; improvement of sledge-cooking apparatus by, 236.
Willow, 74.
Wind. (*See* Gales.)
Winter, approach of, 126.
Winter quarters, precarious nature of at Floe-berg Beach, 126, 132 preparations for, 151 to 254 routine, 160. (*See* Ventilation Warming, Housing, Clothing, Fire-hole, Amusements.)
Wolf, appearance of a, 228, 229.
Wolves, traces of, 60, 107, 321; alarm of, 199.
Woman Islands, 41.
Wood, Sergeant, H.M.S., "Alert," recitation and song by, 216.
Woolley, Wm., H.M.S., "Alert," parts and songs by, 173.
"Woolwich," snow powder storehouse at winter quarters so called, 154; dismantling of, 227.
Wootton, Mr., engineer, H.M.S. "Alert," adventure in a kayak, 30; his lecture on steam, 169, 175; glee sung by, 216.

York, Cape, 47, 49.
Young, Sir Allen, gratitude to, for bringing out letters, 358, 362.

THE END.

PRINTED BY WILLIAM CLOWES AND SONS, LIMITED, LONDON AND BECCLES.

www.ingramcontent.com/pod-product-compliance
Lightning Source LLC
Chambersburg PA
CBHW022111290426
44112CB00008B/635